Pressing Problems in Modern Organizations
(That Keep Us Up at Night)

Pressing PROBLEMS

IN Modern

Organizations

(THAT KEEP US UP AT NIGHT)

TRANSFORMING
AGENDAS FOR RESEARCH
AND PRACTICE

Robert E. Quinn, Regina M. O'Neill,
and Lynda St. Clair, Editors

AMACOM
American Management Association
New York· Boston · Chicago · Kansas City· San Francisco· Washington, D.C.
Brussels· Mexico City· Tokyo· Toronto

Special discounts on bulk quantities of AMACOM books are available to corporations, professional associations, and other organizations. For details, contact Special Sales Department, AMACOM, an imprint of AMA Publications, a division of American Management Association, 1601 Broadway, New York, NY 10019. Tel.: 212-903-8316   Fax: 212-903-8083

This publication is designed to provide accurate and authoritative information in regard to the subject matter covered. It is sold with the understanding that the publisher is not engaged in rendering legal, accounting, or other professional service. If legal advice or other expert assistance is required, the services of a competent professional person should be sought.

Library of Congress Cataloging-in-Publication Data

Pressing problems in modern organizations (that keep us up at night) : transforming agendas for research and practice / Robert E. Quinn, Regina M. O'Neill, Lynda St. Clair, editors.

p.   cm.

Includes index.

ISBN 0-8144-7052-1

1. Industrial management.   I. Quinn, Robert E.   II. O'Neill, Regina M.   III. St. Clair, Lynda, 1960–   .

HD31.P7253   1999

658—dc21   99-32844

CIP

Printing number

10   9   8   7   6   5   4   3   2   1

Contents

Part 2: Process Problems

List of Figures

List of Tables

Preface

As the competitive landscape continues to change at an ever-accelerating rate, many previously useful theories of organization and formerly successful managerial practices are becoming less effective or outmoded. Academic researchers need to develop new theories that can address more appropriately the problems of modern organizations. Likewise, managers today need a different set of tools to help them respond effectively to the rapid changes in their organizational environment. To meet these challenges, this book aims to influence organizational research in three ways.

First, as discussed in the Introduction, we wish to encourage research that is theoretically grounded, methodologically rigorous, and practically relevant. We recognize the tension among these three factors and the challenge of bringing them together. Achieving this interpenetration is a formidable task, but its value is widely recognized because, when properly executed, such research takes on true creative complexity. Thus, the end product increases in quality for both the academic and the practitioner. Each chapter reflects this tripartite approach to organizational research. The authors all address problems that are theoretically interesting and important to practice. In addition, the research agendas developed in each chapter provide a foundation for the type of rigorous analysis necessary for exemplary research.

Second, the eleven core chapters of the book are intended to direct attention to specific pressing problems that clearly need additional research. The problems discussed in this book were selected from a more extensive list of thirty-six problems that was derived by combining insights from a theoretical model of responsive organizations with the practical concerns of senior executives in a variety of organizations. Drawing on a wealth of resources, including published research and interviews with managers, executives, consultants, and change agents, the authors have developed a set of viable agendas designed to guide future research on some of the most pressing problems faced by organizations today.

Third, the Conclusion presents a framework that can be used to identify other potentially pressing organizational problems not discussed in the book. As described in the Conclusion, the responsive organization framework (Quinn and St. Clair 1997) is especially useful for predicting emerging organizational problems of theoretical importance and practical relevance because it was derived by mapping emerging management practices on to a theoretical framework of competing values (Quinn 1988). As organizations attempt to become more responsive to their constantly changing environment, they often find that attempts to be responsive to one aspect of the environment (e.g., customers or suppliers) lead to dysfunctional consequences for another aspect (e.g., employees or processes). Thus, the responsive organization framework can serve as a lens through which one can view current organizational practices and make predictions about the likely dysfunctional consequences of those practices.

Given the goals of this book, we expect that it will be of interest primarily to researchers who wish to push beyond the boundaries of organizational studies. We also believe that it has much to say to practitioners who are struggling to understand and resolve the types of pressing problems described in the book.

It is our hope that *Pressing Problems in Modern Organizations (That Keep Us Up at Night): Transforming Agendas for Research and Practice* will unite researchers and practitioners in the quest for viable solutions to the vexing problems encountered by organizations faced with perpetually changing environments. Such a partnership is necessary if we hope to improve organizational processes and performance while enhancing the quality of life for people working in organizations today.

July 1998

Robert E. Quinn
Ann Arbor, Michigan
Regina M. O'Neill
Boston, Massachusetts
Lynda St. Clair
Smithfield, Rhode Island

References

Quinn, R. E. 1988. *Beyond Rational Management: Mastering the Paradoxes and Competing Demands of High Performance.* San Francisco: Jossey-Bass.

Quinn, R. E. and St. Clair, L. 1997. "The Emerging Professional Adhocracy: A General Framework of Responsive Organizing." *Consulting Psychology Journal: Practice and Research* 49(2), 152–61.

Editors and Contributors

Robert E. Quinn holds the M. L. Tracy Collegiate Professorship of organizational behavior and human resource management at the University of Michigan Business School. He received his Ph.D. from the University of Cincinnati and his M.S. and B.S. from Brigham Young University. His research interests focus on organizational change, leadership, competing values model of organizations, executive skill development, and personal growth and transformation. Professor Quinn is the author of numerous academic articles and books, including *Beyond Rational Management: Mastering the Paradoxes and Competing Demands of High Performance, Becoming a Master Manager: A Competency Based Framework,* and *Deep Change: Discovering the Leader Within.*

Regina M. O'Neill is assistant professor of management at the Sawyer School of Management at Suffolk University in Boston. She received her Ph.D. in 1997 from the University of Michigan Business School in organizational behavior and human resource management. She received her MBA in 1990 from the Amos Tuck School of Business at Dartmouth College and her B.S. in management in 1982 from the University of Massachusetts. Her research interests focus on professional and personal relationships in organizations and the ways these relationships shape and are shaped by individual and organizational factors. Her work considers conceptual and methodological issues in mentoring and social support; issue selling in organizations; and individual and organizational predictors of empowerment, well-being, and career success. Her research has been published in *Strategic Management Journal, Educational and Psychological Measurement,* and *Human Resource Management Journal.*

Lynda St. Clair is assistant professor of management at Bryant College in Rhode Island. She earned her Ph.D. in 1994 from the University of Michigan Business School in organizational behavior and human resource management. She earned an M.P.A. in 1983 from the University of Texas at Austin in consulting and accounting information systems and a B.S. in business management from Louisiana Tech University in 1981. She is a member of the National Academy of Management and the Eastern Academy of Management. She coedited, with Noel M. Tichy and Andrew R. McGill, *Corporate Global Citizenship: Doing Business in the Public Eye*. Her research interests center on the relationship between the individual and the organization and how that relationship changes over time. Most recently she has been studying the concept of the psychological contract with respect to expectations about corporate social responsibility and community service. Her research has been published in *Academy of Management Journal, Journal for the Theory of Social Behaviour, Organizational Dynamics,* and *Handbook of Business Strategy*.

Pyrra Alnot is a doctoral student in organizational psychology at the University of Michigan. She earned her B.A. in 1996 in psychology at Macalester College, St. Paul, Minnesota. Her research interests include organizational boundary crossing, organizational identification, self-presentation, and temporary work.

Aimee Arlington is an internal consultant in the executive and organization development department of Dell Computer Corporation. She is a 1998 M.B.A. graduate of the University of Michigan Business School with a concentration in organizational behavior. Aimee received her Bachelor's of Business Administration in 1993 from Southern Methodist University.

Jeffrey M. Bacidore is visiting assistant professor of finance at the University of Michigan Business School. He received his bachelor's degree in economics from Knox College (1992) and his M.S. (1996) and Ph.D. (1998) in finance from Indiana University. His research interests include asset pricing, corporate finance, and market microstructure.

Wayne E. Baker is associate professor of organizational behavior at the University of Michigan Business School and faculty associate at the University of Michigan Institute for Social Research. He earned his Ph.D. in sociology from Northwestern University. His research interests include economic sociology, culture, networks, organizational theory, and innovative management practices.

Karen A. Bantel is a faculty member at the University of Michigan Business School, where she received her Ph.D. in strategy and organizational behavior in 1987. She earned both her B.A. and M.B.A. from the University of Michigan. Her work is on top management teams in relation to strategic outcomes for their firms, with particular interest in strategic innovation and change. Recent work focuses on strategic issues for technology-based entrepreneurial firms.

Mary Yoko Brannen is associate professor of international business at San Jose State University and adjunct associate professor of executive education at the University of Michigan Business School. She received her Ph.D. in organizational behavior, with a minor in anthropology, and an M.B.A. from the University of Massachusetts School of Management. She has a B.A. in comparative literature from the University of California at Berkeley. She specializes in ethnographic approaches to understanding the effects of changing cultural contexts on technology transfer, work organization, and individuals' assumptions regarding work.

Kim S. Cameron is Dean and Albert J. Weatherhead III Professor of Management at the Weatherhead School of Management at Case Western Reserve University. He received bachelors and masters degrees from Brigham Young University and masters and doctoral degrees from Yale University. His current research focuses on organizational downsizing, cultural and quality change, and virtues in organizations such as forgiveness, compassion, and integrity.

Paul R. Carlile is assistant professor of organizational studies at MIT's Sloan School of Management. He received his Ph.D. in organizational behavior and theory from the University of Michigan Business School in 1997. He earned both his B.A. in philosophy and anthropology and his master's degree in organizational behavior from Brigham Young University. Paul's interests focus on how knowledge is structured within organizations and how an understanding of that structuring process provides insight into the creation of various "organizing tools" to facilitate the flow of knowledge and its transformation across the knowledge boundaries that demarcate the distributed nature of organizations.

Deborah Duarte is a faculty member at The George Washington University and also teaches at the Singapore Institute of Management and at the

International Space University in France. She holds a doctorate in human resource development from George Washington University. She is an expert in the areas of leadership development, project management, global and virtual project teams, leadership development, organizational learning, and organizational culture change activities and consults with a number of private and public organizations.

Jane E. Dutton is the William Russell Kelly Professor of Business Administration at the University of Michigan and an associate professor of psychology. Jane received her Ph.D. from the Kellogg Graduate School of Management at Northwestern University. Her research focuses on the processes by which people are valued and devalued at work. She is researching the kinds of relational knowledge that people acquire in low-power positions, and how this knowledge is used for individual and organizational effectiveness.

Rachel K. Ebert is an HRIS specialist with Marketing Specialists Sales Company in Dallas, Texas. She was assistant to Professor Robert E. Quinn from 1994 to 1997. In 1997 she received her bachelor's degree in language and international trade from Eastern Michigan University. Her research interests include work-life issues, gender, and intercultural communications.

Daniel C. Feldman is Distinguished Business Partnership Foundation Fellow and professor of management at the University of South Carolina College of Business Administration. He received his Ph.D. in organizational behavior from Yale University. Professor Feldman has published extensively in the area of career development in organizations. His most recent book, *Coping with Job Loss,* examines individual reactions to layoffs and organizational strategies for downsizing.

Jeffrey A. Martin is a Ph.D. student in organizational behavior at the Stanford School of Industrial Engineering and Engineering Management. He received his bachelor's degree in computer science from Brigham Young University in 1984 and his M.B.A. from the University of Michigan in 1996. His research interests focus on the phenomena of organizational change, specifically in the areas of innovation and learning across organizational, cultural, and geographic boundaries.

Laura M. Morgan is a doctoral student in organizational psychology at the University of Michigan. She received her bachelor's degree in psychology from the University of Virginia in 1996. Her primary research interests are career development (aspirations and dealing with obstacles) among nonmanagers, women, and people of color.

Nancy Tennant Snyder is the chief learning officer for Whirlpool Corporation. She also heads the Brandywine Creek Performance Centre, Whirlpool's Corporate University. She holds a doctorate in organizational behavior from George Washington University. Her research interests include globalization, organizational learning, and culture change. She also has a forthcoming book, *Mastering Virtual Teams.*

Gretchen M. Spreitzer is associate professor at the University of Southern California Marshall School of Business Administration and a faculty affiliate of the Center for Effective Organizations and the Leadership Institute. She received her Ph.D. in organizational behavior and human resource management from the University of Michigan. She earned a B.S. in systems analysis from Miami University of Ohio. Her research interests focus on employee empowerment and management development, particularly within the context of strategic and organizational change.

Kathleen M. Sutcliffe is assistant professor of organizational behavior and human resource management at the University of Michigan Business School. She received her Ph.D. in organizational behavior and theory from the University of Texas at Austin. Her research program has been devoted to investigating how contexts become known; how contexts influence organizational forms and organizational actions/responses; and how organizations and their units can be designed to help members better sense, cope with, and respond to contextual requirements.

Anjan V. Thakor is Frey Professor of Banking and Finance at the University of Michigan Business School. He received his Ph.D. in finance from Northwestern University. His research interests focus on corporate finance, financial intermediation, and the economics of asymmetric information. He coauthored (with Stuart Greenbaum) *Contemporary Financial Intermediation,* a bank management text.

Michael Thompson is associate professor in the Marriott School of Management at Brigham Young University. He holds an undergraduate degree in classics from Brigham Young University and a Ph.D. in rhetoric from Rennsselaer Polytechnic University. His research has focused primarily on the role of communication in organizational change and learning.

Markus Vodosek is a Ph.D. candidate in the department of organizational behavior and human resource management at the University of Michigan. He received his engineering degree in media technology from the Hochschule für Druck und Medien in Stuttgart, Germany in 1990, and his M.B.A. from Portland State University in 1992. His research interests include the dynamics of interpersonal relationships within organizations, intraorganizational social networks, and the perception and interpretation of information by organizational members.

Julia A. Welch is a Ph.D. candidate in the department of organizational behavior and human resource management at the University of Michigan. In 1994 she received her bachelor's degree in economics from Eckerd College. Her research interests include work-life issues, stress, burnout, and perceptions of success.

Rebecca S. Wells is a doctoral student in the department of health management & policy in the school of public health at the University of Michigan. She earned her B.A. degree in public and international affairs at Princeton University in 1988 and is completing a masters degree in health care management. Her research interests focus on strategic processes as well as environmental constraints on managerial effectiveness.

Michele Williams is a Ph.D. candidate in the department of organizational behavior and human resource management at the University of Michigan. She received her bachelor's degree in psychology from Johns Hopkins University and her master's degree in education from Teachers College, Columbia University. Her research interests include hurtful relationships at work, emotion, and the processes through which trust is built and maintained.

The Pressing Problems of Modern Organizations: Theoretical, Methodological, and Practical Approaches

REGINA M. O'NEILL, LYNDA ST. CLAIR, *and* ROBERT E. QUINN

Truly valuable organizational research rests on three supporting pillars: meticulous theoretical conceptualization, rigorous systematic analysis, and critical practical applications. Within the academic profession, there is a long history of tension among these three elements. Often only one is represented in a given research effort. In terms of academic education, for example, apprentice scholars often find themselves pulled between expectations of meticulous theoretical conceptualization and the demands of rigorous systematic analysis. It is not unusual for a young researcher to reach the dissertation stage with great strengths in analysis or conceptualization. It is much rarer to find doctoral candidates equally strong in both of these dimensions. Unaddressed, this imbalance often leads to rigorous analysis of conceptually barren questions or unsound analysis of theoretically rich questions. It is only when these two characteristics are integrated that the current research takes on true creative complexity and improves in quality. Achieving this interpenetration is a challenge, but its value is commonly recognized.

Less frequently recognized in academic education is the importance of the third factor—critical practical applications. Simply put, an emphasis on practical relevance is often lacking in our efforts to develop future organizational researchers. Much of the current research tends to fall into one of two quite different categories: (1) research that is practically useful, but is not academically rigorous, and (2) research that is theoretically and methodologically precise, but is inconsequential to the real world. When meticulous theoretical conceptualization and rigorous systematic analysis are combined with the examination of a relevant pressing organizational problem, however, the work is usually more widely recognized and highly valued. Because it has an impact on both scholarship and practice, this type of work demands the attention of academics and practitioners alike. Thus, instilling in organizational scholars an appreciation for practical relevance as well as a devotion to theoretical and analytical rigor is often desirable.

This book was undertaken with the hope that it could serve as both a model and a guide for organizational research. First, we see it as a model because it was conceived with the kind of blending of theory and practice that we believe is necessary to make organizational research valuable. Our premise is similar to that of Lawler et al. (1990) in that we assume organizational research can and should be of interest to not only the academic research community but also to practitioners who can benefit from research focused on helping to make their organizations more effective.

The book is also intended to be a guide for organizational research. The chapters on pressing problems are designed to direct future research efforts toward fruitful avenues that combine conceptual richness, methodological rigor, and real-world application. We believe that research of this type will prove to be abundant in terms of meaningful advances in theory as well as important improvements in practice.

The purpose of this book is to influence the agenda of researchers at all stages, from scholars-in-training to established veterans in the field. We particularly seek to enrich the research process by facilitating the interpenetration of theoretical conceptualization, rigorous analysis, and practical application. It is not our intent to devalue work of a purely theoretical orientation. Indeed, we think basic research is clearly valuable. We simply believe that much work in the organizational sciences would improve in quality if it were tied to relevant problems. Our intent, then, is to provide insights that may assist researchers in establishing more grounded research agendas. Once established, these agendas can drive systematic and rigorous empirical examination of topics that are important to both scholars and practitioners.

Our premise is that by examining real-time pressing problems of modern organizations, academic researchers will uncover fertile ground that will lead to new and interesting theoretical perspectives. Thus, we anticipate that this book will be of interest to academics who wish to push the frontiers of research beyond the boundaries of practice.

Identification of Pressing Problems

The process for identifying the pressing problems discussed in this book is grounded in both practice and theory. In previous research, Quinn and St. Clair (1997) developed a theoretical model designed to identify potential problems organizations might encounter as they attempt to become more responsive in today's competitive environment (see also Conclusion). Then, to build on this theoretical work and keep it relevant, the senior editor conducted interviews with senior executives from several companies. The discussions helped refine and extend the original work. Based on the interviews and observations, the senior editor developed a list of thirty-six problems.

To assess the importance of these problems, the editors administered a survey to managers from 117 organizations. The results of the ensuing analyses suggested that there were twenty-one particularly common pressing problems (see Appendix). In planning this book, we presented this list to a group of researchers and asked them to select the problems that were of greatest interest to them. The eleven topics presented in this book represent their final choices.

Overview of the Book

The chapters in this book have been prepared as guides for future organizational research. Each chapter begins with a description of a pressing problem experienced by organizations today. Following the problem statement is a richly blended mixture of qualitative interview data from practitioners, consultants, and academics, as well as a discussion of the relevant research literature. By combining these sources of insights, the authors have developed useful conceptualizations of these problems and provided agendas for future research.

The book is divided into two parts. Part 1 focuses on people problems in modern organizations that have resulted from companies demanding better performance from their employees while providing them with less security in an environment filled with ambiguity and uncertainty. Part 2 focuses on process problems that have resulted from companies demanding innovation, flexibility, improved quality, and faster production in an environment of cost cutting, downsizing, and continuous revamping of operations.

Chapter 1 explores negative political behaviors and the corrosive political environments in which they flourish. The authors discuss how the frequency and extensiveness of negative political behavior can inflict shock, confusion, and other emotional tolls on individuals. They also consider how these behaviors can hurt an organization's capacity to remain coherent and effective. The authors synthesize the organizational literature to consider some common assumptions and conditions that contribute to negative political behaviors. Building on existing research, they propose a promising new model that focuses on the previously unexplored relationship between negative political behavior and issues of trust. These sections provide the foundation for the authors to describe an agenda for future research that considers individuals' emotional responses to negative political behavior as well as some micro- and macrolinking mechanisms that affect perceptions of negative political behavior. Finally, the authors identify the practical issues associated with managing negative political behaviors.

Chapter 2 addresses the problem of multiple accountabilities. Using interview data and existing research, the authors begin by identifying the reasons that the use and practice of multiple accountabilities have substantially increased as well as the negative individual and organizational consequences that can result from multiple reporting relationships. The authors take a different perspective on this problem, moving away from the typical conclusion that multiple reporting relationships are inevitably problematic; instead, they propose a new paradigm that considers the promise and potential of multiple accountabilities. Recognizing that more people are engaged in multiple reporting relationships than ever before, the authors then suggest ways for individuals and organizations to meet the challenges of serving multiple masters. By proposing a fundamental shift in management paradigms, they present several future research directions that align practical concerns with theoretical richness.

Chapter 3 addresses the problem of overwork, an issue often associated with the problem of multiple accountabilities. While many companies are expecting employees to work longer hours, the number of dual-career families and working parents continues to grow, exacerbating the problem of overwork for many people. Given these issues, the authors consider the problem of overwork from a whole-life perspective. They begin by explaining the fundamental lack of agreement among both scholars and practitioners on how to define overwork. The authors then consider the concept of overwork from a number of perspectives including research on role overload, downsizing, and work and family. They then propose an agenda for future research that addresses the nature of overwork as well as some potential levers for reducing it. One possible lever, psychological empowerment, is explored in some detail as a way of reducing feelings of overwork.

In contrast to the problem of overwork, Chapter 4 considers the problem of underemployed human resources—employees who are not contributing or adding value to their organizations. While the problem of underemployed human resources has traditionally been addressed by taking into account motivation and the effects of reward systems, the authors propose an alternative explanation. Specifically, they suggest that organizational constraints may prevent employees from working to their full potential, resulting in underutilization of employee skills. Thus, employees are psychologically demotivated, leading to their failure to contribute to the organization. Although little attention has been paid to underemployment as an organizational problem, the authors identify its direct and indirect consequences on organizational performance. Their research agenda is supported by the identification of societal factors that affect an organization's propensity to have an underemployed workforce, and organizational factors that affect an employee's propensity for becoming underemployed.

Chapter 5 considers the problem of cultural misunderstandings. One of the major forces influencing organizations today is globalization. Many organizations are now made up of members from a variety of national and ethnic cultural backgrounds. The combination of these forces has resulted in an increase in misunderstandings, communication problems, and interpersonal conflicts. The authors use detailed interviews to examine the issue of misunderstandings in globally diverse organizations that arise due to differences in language and cultural backgrounds. They then discuss the different ways that executives, managers, change agents, and consultants have each approached the problem and the implications of those differences in perceptions. This discussion, combined with a comprehensive literature review, provides a strong foundation for the authors to propose new perspectives that will prove helpful to both scholars and practitioners interested in investigating and mitigating cultural misunderstandings.

Finally, Chapter 6 considers chaotic role movement. The authors introduce this problem by considering the rapid movement of professionals into new roles within a company in which the number of roles exceeds the number of qualified people available. In contrast to the problem of cultural misunderstandings discussed in Chapter 5, however, the authors underscore that not all consequences of chaotic role movement are negative. They then provide insightful perspectives on both the positive and negative consequences of chaotic role movement. Drawing connections to the changing concept of the career from both the individual and organizational perspective, the authors present a comprehensive literature review that focuses on open systems theory to bring a broad conceptual framework to the topic of chaotic role movement. Finally, they present future research strategies that emphasize improving our understanding and measurement of chaotic role movement and assessing its impact at the organizational level.

Part 2 examines process problems. Chapter 7 considers the failure of most organizations to achieve either explicit or implicit change in organizational processes. The authors argue that organizations are bundles of processes and that organizational success depends on agility, or the capacity to respond quickly to changes in the environment. Building on the literature on change efforts aimed at redesigning organizational processes, they propose a new framework of communities-of-practice and organizational learning that helps organize perspectives on process problems. They then propose new research directions of interest to researchers and practitioners alike. Specifically, the authors suggest that practice theory and communities-of-practice can provide a robust way to examine process problems, thus providing insights into ways to create agile organizations through the design and implementation of effective organizational processes.

Chapter 8 deals with the problem of overemphasis on analysis. As with Chapter 7, the authors accept the premise that modern organizations need to become more agile. They then take a new perspective and focus specifically on how overemphasis on analysis inhibits agility, thereby preventing organizations from responding quickly in a dynamic and competitive environment. They consider how organizations must balance the need for speed in decision making with the increasing complexity of the decision-making context. The authors also consider the impact of accountability for decision-making and information processing behaviors (e.g., rejecting important information and relying on unimportant information) based on the probability that organizations will tend to overemphasize analysis in their decision-making processes. By challenging traditional assumptions about decision making, the authors provide a foundation to propose previously unexplored avenues for future research that are of both theoretical and practical importance.

Continuing the theme of increasingly complex decision-making contexts, Chapter 9 considers the problem of competitive external pressures and the role of top management teams. The authors present case studies of firms that share the challenges of complexity, scarcity, and unpredictable change. In particular, they focus on ways to build top management teams with the ability to make strategic decisions that sustain a firm's competitive advantage in spite of the challenges of operating in these complex, resource-scarce, and dynamic environments. The authors discuss the need for top management teams to create competencies, proposing the concept of team-level cognitive complexity as a potential antecedent of sustained competitive advantage. Their future research agenda, of concern to organizational scholars and practitioners alike, includes a discussion of the need to develop measures of team-level cognitive complexity that can assess the extent to which top management teams successfully balance differentiation and integration when evaluating alternative competitive strategies.

Chapter 10 addresses the problem of poor financial performance. It first focuses on evaluating an important question: Why do firms perform poorly? Drawing on existing literature, the authors discuss several different organizational causes of poor financial performance and highlight some of the serious consequences of sustained poor financial performance for both individuals and organizations. Then, the authors turn to identifying the most appropriate measure for evaluating a company's financial performance. Their critique of existing measures of financial performance provides the foundation for developing a useful new measure of company financial performance. In particular, they propose using Refined Economic Value Added (REVA) as an appropriate measure to assess period-by-period company financial performance. Their future research agenda discusses the importance of continuing research both on REVA as a measure of company performance and on corporatewide pay-for-performance compensation systems.

Chapter 11 considers the problem of quality. Specifically, the authors focus on total quality management (TQM) in response to fundamental organizational issues of quality, recognizing that quality and TQM are used interchangeably. They begin by identifying a critical paradox: Although practitioners have come to realize that quality must be a given in their organizations, we still lack a clear understanding of the nature and scope of quality. The authors summarize the existing literature, which includes numerous approaches to and definitions of quality, but provides little direction on how to integrate these diverse concepts. To help improve our understanding of the concept of quality, the authors discuss its relationship with organizational effectiveness, customer satisfaction, and productivity. The chapter concludes with a series of future research questions on defining, measuring, and understanding TQM in a way that is of real-world consequence.

The contributors to this book have each considered a different pressing problem and have offered exciting new ideas for future research that can combine rigorous analysis with research that is conceptually strong and practically relevant. Naturally, the chapters in this book consider only a small portion of the problems of modern organizations. To further expand the potential scope of future research, the Conclusion provides a theoretical framework for thinking about other problems that are likely to be encountered by modern organizations. The Conclusion begins with a presentation of Quinn and St. Clair's (1997) responsive organization framework. Next, the authors demonstrates how each of the eleven problems described in this book fits within that framework. Finally, they emphasize the dynamic nature of the responsive organization framework and its value for identifying pressing problems of modern organizations.

Although there is clearly still much fertile ground to be covered, we feel that this book makes an important contribution to developing research agendas that are both theoretically significant and practically relevant. It is our hope that this book will be a catalyst for future research on the organizational problems presented in the following chapters as well as other pressing problems in today's organizations. Such research is needed not merely to improve organizational processes and performance, but also to enhance the quality of life for people working in organizations today and help all of us get to sleep at night.

References

Lawler, E. E., Mohrman, A. M., Mohrman, S. A., Ledford, G. E., Cummings, T. G., and Associates. 1990. *Doing Research That Is Useful for Theory and Practice.* San Francisco: Jossey-Bass.

Quinn, R. E. and St. Clair, L. 1997. "The Emerging Professional Adhocracy: A General Framework of Responsive Organizing." *Consulting Psychology Journal: Practice and Research* 49(2), 152–61.

PART 1

People Problems

Chapter 1

Corrosive Political Climates: The Heavy Toll of Negative Political Behavior in Organizations

Michele Williams *and* Jane E. Dutton

F ive middle managers in five different settings put into words what most employees feel when they find themselves exposed to episodes of negative political behavior in their work organizations:

"I was astonished, appalled, angry, shocked!" (team member, small publishing company)

"The tension. I feel it." (staff member, mid-size information technology subcontractor)

"We're still trying to make sense of it. We felt bad as a group." (team leader, Fortune 500 high-technology company)

"You have to be on guard all of the time here. You can't trust anyone in this place. (team leader, Fortune 500 high technology company)

"Remember I told you that nothing shocks me anymore? Well, this shocked me." (manager, national headquarters of a large non-profit organization)

*The authors wish to thank Regina M. O'Neill and Lynda St. Clair for helpful comments on an earlier draft of this chapter.

3

Corrosive political climates in organizations are marked by frequent episodes of negative political behavior. Negative political behavior describes the actions taken by individuals that result in hurtful outcomes for organizational members, and for the organization more broadly. Negative political behaviors are a subset of what researchers have called *political behaviors*—those that are "informal, ostensibly parochial, typically divisive, and above all, in a technical sense, illegitimate—sanctioned neither by informal authority, accepted ideology nor certified expertise" (Mintzberg 1983, 172). Political behaviors are marked by an actor's attempt to conceal the motive for the behavior, implicitly aware of its unacceptability (Pfeffer 1981). Negative political behaviors take many forms including showing favoritism in promotions, purposefully withholding information, feigning attitudes in an opportunistic fashion, taking credit for other people's work (Ferris and King 1991), or taking actions that put personal power ahead of organizational good. Negative political behaviors often involve conflicts that produce outcomes that are detrimental to other individuals or groups (Drory and Romm 1990). The self-serving motives of the members engaging in negative political behaviors result in outcomes that hurt the organization.

Evidence shows that negative political behaviors inflicted on individuals and the corrosive political climates that create and sustain them are harmful. The expressed shock, confusion, and tension reveal the negative emotional toll levied on individuals who endure in these kinds of contexts. Individuals' attachments to organizations weaken. Uncertainty and ambiguity flourish. A sense of personal vulnerability, hurt, and a weakened sense of control may ensue. These individual reactions contribute to group and organizational-level consequences. Research suggests that individuals become less focused on organizational goals (Madison et al. 1980), the flow of information becomes restricted and decision speed slows (Eisenhardt and Bourgeois 1988), excitement about innovation dampens (Parker, Dipboye, and Jackson 1995), members withdraw psychologically and physically (e.g., Cropanzano et al. 1997; Ferris et al. 1996), employee stress increases (Cropanzano et al. 1997; Ferris et al. 1996), critical employee attitudes such as job involvement and satisfaction decline (Cropanzano et al. 1997; Gandz and Murray 1980), and valuable employees exit the organization (Pfeffer 1992). Clearly, the frequency and extensiveness of negative political behavior can harm an organization's capacity to remain coherent and effective. Mintzberg (1991) describes the consequences quite graphically: "At the limit, the organization dominated by politics goes out of control by exploding. Nothing remains at the core—no central direction, no integrating ideology, and therefore, no directed effort at efficiency or proficiency or innovation" (p. 65).

This chapter builds a research agenda around the issue of negative political behavior and the corrosive political environments in which it flourishes. To do so, we begin with a discussion of why this problem is now so compelling for research and practice. Building on this call for understanding, we turn to the organizational literature to consider common assumptions and conditions that contribute to negative political behavior. We identify a significant gap in current research and propose a model that focuses on the critical relationship between negative political behavior and issues of trust. The following sections provide a foundation to consider the practical issues of managing negative political behaviors and to describe an ambitious agenda for future research that is useful for practitioners and organizational scholars alike.

Getting Serious about the Downsides of Negative Political Behavior

Negative political behaviors are ubiquitous in organizational life. However, the consequences of these behaviors are amplified in fast-paced, globally competitive environments in which work is increasingly more interdependent within and across organizational boundaries. Three arguments compel practitioners and scholars to become serious about actively managing the occurrence of negative political behaviors in organizations: dynamic capabilities, collaborative potential, and changing employee contracts.

The competitive conditions facing organizations are increasingly dynamic: "There is rapid change in technology and market forces, and 'feedback' effects on firms" (Teece, Pisano, and Shuen 1997, 512). Under these competitive conditions, an organization's capacity to build and sustain dynamic capabilities is key. In today's world, the organization must be capable of "adapting, integrating, and reconfiguring internal and external organizational skills, resources, and functional competencies to match the requirements of changing environment" (Teece, Pisano, and Shuen 1997, 515). This achievement rests critically on "business processes' market positions, and expansion paths" (Teece, Pisano, and Shuen 1997, 515) that are enabled and sustained by the behaviors and commitments of employees. It is the behaviors and commitments of employees that compose the "organizational structures and managerial processes which support productive activity" (Teece, Pisano, and Shuen 1997, 517).

Trust is critical to these processes. Interpersonal trust permits flexibility in responding to dynamic conditions. It allows for greater interdependence, promotes the free flow of information (Powell and Smith-Doerr 1994), and enhances constructive interpersonal contributions (McAllister 1995). Likewise, employees' trust in their organization increases commitment, job involvement, and civic contributions (Robinson 1996). Our basic argument is that corrosive political environments undermine trust, cutting away at an organization's dynamic capabilities, weakening its basis for competitive survival.

In particular, an organization's capability for collaboration both within and across its boundaries relies on the development of reliable routines and the creation and maintenance of trust. Trust is particularly important because companies are moving toward less hierarchical forms of governance. Less hierarchy leaves individuals and organizations more dependent on others over whom they have no legitimate authority (Pfeffer 1992). Trust facilitates collaboration among peers because it reduces the need to monitor others' behavior, formalize procedures, and create completely specified contracts (Macauley 1963; Williamson 1975). Trust building is valuable to any organization that depends on long-term nonhierarchical relationships (Powell 1990).

For example, a network company's competitive advantage in terms of flexibility, access to tacit knowledge, and richer-freer information (Powell and Smith-Doerr 1994; Zajac and Olsen 1993) depends on a foundation of trust (Powell 1990; Ring and Van de Ven 1994). When parties trust one another, they can adjust to unanticipated contingencies in jointly optimal ways without having to renegotiate with opportunistic partners (Lorenz 1988). In addition, trust facilities parties' use of informal agreements that enhance the flexibility of formal procedures, thereby promoting collaboration (Ring and Van de Ven 1994).

Negative political behaviors pose a serious threat to the development and maintenance of trust both within and between organizations because they inflict harm on individuals. Trust is based on expectations that another party will behave in ways that are helpful or at least not harmful (Gambetta 1988). Because negative political behaviors are harmful, they can not only inhibit the development of trust but destroy existing trust.

Thus, negative political behaviors are detrimental to the trust creation process, hampering the conduct of vital collaborative work.

Finally, evidence abounds that employees' loyalty at any organization is and will become increasingly fragile (Stroh and Reilly 1997). Employees' satisfaction with their jobs, their loyalty, and commitment are no longer guaranteed by either psychological or instrumental contracts. In addition, employees' perceptions of their obligations to their employers have been significantly decreased by their employers' failure to uphold commitments (Robinson 1996). In organizations in which negative political behavior is pervasive, loyalty accrues to individual people as opposed to whole organizations (McGrath 1995). This kind of outcome is particularly damaging when organizational loyalty is in short supply and crucial for attracting and retaining employees. In short, conditions such as a corrosive political climate that sever or damage fragile employee attachments put organizations at risk in terms of both higher costs and limited flexibility.

A View of Negative Political Behavior from the Literature

Research on negative political behavior in organizations has taken two distinct trajectories. The first examines occurrences of such behavior from the point of view of resource dependence, focusing on how and why these kinds of tactics are used. For the most part, researchers from this vein consider both the positive and negative effects of political behavior. They investigate political behaviors that are not inherently negative but that can adversely affect organizational decisions and performance. For example, when resources are scarce, coalition building can contribute to a project's success by rallying needed support (Brown 1995). By contrast, in a rapidly changing but otherwise munificent environment, coalition building may result in failure by slowing down and lowering the quality of decision making (Pfeffer 1992).

The second research path focuses on perceptions of negative political behavior—both on political behaviors that are inherently harmful and on the negative effects of neutral political behaviors. This path was blazed by researchers interested in the antecedents and outcomes of perceptions of political behavior in organizations. These researchers consider the targets of negative behavior: what they see and how they respond.

Both research camps share four assumptions about negative political behavior. First, all researchers agree that political behavior in organizations is a normal part of conducting business. Politics infect strategic decision making (Eisenhardt and Bourgeois 1988), the allocation of budgets (Pfeffer and Salancik 1974), human resource decisions (Ferris and King 1991), the collection and use of information used for forecasting and modeling (Davenport, Eccles, and Prusak 1992), and the innovation process (Kiechel 1988). Furthermore, political actors can be specific individuals or intact formal or informal groups (Cobb 1986; Drory and Romm, 1990). Second, many adopt what is called a *constructionist perspective,* which assumes that perceptions of behavior as political are important for understanding employee behavior, rather than objective behaviors. These perceptions are complex and fluid, being highly sensitive to the changing conditions in a potentially political situation and to the characteristics of the observer (Drory and Romm 1988). Third, both camps acknowledge that politics are in and of themselves not bad. Rather, certain types of actions and behaviors generate more destructive and hurtful consequences than others. Fourth, most researchers agree that the negative side of political behavior may be most apparent under conditions in which resources become scarce, outcomes are uncertain, and there is limited sanctioning of political behavior.

Contributors to Negative Political Behavior

The two research paths on the occurrence and perceptions of politics in organizations identify two distinctly different sets of contributors. For researchers interested in the frequency of actual political actions in organizations, the findings are consistent with what is typically called the strategic contingencies view of power (Hickson et al. 1971). In general, political behavior is more likely to occur when uncertainty is present, the situation is important to the organization, the issue is salient and important to the individuals involved (Madison et al. 1980), and conflicting interests exist such that individuals or groups are differentially affected by the situation (Pfeffer 1992).

Researchers frequently cluster the probable causes of perception of negative political behavior into three categories: (1) organizational-level factors, (2) job or work environment factors, and (3) personal-level contributors to the perception and, by implication, execution of negative political behavior. A large number of studies have been tests of a framework proposed by Ferris, Russ, and Fandt (1989), who first presented this tripartite classification scheme. The findings from this research suggest the following:

▲ At the organizational level, power concentrated at the top, lower levels of formalization, and higher levels in the hierarchy are correlated with stronger perceptions of political behavior (Ferris et al. 1996; Parker et al. 1995).

▲ Job and work environment conditions also contribute to the perception of negative political behavior. Restricted job autonomy, reduced career development opportunities, lower job variety, less job feedback, restricted advancement opportunity, a perception of unfair reward practices, lower levels of intergroup cooperation across units, and poor quality of interactions with coworkers and supervisors have contributed to stronger perceptions of political behavior (Ferris and Kacmar 1992; Ferris et al. 1996; Parker et al. 1995).

▲ Empirical support for when and how personal-level variables predict perceptions of political behavior has been uneven. Some studies have supported the idea that men see more political behavior in their organizations than women (Drory and Beaty 1991; Ferris et al. 1996), and that persons of minority status see political behavior more than nonminority status individuals (Parker et al. 1995), as do people who are younger (Ferris et al. 1996). However, the mixed support for these findings makes it difficult to draw any firm conclusions about how these attributes contribute to perceptions of political behavior.

Negative Political Behavior: The Process Gap

Although researchers have been diligent about identifying possible contributors to the occasion of and perception of negative political behavior, they have been silent about the interpersonal processes through which negative political behavior affects critical employee attitudes and important organizational processes. In this section, we discuss the influence of negative political behavior on trust as one of these crucial interpersonal processes and present a model of this relationship. We propose that the impact of negative political behavior on employees' trust in one another as well as in their organization exacts a heavy toll on organizational functioning.

Current research only mentions in passing that negative political behaviors destroy trust and damage interpersonal relationships (e.g., Ferris and Kacmar 1992; Madison et al. 1980; Vredenburgh and Maurer 1984). This is surprising considering that recent work on violations of trust investigates many behaviors that are also classified as negative political behaviors, such as promoting someone who does not meet the necessary criteria, stealing ideas or credit, and using confidential information to a person's own advantage (Bies and Tripp 1996). The overlap between negative political behaviors and violations of trust is significant because the research on violations of trust (e.g., Bies and Tripp 1996; Morrison and Robinson 1997; Robinson 1996) provides insight into the interpersonal processes through which negative political behavior influences important organizational processes. Figure 1-1 provides an overview of our model.

Negative Political Behavior and the Heavy Toll of Distrust

Trust is one party's willingness to rely on the actions of another in a situation involving the risk of the other's opportunistic behavior (Mayer, Davis, and Schoorman 1995; Zand 1972). Trust is violated when expectations that another party will act in trustworthy, nonopportunistic ways are not met.

When trust is violated, individuals experience anger, hurt, fear, and frustration, causing them to reassess their feelings about the violator (Lewicki and Bunker 1996). Violations of trust often increase individuals' perceptions that another party is untrustworthy and cause negative emotions that decrease their emotional bond to that party. Consequently, violations cause cognitive and emotional responses that may decrease individuals' trust in others.

Although all violations of trust may reduce trust, negative political behavior is particularly likely to do so because perceptions of negative political behavior are associated with attributions of self-serving motives. While some violations of trust may be attributed to extenuating circumstances and, therefore, not affect trust (Sitkin and Roth 1993), negative political behavior is attributed to agents' political motives. And this internal attribution for the cause of the violation should consistently result in targets' decreased trust in agents (Sitkin and Roth 1993).

Negative political behavior is also likely to influence targets' trust in

Figure 1-1. Negative political behavior and outcomes of trust.

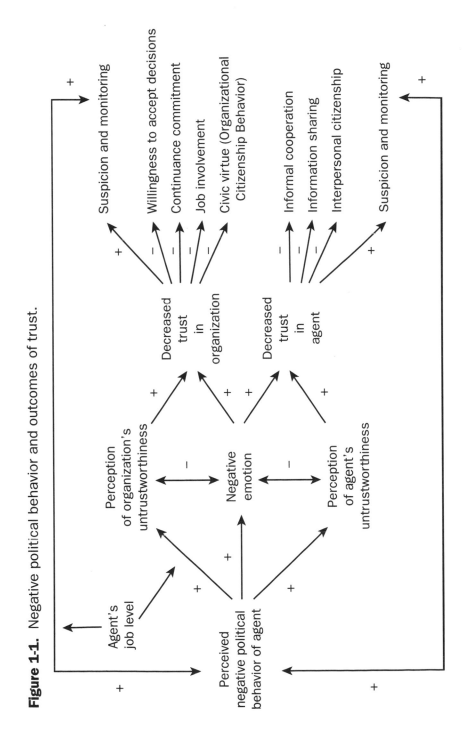

their organization (e.g., organizational trust). Organizational trust decreases when targets attribute some of the responsibility for the agent's actions to the organization (e.g., systemic responsibility attributions; Bies and Tripp 1996). Through rumination about an organizational incident, targets often come to believe that the individuals in authority are partially responsible for the incident because these individuals have encouraged or failed to curb the agent's untrustworthy behavior (Bies, Tripp, and Kramer 1996).

Although systemic responsibility attributions can result from the behavior of any organizational member, people in higher authority positions than the target more often elicit systemic attributions because targets regularly view individuals in these positions as organizational representatives. Thus, an agent's position in the organization may moderate the relationship between negative political behavior and perceptions of an organization's trustworthiness. When agents are more powerful than targets, it is more likely that perceptions of the agent's negative political behavior will decrease the target's trust in the organization.

The adverse effects of negative political behavior on both interpersonal and organizational trust are critical because of their links to organizationally relevant outcomes. Figure 1-1 depicts relevant outcomes that are negatively affected by decreased trust, such as job involvement (Robinson 1996), the willingness of employees to accept decisions (Tyler and Degoey 1996), information sharing (Currall and Judge 1995; Powell 1990; Ring and Van de Ven 1994), and interpersonal citizenship (McAllister 1995).

Furthermore, negative political behavior can create a vicious feedback loop between low trust and suspicion. In corrosive political environments, for example, negative political behavior decreases both interpersonal and organizational trust, which increases suspicion. Subsequently, suspicion makes the perception of self-serving, political motives more likely because it fosters the tendency to frame social situations negatively and to make overly personalistic attributions for the causes of events. Thus, negative political behavior can create a vicious cycle by decreasing trust, increasing suspicion, and increasing the likelihood that future behavior will be perceived as political.

In summary, we have asserted that negative political behavior affects organizational processes through trust. We proposed that through its effect on interpersonal trust and employees' trust in their organizations, negative political behavior affects organizational functioning, exacting a heavy toll on organizations' dynamic capabilities, collaborative potential, and employee loyalty. The following sections build on this foundation by describing an ambitious agenda for future research and by considering the practical issues of managing negative political behaviors.

Looking Toward the Future: A Research Agenda

Future research should consider two critical areas: (1) individuals' emotional responses to negative political behavior, and (2) cross-level effects of and influences on negative political behavior. We chose these two areas to challenge researchers to investigate the complicated ways in which negative political behavior affects individuals and organizations.

Individual Emotional Responses and Negative Political Behavior

In our model, we illustrate how microprocesses including emotion link negative political behavior to trust and thereby to organizational outcomes. This model provides a springboard for investigating the broader question, What are the emotional consequences of negative political behavior for individuals, their relationships, and the organization? Three additional questions must be addressed:

1. What situational, relational, and person-level factors affect individuals' emotional responses to political behavior?
2. What conditions cause negative political behavior to lead to different emotions such as anger versus fear or frustration?
3. Under what circumstances do negative emotions lead to constructive outcomes, such as people speaking out and engaging in relational work that allows them to resolve interpersonal problems and reconcile divergent perspectives?

Recent work on coercion provides a starting point for investigating the emotional experience of negative political behavior. This research investigates many behaviors that can also be classified as negative political behaviors. Negative political behaviors that intentionally impose harm or force compliance are, by definition, coercive acts (e.g., threatening, blaming, and denigrating others; Tedeschi and Felson 1994). Although all negative political behaviors are not coercive acts (i.e., some do not intentionally cause harm), coercive acts prompt attributions of blame and perceptions of injustice, which are associated with anger (Tedeschi and

Felson 1994). Thus, negative political behaviors should frequently trigger anger (although this anger may not be expressed toward the agent).

Expressed or not, anger is energizing, prompting action but disrupting and disorganizing cognitive processes, reducing attention to social skills and long-term consequences (Tedeschi and Felson 1994). Moreover, anger focuses targets' attention on the anger-inducing incident and their victim status. The potential negative organizational impact of anger is clear. Angry employees may be less able and willing to perform due to anger-induced cognitive deficits and distraction. This may be a particularly important consequence for knowledge workers whose work is highly contingent on cognitive capacity and engagement. In addition, anger can lead to self-defeating behavior; individuals may take unreasonable risks because they fail to consider the long-term consequences of their actions (Leith and Baumeister 1996). Furthermore, because anger reduces attention to social skills (Tedeschi and Felson 1994), target individuals who are angry may inadvertently damage their relationships with co-collaborators, thus affecting an organization's collaborative potential.

However, anger also has potentially positive effects. Expressed anger can focus attention on issues that concern the aggrieved individual and thereby serve the constructive function of prompting solutions to interpersonal problems (Tedeschi and Felson 1994). Unfortunately, the positive potential of anger within organizations may go largely unrealized. For instance, Felson (1984) found that anger was often not expressed toward other individuals in the work setting.

Hochschild (1983) also captured this phenomenon in her concept of "feeling rules," which she found generally inhibited employees from expressing negative emotions. Furthermore, these feeling rules may apply differentially to individuals based on their gender or power position within an organization (Pierce 1995). For example, Pierce (1995) found that litigation lawyers were expected to express negative emotions, whereas paralegals were not. Similarly, Tedeschi and Felson (1994) note that "in many cases the unjust person has superior status to the grievant and cannot be challenged without incurring unacceptable costs" (p. 237).

Thus, people often do not express anger in order to avoid damaging their relationship with the individual who has provoked them (Deshields, Jenkins, and Tait 1989). However, unexpressed anger may be costly; an individual's energy level may decrease, making it difficult for him or her to persist with other tasks (Baumeister et al. 1998). For instance, Baumeister et al. (1998) found that suppressing emotion led to a subsequent drop in performance. Thus, the anger induced by negative political behavior can prompt a wide range of responses that can significantly influence organizational functioning. And, the ability to express and use anger constructively may be constrained by contextual, relational, and personal factors, which need to be elaborated through future research.

Cross-Level Effects on Negative Political Behavior

The model we have presented in this chapter proposes how negative political behavior can affect individuals' trust in one another and in their employing organization. In addition to our model-specific hypotheses, we have selected several other important cross-level issues that warrant research attention. The critical research questions we pose in this section are as follows:

1. How does negative political behavior escalate?
2. When and how does it become a threat to the organization?
3. How do events external to the organization influence the political climate within the organization?

To address these questions, we explore the possibility of micro- and macrolinking mechanisms that affect perceptions of negative political behavior across levels of analysis. Microlinking mechanisms connect negative political behaviors that occur between individuals to groups, the organization, and interorganizational relationships. Three such mechanisms are social identity, ambient emotion, and social rumination. We also contend that there are macromechanisms at the organizational and extraorganizational levels of analysis that influence perceptions of negative political behavior at the interpersonal level, for example, adaptive cycles and meta-narratives. Taken together, these five cross-level mechanisms and their interrelationships represent a next crucial step in understanding the effects of political behavior.

Micro Cross-Level Influences on Negative Political Behavior

Negative political behaviors such as scapegoating and intimidation are often social episodes that have many witnesses (Harvey 1989; Jackall 1988). However, the processes through which an episode of negative political behavior between two individuals affects larger numbers of employees are rarely investigated. Social identification is one such process. Social identification refers to "the perception of oneness with or belongingness to some human aggregate" (Ashforth and Mael 1989, 22). Organizational members have multiple group memberships. They may strongly identify with groups based on demographic categories such as race, gender, or nationality; professional categories such as accountant or engineer; and organizationally specific groups such as a product development team, profit center, or the organization itself. When an agent threatens the identity of a member of a group through negative political behavior (Bies et al. 1996), the emotional and cognitive consequences may also affect other members who strongly identify with that group (Dutton, Dukerich, and Harquail 1994). Moreover, this threat may have different effects depending on the agent's power and whether he or she is also a group member. For instance, negative political behavior by a low-powered in-group member may be ignored, whereas negative political behavior by a high-powered in-group member may be seen as the ultimate betrayal of the in-group, causing anger, confusion, and disillusionment.

A second process with cross-levels effects is emotion. Emotions can permeate a social environment. For example, political behavior can lead to tension so palpable that employees "can cut it with a knife" or fear that causes everyone "to walk on egg shells." Often these feelings of tension and fear become disembodied. These emotions seem to be an ambient property of the workplace rather than feelings about or between specific individuals. Furthermore, different emotions may have significantly different effects when they permeate an organization. For example, contextualized fear may paralyze decision making (Pfeffer 1992), whereas contextualized anger may lead to organizationally motivated aggression (Andersson and Pearson, 1997). This phenomenon of ambient emotion leads us to ask, How do the negative emotions generated by political behavior become an integral part of employees' shared work experience?

A third cross-level process is social rumination. Negative political behavior often leads to social rumination, a process in which the target and observers try to make sense of the event by discussing it with coworkers and friends (Bies et al. 1996). Because social rumination often reinforces the initial suspicion, decreased trust, and outrage triggered by an episode (Bies and Tripp 1996), it may cause distrust to spread beyond targets, to observers and others who indirectly hear about episodes of negative political behavior.

In addition, social rumination creates suspicion, which may have other important effects across organizational levels. For instance, people view individuals within their own group as more trustworthy than those in other groups (Brewer 1979; Kramer, Brewer and Hanna 1996). Therefore, when individuals are suspicious of members within their own group, they are likely to become suspicious of individuals from other groups within and among organizations.

In sum, the potential for social identification, emotion, and social rumination to spread the effects of negative political behavior across levels of analysis has not received much attention. We propose that understanding how suspicion, negative emotion, and distrust spread is critical to understanding how and when organizations reach the "tipping point," the point when negative political behavior within an organization escalates into a corrosive political climate and threatens organizational functioning.

Macro Cross-Level Influences on Negative Political Behavior

Although researchers rarely investigate macrolevel influences on individuals' perceptions of negative political behavior, we believe that investigating how events external to organizations influence the political climate within organizations is a promising future research direction. We propose that adaptive cycles and meta-narratives are two factors that may influence perceptions of negative political behavior among individuals. *Adaptive cycles* refer to organization-level cycles that influence the ability of individuals within organizations to react constructively to political behavior. For instance, researchers might investigate whether different organizations have cycles of increased and decreased workload and time pressure that cause people to perceive political behavior differently. For example, during income tax time in a public accounting firm, potentially political behavior may be attributed to external unstable factors associated with time pressure rather than to self-serving motives. Thus, organizations may have their own narrative accounts that excuse certain types of behavior at certain times by attributing the blame to external forces.

Meta-narratives are stories about common or current events that are widely accepted as part of popular discourse and reflect a society's values and beliefs. For example, meta-narratives about U.S. business and global competition may explain why organizations need to downsize or why union workers should make wage concessions.

The effects of meta-narratives on employees' perceptions of what constitutes fair, appropriate, apolitical behavior have not been investigated. For example, changes in the dominant meta-narratives about gender, ethnicity, sexual orientation, and class may affect people's perceptions of political behavior and the accounts they use to explain their experience. Researchers might ask, How have the meta-narratives about the "glass ceiling," sexual harassment, or affirmative action influenced employees' interpretations of and perspectives on negative political behaviors? Likewise, researchers might look at the influence of cyclical trends in management meta-narratives (e.g., philosophies; Abrahamson 1996) on employees' perceptions of how they should be treated and what constitutes self-serving versus justified behavior.

Research Implications

Implementing the research agenda we have presented requires research methodologies that are not traditionally used by researchers investigating negative political behavior. In this section, we present research methodologies to complement our research agenda. Table 1-1 summarizes our proposed research questions and methodological suggestions.

The first item on our agenda focused on individual's emotional responses to negative political behavior. Research on stressful life events (Harvey, Orbuch, and Weber 1990), violations of trust (Bies and Tripp 1996), and anger-inducing incidents (Baumeister, Stillwell, and Wotman 1990) suggests that accounts or micro-narratives are a research methodology that will shed light on individuals' emotional experiences of negative political behavior.

Accounts are "story-like constructions that contain individuals' recollections of events, including plot, story line, affect, and attributions" (Orbuch 1997, 459). They allow researchers to examine how individuals experience events, provide a fuller understanding than standard surveys (Orbuch 1997), and have high external validity (Baumeister, Stillwell, and Wotman 1990). In addition, because accounts include both emotive information and attributions about a specific event, they are particularly well-suited to the study of negative political behavior that triggers emotion and depends on attributions of self-serving motives. Moreover, accounts can be used to answer a variety of research questions because once accounts are coded, they can be analyzed qualitatively (Harvey, Orbuch, and Weber 1990) or treated as quantifiable categories (e.g., Baumeister, Stillwell, and Wotman 1990).

The second part of our research agenda focused on three cross-level mechanisms: social identity, ambient emotion, and social rumination. In addition to the insights that accounts can provide, questions relating to how each of these mechanisms extends the effects of political behavior between individuals to groups, the organization, and interorganizational relationships can be better understood using network analysis. A modified version of a network survey would permit researchers to determine whom people speak with about political episodes, whom they go to when negative emotional events occur, and how networks of social rumination and negative emotion are influenced by social identification. Moreover, once researchers have described organizational networks, they are in a position to investigate who in the network is affected by various political episodes and how emotional responses to events vary with individuals' network positions (see Wasserman and Faust 1994 for detailed information on network methodology).

Of course, other methodologies such as interviews, standard surveys, and observations are feasible. For example, observation may be invaluable in understanding the process of social rumination in organizations. Likewise, standard surveys may allow estimation of individuals' salient group identifications.

The third part of our research agenda focused on macro cross-level effects. For investigating the effect of adaptive cycles on perceptions of political behavior, interviews could determine what cycles exist. Then surveys using vignettes could be used to determine whether employees perceive the same behaviors differently when they occur during different cycles.

For investigating the effect of meta-narratives on perceptions of political behavior, archival data could be used. Popular literature could be used to determine the dominant meta-narratives in different time periods, and data on negative behaviors such as those documented in grievances, lawsuits, and exit interviews could be used to determine changing perceptions of negative political behavior.

In sum, we propose that accounts, network analysis, vignettes, and archival data represent important methodologies for future research on negative political behavior.

Getting Practical: Dealing with Negative Political Behavior in Practice

We see three different areas where managers can make a meaningful difference in reducing the toll from corrosive political environments by both

Table 1-1. Directions for Future Research

Sample Questions	Research Methodologies	Methodologically Relevant Sample Studies
1. *Emotional response*	Accounts, interviews	*Accounts*
▲ What are the emotional consequences of negative political behavior for individuals, their relationships, and the organization?		Baumeister, Stillwell, and Wotman (1990); Bies and Tripp (1996); Harvey, Orbuch, and Weber (1990)
▲ What situational, relational, and person-level factors affect individuals' emotional responses to political behavior?		
▲ What conditions cause negative political behavior to lead to different emotions such as anger, rather than fear or frustration?		
▲ Under what circumstances do negative emotions lead to constructive outcomes?		
2. *Micro cross-level effects*	Network survey methodology, interviews, accounts	*Network analysis*
▲ How and when do the negative political behaviors that occur between individuals affect groups, the organization, and interorganizational relationships?		Burt and Knez (1996); Ibarra (1992); Krackhardt (1992); Wasserman and Faust (1994) for network methodology
a. *Social identity*	Network survey methodology, interviews, accounts; also standard surveys	
▲ How does social identification with the target or agent of political behavior affect the observers of political episodes?		

b. *Emotion*
  ▲ How do the negative emotions generated by political behavior become an integral part of employees' shared work experience?

  Network survey methodology, interviews, accounts

c. *Social rumination*
  ▲ How does social rumination (i.e., the collective narration of political episodes) influence the components of a corrosive political climate, for instance, suspicion and distrust?
  ▲ How does social rumination interact with social identification and emotion to create corrosive political climates?

  Network survey methodology, interviews, accounts; also observation

3. *Macro cross-level effects*
  ▲ How do events external to the organization influence the political climate within the organization?

  See below

a. *Adaptive cycles*
  ▲ How have the meta-narratives about the "glass ceiling," sexual harassment, or affirmative action influenced employees' interpretations of and perspectives on negative political behaviors?

  Interviews, survey methodo ogy (vignettes)

  Vignettes
  Heilman, Block, and Sta- thatos (1997)

b. *Meta-narratives*
  ▲ How and under what conditions do organization-level cycles of workload and time pressure influence individuals' reactions to potentially political behavior?

  Archival data

  Archival data/cycles
  Abrahamson (1996)

reducing the incidence of negative political behaviors in organizations and thinking proactively about how to equip people to deal more effectively with these types of behaviors:

1. *Building Awareness.* Although it is common knowledge in most organizations that political behaviors are exhibited, knowledge regarding the damage caused by negative political behavior is not commonly known nor discussed. Managers would benefit from building awareness of both the consequences of outbreaks of negative political behavior and the conditions that encourage these outbreaks.

Building awareness is important because managers often underestimate the impact of negative political behavior. In most cases, the effects of incidences of negative political behavior are felt most acutely at lower levels of the organization, where individuals have fewer opportunities and resources to combat such occurrences or deal with their aftereffects. Upper management may not be aware of the true consequences of such episodes. As Spitzer (1995) describes the awareness gap: "They (managers) underestimate the importance of what they consider to be 'minor irritations' in their organizations; they don't realize how large these irritations loom in the subjective experience of employees" (p. 57).

Creating an awareness of negative political behavior and its potential damage is difficult because people "see" incidents of negative political behavior differently. The research results on political perceptions showed that what one "sees" depends greatly on where one sits in the organization. As a result, managers must work hard to create common awareness and understanding of the negative fallout from negative political behavior. It is important to build awareness that acting quickly to deal directly with the causes of negative political behavior reduces the emotional and behavioral toll from these kinds of behavioral outbreaks.

2. *Allowing Expression.* This chapter has emphasized the emotional pain experienced by organizational members who are targets of negative political behavior. At a practice level, organizational practices and individuals' reactions to negative political behavior can amplify or depress the negative emotional toll by allowing for expression of the affect or feelings induced by these behaviors. Research on stress and burnout in organizations suggests the heavy toll paid by individuals who work in organizational contexts that treat these conditions as emotional states that need to be snuffed out or suppressed (Meyerson 1998). Instead, at a practical

level, organizations could work toward honoring the feelings of individuals who work in settings infected by negative political behaviors or who have to deal with work transations where emotions are traditionally suppressed. "Rather than developing procedures to produce phony smiles or prevent the showing of emotion, training programs might help employees to develop their individual response styles and to understand their ongoing social and task conditions" (Mumby and Putnam 1992, 478). This kind of reaction to negative political behavior may mean that organizations and the people within them will need to provide significant relational work (Fletcher 1994; Jacques 1996) or caregiving to restore and repair the damage caused by acts of negative political behavior (see also Meyerson 1998).

3. *Encouraging Action.* Organizations can behave in ways that prevent or respond to negative political behavior. We consider both. In both cases, we urge practitioners to reframe the role of managers in creating the conditions for negative political behaviors to flourish. Rather than thinking of managers as politicians, we would like to consider managers as architects of contexts that either encourage or discourage negative political behavior and, in so doing, damage or sustain corrosive political climates in organizations.

Preventative Actions

Three preventative zones stand out as possibilities for reducing the frequency or severity of negative political behavior in organizations. None are easy to execute and all take time and substantial effort to sustain. However, none of these preventative actions can alone alter what Frost (1987) calls the "deep structure games" of politics in organizations, which are often embedded in rules and other structures that transcend any particular organization. But, within a particular organization, there are actions that can alter the political system. First, politics in general, and negative political behavior in particular, are less likely when there is a clear correspondence between performance and rewards and when performance criteria are objective and measurable; there are simply fewer opportunities for individuals to seek rewards for actions other than good performance, and agreement about what is good performance or not is more easily achieved. Thus, a significant deterrent to negative political behavior is a careful and clearly designed performance evaluation and reward system.

Second, negative political behavior is less likely when norms encourage opposite behavior. For example, Covey (1993) argues that cultural practices sustained by clear, collective norms are critical to creating organizations with affirmative values. Where these values thrive, negative political behaviors are less likely to emerge or be tolerated if they do. He suggests making norms explicit. For example, members of an organization could declare that "we will not talk about each other behind each other's back" as a step toward moving away from a "swamp culture," where adversarialism, legalism, protectionism, and politics run rampant, toward an "oasis culture," where such behaviors are far less likely (Covey 1993). Of course, clear norms for behaviors that counteract negative political behavior only work if norm compliance is rewarded and norm deviance is punished. Thus, there must be clear and compelling consequences associated with the perpetrators of negative political behavior.

A third preventative measure focuses on designing lines of communication so that organizational members know that there are "safe" avenues to share information on negative political behavior and that perpetrators will suffer the consequences of their actions. In addition to encouraging the raising of potentially critical information, "opening up lines of communication helps to diminish the value of the network that politically-oriented middle managers rely on for their power base" (McGrath 1995, 53). Thus, there is a twofold value in carefully architecting lines of communication that encourage information sharing about negative political behavior.

Responsive Actions

Not all negative political behavior can be prevented. In fact, it is highly unlikely that the design of any system of rewards, norms, or communication lines can extinguish outbreaks of negative political behavior in organizations. Thus, managers would be well-advised to consider when and how to respond once such behaviors come forth. We suggest three strategies.

First, as we have already mentioned, it is important that incidences of negative political behavior be acknowledged and responded to with quick and decisive negative sanctions. Second, in addition to providing sanctions for agents, managers should also provide emotional support for targets. Expressions of care, sensitivity, and understanding may lessen employees' negative emotional response to perceived negative political behavior and mitigate the adverse effects of such behavior on employees' trust in their organization. Third, managers may offer understanding to agents. Offering the understanding that all employees are fallible may reduce agents' defensive behavior, allowing a more constructive dialogue between targets and agents, while increasing the likelihood that agents will apologize or work hard to repair the relationship. Managerial behaviors that facilitate apologies are important because apologies often reduce the adverse impact of negative actions (e.g., destructive criticism; Baron 1990).

Conclusion

Corrosive political climates and the negative political behaviors that create them are a pressing problem for organizations. While always an empirical fact, the toll paid by organizations for the damage caused by negative political behaviors has skyrocketed. We can only imagine that the cost will intensify with "mergers, restructuring and other reorganizations that create fertile ground for politics to grow and prosper" (McGrath 1995). Given this forecast, we see this chapter as an urgent call for meaningful research and informed practice that takes seriously what we currently know and are seeking to learn about the causes, consequences, and processes of negative political behavior in organizations. We believe that understanding the processes through which negative political behavior affects individuals, groups, and interorganizational relationships will enable organizations to prevent, contain, and mitigate the adverse effects of such behavior for individuals and organizations.

References

Abrahamson, E. 1996. "Management Fashion." *Academy of Management Review* 21, 254–85.

Andersson, L. M. and Pearson, C. M. 1997. "Tit-For-Tat: The Spiraling Effect on Incivility in the Workplace." Paper presented at the 57th Annual Meeting of the Academy of Management, Boston, August.

Ashforth, B. E. and Mael, F. 1989. "Social Identity Theory and the Organization." *Academy of Management Review* 14, 20–39.

Baron, R. A. 1990. "Countering the Effects of Destructive Criticism: The Relative Efficacy of Four Interventions." *Journal of Applied Psychology* 75(3), 235–45.

Baumeister, R. F., Bratslavsky, E., Muraven, M., and Tice, D. M. 1998. "Ego Depletion: Is the Active Self a Limited Resource?" *Journal of Personality and Social Psychology* 74(5), 1252–65.

Baumeister, R. F., Stillwell, A., and Wotman, S. R. 1990. "Victim and Perpetrator Accounts of Interpersonal Conflict: Autobiographical Narratives about Anger." *Journal of Personality and Social Psychology* 59(5), 994–1005.

Bies, R. J. and Tripp, T. M. 1996. "Beyond Trust: 'Getting Even' and the Need for Revenge." In R. M. Kramer and T. R. Tyler (eds.), *Trust in Organizations: Frontiers of Theory and Research.* London: Sage.

Bies, R. J., Tripp, T. M., and Kramer, R. M. 1996. "At the Breaking Point: Cognitive and Social Dynamics of Revenge in Organizations." In R. A. Giacalone and J. Greenberg (eds.), *Antisocial Behavior in Organizations.* Thousand Oaks, CA: Sage.

Brewer, M. B. 1979. "In-Group Bias in the Minimal Intergroup Situation: A Cognitive-Motivational Analysis." *Psychological Bulletin* 86, 302–24.

Brown, A. D. 1995. "Managing Understanding: Politics, Symbolism, Niche Marketing and the Quest for Legitimacy in IT Implementation." *Organization Studies* 16(6), 951–69.

Burt, R. S. and Knez, M. 1996. "Trust and Third-Party Gossip." In R. M. Kramer and T. R. Tyler (eds.), *Trust in Organizations: Frontiers of Theory and Research.* London: Sage.

Cobb, A. T. 1986. "Informal Influence in the Formal Organization." *Group and Organization Studies* 11, 229–53.

Covey, S. R. 1993. "Transforming a Swamp." *Training and Development* 47(May), 42–46.

Cropanzano, R., Howes, J. C., Grandey, A. A., and Toth, P. 1997. "The Relationship of Organizational Politics and Support to Work Behaviors, Attitudes, and Stress." *Journal of Organizational Behavior* 18, 159–80.

Currall, S. C. and Judge, T. A. 1995. "Measuring Trust between Organizational Boundary Role Persons." *Organizational Behavior and Human Decision Making* 64, 151–70.

Davenport, T. H., Eccles, R. G., and Prusak, L. 1992. "Information Politics." *Sloan Management Review* 34(1), 53–65.

Deshields, T. L., Jenkins, J. O., and Tait, R. C. 1989. "The Experience of Anger in Chronic Illness: A Preliminary Investigation." *International Journal of Psychiatry in Medicine* 19, 299–309.

Drory, A. and Beaty, D. 1991. "Gender Differences in the Perception of Organizational Politics." *Journal of Organizational Behavior* 12, 249–58.

Drory, A. and Romm, T. 1988. "Politics in Organization and Its Perception Within the Organization." *Organization Studies* 9(2), 165–79.

———. 1990. "The Definition of Organization Politics: A Review." *Human Relations* 43(1), 1133–54.

Dutton, J. E., Dukerich, J. M., and Harquail, C. V. 1994. "Organizational Images and Member Identification." *Administrative Science Quarterly* 39, 239–63.

Eisenhardt, K. M. and Bourgeois, L. J., III. 1988. "Politics of Strategic Decision Making in High-Velocity Environments: Toward a Midrange Theory." *Academy of Management Journal* 3(4), 737–70.

Felson, R. B. 1984. "Pattern of Aggressive Interaction." In A. Mummendey (ed.), *Social Psychology of Aggression: From Individual Behavior to Social Interaction.* Berlin: Springer-Verlag.

Ferris, G. R., Frink, D. D., Galang, M. C., Zhou, J., Kacmar, K. M., and Howard, J. L. 1996. "Perceptions of Organizational Politics: Prediction, Stress-Related Implications, and Outcomes." *Human Relations* 49(2), 233–66.

Ferris, G. R. and Kacmar, K. 1992. "Perceptions of Organizational Politics." *Journal of Management* 18(1), 93–116.

Ferris, G. R. and King, T. R. 1991. "Politics in Human Resource Decisions: A Walk on the Dark Side." *Organization Dynamics* 20(autumn), 59–71.

Ferris, G. R., Russ, G. S., and Fandt, P. M. 1989. "Politics in Organizations." In R. A. Giacalone and P. Rosenfeld (eds.), *Impression Management in the Organization.* Hillsdale, NJ: Lawrence Erlbaum.

Fletcher, J. K. 1994. "Toward a Theory of Relational Practice in Organizations: A Feminist Reconstruction of 'Real' Work." Ph.D. diss., Boston University.

Frost, P. J. 1987. "Power, Politics, and Influence." In F. M. Jablin, L. L. Putnam, K. H. Roberts, and L. W. Porter (eds.), *Handbook of Organizational Communications: An Interdisciplinary Perspective.* Newbury Park, CA: Sage.

Gambetta, D. 1988. "Can We Trust?" In D. Gambetta (ed.), *Trust: Making and Breaking of Cooperative Relations.* New York: Basil Blackwell.

Gandz, J. and Murray, V. V. 1980. "The Experience of Workplace Politics." *Academy of Management Journal* 23(2), 237–51.

Harvey, J. B. 1989. "Some Thoughts about Organizational Backstabbing." *Academy of Management Executive* 3(4), 271–77.

Harvey, J. H., Orbuch, T. L., and Weber, A. L. 1990. "A Social Psychological Model of Account-Making in Response to Severe Stress." *Journal of Language and Social Psychology* 9(3), 191–207.

Heilman, M. E., Block, C. J., and Stathatos, P. 1997. "The Affirmative Action Stigma of Incompetence: Effects of Performance Information Ambiguity." *Academy of Management Journal* 40, 603–25.

Hickson, D. J., Hinings, C. R., Lee, C. A., Schneck, R. E., and Pennings, J. M. 1971. "A Strategic Contingencies Theory of Intraorganizational Power." *Administrative Science Quarterly* 11, 216–29.

Hochschild, A. R. 1983. *The Managed Heart.* Berkeley: University of California Press.

Ibarra, H. 1992. "Homophily and Differential Returns: Sex Differences in Network Structure and Access in an Advertising Firm." *Administrative Science Quarterly* 37, 422–47.

Jackall, R. 1988. *Moral Mazes.* Oxford: Oxford University Press.

Jacques, R. 1996. *Manufacturing the Employee: Management Knowledge from the 19th to the 21st Century.* Thousand Oaks, CA: Sage.

Kiechel, W., III. 1988. "The Politics of Innovation." *Fortune* 117(8), 131–32.

Krackhardt, D. 1992. "The Strength of Strong Ties: The Importance of Philos in Organizations." In N. Nohria and R. G. Eccles (eds.), *Networks and Organization: Structure, Form, and Action.* Boston: Harvard Business School Press.

Kramer, R. M., Brewer, M. B., and Hanna, B. A. 1996. "Collective Trust and Collective Action: The Decision to Trust as a Social Decision." In R. M. Kramer and T. R. Tyler (eds.), *Trust in Organizations: Frontiers of Theory and Research.* London: Sage.

Leith, K. P. and Baumeister, R. F. 1996. "Why Do Bad Moods Increase Self-Defeating Behavior? Emotion, Risk Taking, and Self-Regulation." *Journal of Personality and Social Psychology* 71(6). 1250–67.

Lewicki, R. J. and Bunker, B. B. 1996. "Developing and Maintaining Trust in Working Relationships." In R. M. Kramer and T. R. Tyler (eds.), *Trust in Organizations: Frontiers of Theory and Research.* London: Sage.

Lorenz, E. H. 1988. "Neither Friends nor Strangers: Informal Networks of Subcontracting in French Industry." In D. Gambetta (ed.), *Trust: Making and Breaking of Cooperative Relations.* New York: Basil Blackwell.

Macauley, S. 1963. "Non-Contractual Relations in Business: A Preliminary Study." *American Sociology Review* 28, 55–67.

Madison, D. L., Allen, R. W., Porter, L. W., Renwick, P. A., and Mayes, B. T. 1980. "Organizational Politics: An Exploration of Managers' Perceptions." *Human Relations* 33(2), 79–100.

Mayer, R. C., Davis, J. H., and Schoorman, F. D. 1995. "An Integrative Model of Organizational Trust." *Academy of Management Review* 20, 709–34.

McAllister, D. J. 1995. "Affect- and Cognition-Based Trust as Foundations for Interpersonal Cooperation in Organizations." *Academy of Management Journal* 38, 24–59.

McGrath, N. 1995. "Scheming Workers Can Ruin Business." *Asian Business* 31(September), 50–54.

Meyerson, D. 1998. "Feeling Stressed and Burned Out: A Feminist Reading and Revisioning of Stress-Based Emotions Within Medicine and Organization Science." *Organization Science.* 9(1), 103–118.

Mintzberg, H. 1983. *Power in and Around Organizations.* Englewood Cliffs, NJ: Prentice Hall.

———. 1991. "The Effective Organization: Forces and Forms." *Sloan Management Review* 32(2), 54–67.

Morrison, E. W. and Robinson, S. L. 1997. "When Employees Feel Betrayed: A Model of How Psychological Contract Violation Develops." *Academy of Management Review* 22(1), 226–56.

Mumby, D. K. and Putnam, L. L. 1992. "The Politics of Emotion: A Feminist Reading of Bounded Emotionality." *Academy of Management Review* 17, 465–86.

Orbuch, T. L. 1997. "People's Accounts Count: The Sociology of Accounts." *Annual Review of Psychology* 23, 455–78.

Parker, C. P., Dipboye, R. L., and Jackson, S. L. 1995. "Perception of Organizational Politics: An Investigation of Antecedents and Consequences." *Journal of Management* 21(5), 891–912.

Pfeffer, J. 1981. *Power in Organizations.* Marshfield, MA: Pitman.

———. 1992. *Managing With Power: Politics and Influence in Organizations.* Boston: Harvard Business School Press.

Pfeffer, J. and Salancik, G. R. 1974. "Organizational Decision Making as a Political Process: The Case of University Budgeting." *Administrative Science Quarterly* 19, 135–51.

Pierce, J. L. 1995. *Gender Trials.* Berkeley: University of California Press.

Powell, W. W. 1990. "Neither Market nor Hierarchy: Network Forms of Organization." In B. M. Staw and L. L. Cummings (eds.), *Research in Organization Behavior.* Vol. 12. Greenwich, CT: JAI.

Powell, W. W. and Smith-Doerr, L. 1994. "Networks and Economic Life." In N. J. Smelser and R. Swedberg (eds.), *The Handbook of Economic Sociology.* Princeton, NJ: Princeton University Press.

Ring, P. S. and Van de Ven, A. H. 1994. "Developmental Processes of Cooperative Interorganizational Relationships." *Academy of Management Review* 19, 90–118.

Robinson, S. L. 1996. "Trust and Breach of the Psychological Contract." *Administrative Science Quarterly* 41, 574–99.

Sitkin, S. B. and Roth, N. L. 1993. "Explaining the Limited Effectiveness of Legalistic 'Remedies' for Trust/Distrust." *Organization Science* 4, 367–81.

Spitzer, D. R. 1995. "The Seven Deadly Demotivators." *American Management Association* 84(November), 56–60.

Stroh, L. K. and Reilly, A. H. 1997. "Loyalty in the Age of Downsizing." *Sloan Management Review* 38(4), 83–88.

Tedeschi, J. L. and Felson, R. B. 1994. *Violence, Aggression, and Coercive Actions.* Washington, DC: American Psychological Association.

Teece, D. J., Pisano, G., and Shuen, A. 1997. "Dynamic Capabilities and Strategic Management." *Strategic Management Journal* 18(7), 509–33.

Tyler, T. R. and Degoey, P. 1996. "Trust in Organizational Authorities: The Influence of Motive Attributions on Willingness to Accept Decisions." In R. M. Kramer and T. R. Tyler (eds.), *Trust in Organizations: Frontiers of Theory and Research.* London: Sage.

Vredenburg, D. J. and Maurer, J. G. 1984. "A Process Framework of Organizational Politics." *Human Relations* 37(1), 47–66.

Wasserman, S. and Faust, K. 1994. *Social Network Analysis: Methods and Application.* New York: Cambridge University Press.

Williamson, O. E. 1975. *Markets and Hierarchies: Analysis and Antitrust Implications.* New York: Free Press.

Zajac, E. J. and Olsen, C. P. 1993. "Form Transaction Cost to Transactional Value Analysis: Implications for the Study of Interorganizational Strategies." *Journal of Management Studies* 30, 132–45.

Zand, D. E. 1972. "Trust and Managerial Problem Solving." *Administrative Science Quarterly* 17, 229–39.

Chapter 2

Serving Two (or More) Masters: The Challenge and Promise of Multiple Accountabilities

AIMEE ARLINGTON *and* WAYNE E. BAKER

The problems associated with multiple accountabilities are some of the most frequently cited issues in modern organizations. Those who have multiple reporting relationships express many personal frustrations, such as conflict arising from confusing reporting relationships or having to please multiple bosses with divergent agendas. Multiple accountabilities also create pressing problems for the organization. Organizational-level consequences of conflicting accountabilities include decreased organizational commitment, lower job satisfaction, and increased absenteeism and turnover (e.g., Fisher and Gitelson 1983; Jackson and Schuler 1985; Netemeyer, Burton, and Johnston 1995).

The practice of serving two (or more) masters is a pressing problem in organizations today for two reasons. First, organizational trends indicate a substantial increase in the use and practice of multiple accountabilities, driven by such organizational changes as downsizing, the use of teams, and the emergence of new organizational forms (e.g., the "network" design). More people are engaged in multiple reporting relationships than ever before. This trend implies a concurrent increase in the

*This research was supported in part by the University of Michigan Business School. The authors are grateful to the editors of this book for their helpful and insightful comments on earlier drafts.

personal and organizational problems that result from multiple account-abilities. Our interviews of practitioners, consultants, and researchers who deal with multiple accountabilities in organizations demonstrate the prevalence of the problem.

Second, little has been written about effective strategies for managing multiple accountabilities. As we describe subsequently, researchers and practitioners have always been interested in the concept of multiple accountabilities, but their research has focused on negative consequences, such as role ambiguity and role conflict. Multiple accountabilities are considered illegitimate because the practice violates two traditional principles of organization design: unity of command and span of control. The usual recommendation is to eliminate this deviant practice and reinstate single reporting relationships. Little attention has been given to alternative organizational and management paradigms that would be more informative, realistic, and useful in the 1990s and beyond. A change in perspective is needed, one that sees the promise of multiple accountabilities, while it helps individuals and organizations meet the challenge of serving multiple masters.

Evidence of a Problem

To document the issues associated with multiple accountabilities, we interviewed three groups of individuals: practitioners, consultants, and researchers. Their responses indicate numerous and occasionally intense frustrations associated with this practice. Consider the following three typical cases.

Case 1

A common case involves an employee who feels caught between the conflicting expectations of two bosses. A consultant described a situation involving a person who works for an international pharmaceutical company. This person had only a single reporting relationship for years. When he was placed on a regional product team, he suddenly reported directly to two bosses—one a functional boss who resides in his home office, the other a product team leader who resides in an office abroad. Participation on the product team required that the employee travel quite frequently to New York, where the product team meetings were held. Shortly after joining the team, however, he began receiving negative feedback from his functional boss. This boss was displeased with the amount of time the employee was spending out of town at product meetings. To compensate for his functional boss's concerns, the employee began to lessen his participation on the product team. Not unexpectedly, the product team leader was disappointed in the employee's lack of participation and demanded more attention. This individual's experience is a prime example of *role conflict,* when the expectations of one role (his position in the home office) conflict with the expectations of another role (his position on the product team). Role conflict caused stress for the employee, lowered his morale, and affected his productivity. Much of his time was spent trying to resolve the conflict caused by serving two bosses. Indeed, he was so dissatisfied that he contemplated leaving the organization.

This case describes one of the most common organizational structures causing multiple accountabilities: a matrix organization. This organizational type is organized along two formal dimensions, function and product, giving a person two formally assigned superiors (a functional boss and a product team boss). Power struggles and role conflicts are some of the major problems documented in studies of matrix organizations (e.g., Davis and Lawrence 1978). In theory, each dimension—function and product—should have equal power. However, managers in matrix organizations often struggle with each other, attempting to assert the dominance of the functional or product sides of the organization. This breaks down the matrix structure, frustrates and confuses employees caught in the middle of the struggle, and diverts the attention of organizational members to handling internal strife and politics.

Case 2

We interviewed several secretaries as practitioners who routinely report to multiple bosses. A secretary in a management consulting firm shared her frustrations. At any given time, she is formally assigned to five people: one national partner, a local partner, and three senior managers. In addition, on an informal basis, she handles the requests of any number of staff members who may be in the office and/or working for one of her formal bosses. Several factors complicate the task of managing her multiple accountabilities. First, her accountabilities include individuals at differing levels in the organization. Consequently, she must adapt to requests that differ along many dimensions (e.g., priority, the status of individuals, the amount of work required, the level of explanation given). Second, her many bosses often travel to different client sites. Thus, she must interact with and manage each of these accountabilities from a distance. Third, there is a relatively high level of turnover in the business. This means that she must continually adjust to a new set of accountabilities; as she is reassigned to a different set of managers, she must adapt to the expectations and work style of each new boss.

The secretary described a self-reinforcing cycle of frustration and unmet expectations resulting from unrealistic expectations held by her bosses. Multiple managers assign work to her without fully understanding the other demands of her workload. Likewise, she rarely is given advance notice of upcoming projects and cannot predict future workloads. Therefore, unrealistic deadlines are often established, against which she is ultimately evaluated. Her bosses are disappointed when she is unable to produce the work within the expected time frame. Consequently, when the secretary is unable to meet her bosses' expectations because of circumstances out of her control, she receives negative evaluations, which, of course, she feels is unfair. These problems are compounded when the secretary produces poor-quality work in order to meet the deadlines. Revisions to a poor-quality work product require additional time, which only exacerbates the time pressures and increases her stress.

Case 3

An associate attorney described frustrations resulting from the multiple accountabilities attorneys typically face. As an associate in a large law firm, this person reports to many partners and external clients (as many as twenty attorneys and forty clients). No champions or sponsors are assigned formally; no one feels responsible for the associate's professional development. The associate has watched his career development suffer due to the lack of timely and constructive feedback. In addition, he felt that the law firm suffered by not developing its employees. Many mistakes could be avoided and workmanship enhanced, he felt, if attorneys were not left to "figure it out" on their own.

Another attorney described similar negative consequences experienced by his law firm due to the tension between internal and external accountabilities. In addition, he described the difficulties an associate attorney experiences as he or she attempts to build his or her own client base. Generating new business ("rainmaking") is expected of associates as they grow and develop. But they must balance these efforts against the demands of senior attorneys, who have little tolerance for time spent on clients other than their own. Consequently, the associate attorney faces the dilemma of trying to meet both the expectations of the senior attorney and the overall expectation of building new business. Usually, it is the senior attorney's expectations that are met. Eventually associate attorneys are promoted to the level of partner, but with little experience in generating new business.

Summary of Case Studies

These three cases briefly illustrate some of the troubles suffered by individuals engaged in multiple accountabilities. Organizations also suffer when employees deal with confusion and frustration resulting from conflicting expectations and uncertainty in their jobs. For example, Jackson and Schuler (1985) examined almost one hundred studies conducted between 1967 and 1982 and concluded that both uncertainty about job expectations and conflicting job expectations were negatively correlated with job satisfaction, organizational commitment, job involvement, and, to some extent, performance. As employees become dissatisfied with their jobs, they are less motivated to work harder because they no longer expect that their efforts will result in recognized outcomes. Uncertainty and conflicting expectations are positively correlated with absenteeism and a propensity to leave. Absenteeism raises costs and lowers productivity. When the propensity to leave becomes actual turnover, the organization must bear the added cost of recruiting, hiring, and training new employees.

Historical Presence of Multiple Accountabilities

To understand the broad context of multiple accountabilities, we first must understand the genesis of multiple reporting structures. To accomplish this task, we examine briefly the history of organizational forms. Many researchers have chronicled the evolution of organizational forms, identifying three or four basic models of organization (e.g., Davis, Dieckman, and Tinsley 1994; Fligstein 1990). These histories trace the introduction of multiple accountabilities at least to the 1950s; the historical accounts also depict an increasing number of accountabilities with each new model generated. Mercer (1981) divides the evolution of organizational form into first-, second-, and third-generation structures. First-generation organizational structures resemble a pyramid and operate as a top-down unity-of-command hierarchy. Multiple accountabilities were formalized in second-generation organizational structures more than forty years ago. In response to the complex and time-pressured projects of the aerospace and defense industries, second-generation organizations overlaid a horizontal project-management structure on the traditional vertical hierarchies of first-generation organizations. Employees assigned to project teams had two bosses. The dual reporting relationship was solidified in the third-generation organizational structure, which Mercer (1981) terms a "mature matrix," a permanent project-management structure in which the project manager has at least two bosses.

Similar to Mercer's (1981) account of the evolution of organizations, Miles et al. (1997) trace the development of the matrix organization to the middle of the twentieth century, with popular adoption of the structure in the late 1960s and early 1970s. They attribute changes in organizational structures to the development and demands of new economic eras. Although their account trails slightly behind that of Mercer (1981), Miles et al. (1997) indicate that multiple accountabilities have been in widespread use for thirty years. They trace popular adoption of mixed or matrix structures to the late 1960s, in response to the demands of the Age of Customization. The project structure allowed companies to serve diverse markets, with both standardized and customized products and services. The new form created project groups, composed of members from the different functional divisions. Project members had a dual reporting relationship with a project and a functional leader.

Like Miles et al. (1997), Knight (1976) saw an influx of matrix organizations in the 1960s. He cites many reasons for their introduction, based on his review of the literature on matrix organizations. First, he cites historical reasons similar to those of Mercer (1981). At the time, the U.S. government required that firms vying for research and development contracts use a "project management system." Second, he cites task requirements as reasons for the introduction of matrix organizations. Similar to Miles et al. (1997), he points to increasingly complex environments (internal environments in terms of size and technology and external environments in terms of markets, competitors, and collaboration with other organizations) as the impetus for the development of matrix organizations. Third, he suggests that matrix organizations were introduced for motivational and ideological reasons. He also cites research suggesting that organic forms such as matrix organizations are more suitable for complex rapidly changing environments than mechanistic forms. Thus, according to Knight (1976), multiple accountabilities have been present in the form of matrix organizations for almost forty years.

Not only does organizational theory provide evidence of the historical presence of multiple accountabilities, it also indicates a trend in an increasing number of multiple accountabilities. Miles et al. (1997) demonstrate that the number of relationships in which an employee is accountable continued to expand with the evolution of yet another organizational structure in the late 1970s through the 1980s, the network organization. In response to the demands of the Age of Full (Efficient) Customization, the network organization expands an employee's accountabilities outside the boundaries of the organization to include relationships with other organizations along the value chain (see also Baker 1994). Miles and Snow (1986) describe a new organizational form with not only multiple accountabilities, but a set of accountabilities that is constantly changing with the assembling, disassembling, and reassembling of a *dynamic network*. In the dynamic network, firms are *vertically disaggregated;* that is, functions that used to be performed inside a single organization are now divided among separate organizations. In this situation, people must learn to function in a dynamic network of accountabilities and relationships that extends outside the organization's boundaries (Miles and Snow 1986).

Unlike a bureaucracy in which the organization is a defined set of relationships that handles all problems, the network organization is a dynamic set of relationships that adapts to the needs of unique problems. Within the broad confines set by corporate strategy, employees autonomously create the necessary relationships between people and resources (Baker 1992). These characteristics led Eccles and Crane (1988) to call network organizations "self-designing." Network structures expand the number of accountabilities far beyond the two formal accountabilities (function and product) created by the matrix structure. For example, some network structures are clusters of "knowledge workers" coordinated through cross-functional teams (Nohria 1991). Baker (1994) cites General Electric as a role model of a company that has become the "ultimate network organization," which CEO Jack Welch calls the "boundaryless organization." Baker (1994) describes the "network" or "boundaryless" organization as a seamless network of relationships. The walls that separate people inside the company are torn down; departments and functions are replaced with multidisciplinary project-based teams that form, disband, and reform again in a continual process of change and renewal. The walls between "domestic" and "foreign" are knocked down, producing a genuinely global company. And the barriers separating inside and outside are broken, bonding the organization and its suppliers, customers, investors, and communities in common purpose. (p. 9)

This boundaryless organization implies multiple, dynamic accountabilities for the employee navigating the informal charts of the organization.

Finally, Miles et al. (1997) predict another stage in the evolution of economies: the Age of Innovation. The Age of Innovation is a time in which continuous and efficient innovation is critical for success. Customers demand more than customization. Competitive pressures push companies to use their growing know-how from network alliances to mass produce innovation. The authors speculate that this new age is spawning a new organizational form for the twenty-first century: the cellular organization. In an era of continuous innovation, the cellular organization will be able to adapt and generate innovations according to the changes in the marketplace. Of the structures we have discussed, the organic structure may be the most demanding on the employee. The informal and constantly adapting nature of the structure requires that an employee manage more accountabilities and dynamic networks than ever before.

Research on Multiple Accountabilities

Our review of prior research reveals an overemphasis on the negative consequences of multiple accountabilities, as well as a gap in research on effective strategies for dealing with them. In reviews of the matrix and project management literatures, Knight (1976) and Ford and Randolph (1992) cited examples of organizational approaches to making matrix organizations operate effectively, but neither review found evidence of empirical studies identifying effective strategies for managing the multiple accountabilities created by such structures. Two recent studies, however, have begun testing strategies for managerial effectiveness in dealing with role conflict resulting from the incompatible expectations of multiple accountabilities (Tsui and Ashford 1994; Tsui et al. 1995).

Role Theory

Many of the studies analyzing the negative consequences of multiple accountabilities have been derived from role theory. Role theory dates from the 1930s, when *role* was first used as a technical term. Anthropologist Ralph Linton's (1936) classic work has shaped much of the research on roles conducted in the field to date. He distinguishes between status (or position) and role (Biddle and Thomas 1979):

> A *status,* as distinct from the individual who may occupy it, is simply a collection of rights and duties. . . . A *role* represents the dynamic aspect of a status. The individual is socially assigned to a status and occupies it with relation to other statuses. When he puts the rights and duties which constitute the status into effect, he is performing a role. . . . Every individual has a series of roles deriving from the various patterns in which he participates and at the same time a role, general, which represents the sum total of these roles and determines what he does for his society and what he can expect from it. (Linton 1936, 113–14)

Linton's (1936) work made an important link between an individual's behavior (as role performance) and social structure. Merton (1957) extended Linton's work by distinguishing between *role sets* and *status sets* (for recent work and refinements of role theory, see, e.g., Platt and Gordon 1994; Winship and Mandel 1983). Linton (1936) assumed that each status had a distinct role. Merton (1957) explains that, in fact, each status comprises many associated roles. The term he developed to characterize this structure is *role set,* defined as "that complement of role relationships which persons have by virtue of occupying a particular social status" (p. 369). Merton uses as an example the status of a public school teacher, whose role set includes his or her relation to his or her pupils, colleagues, the school principal and superintendent, the Board of Education, Parent-Teachers Associations, and so on. This concept is different from the established term *multiple roles,* used in sociology to mean the roles associated with numerous statuses (e.g., teacher, wife, mother, Catholic, Republican). Merton (1957) termed this array of statuses as the *status set.* The distinction he made between role sets and multiple roles is key to the work that has been done on the conflict caused by differing expectations of role partners in the role set, now known as *role conflict.*

Role Conflict

Prior to the late 1950s and early 1960s, the term *role conflict* had been used to mean many different things (Gross, McEachern, and Mason 1958). Gross, McEachern, and Mason (1958) limited their definition of the term to include the incompatible expectations that were the result of an individual's occupancy of either single or multiple positions (intra- and interrole conflict). Kahn et al. (1964) refined the definition of role conflict to mean the simultaneous occurrence of two (or more) incongruous sets of expectations. They further refined it by identifying several ways in which role conflict is created:

1. Role conflict results from conflicting expectations sent by others *(sent role conflict).*
2. The role requirements of the position are incompatible with the expectations of the role incumbent *(person-role conflict).*
3. Multiple role senders expect a role incumbent to accomplish several tasks, all of which are mutually compatible in the abstract, but impossible to complete in the time given *(role overload).*

Role Ambiguity

Role ambiguity is the degree to which information is lacking with respect to expectations, methods, and consequences for fulfilling the role (Kahn et al. 1964). One could experience role ambiguity in one or all of the following forms: "a) information is unclear regarding which potential role expectation—A, B, or C—should be performed; b) it is understood that expectation A should be met, but information is unclear regarding what behavior will in fact yield A; c) the consequences of behavior A are unclear" (Van Sell, Brief, and Schuler 1981, 11). The problems associated with multiple accountabilities can result from such role ambiguity, role conflict, or both. For our purposes, we use the term *role strain* to include both role ambiguity and role conflict.

Link between Organizational Structure and Role Strain

Implicit in role theory is the assumption that organizational structure (e.g., work group size, formal reporting relationships, number of bosses, number of subordinates) is a means by which role expectations are conveyed. Several studies have been conducted that examine the causal relationship between elements of organizational structure and role strain. One such study explored the simultaneous impact of distinct structural elements, such as work group size, span of subordination, supervisory span, functional dependence, participation in decision making, and formalization (Morris, Steers, and Koch 1979). The study concluded that, among other organizational structure elements, an employee's span of subordination (the number of supervisors to whom a subordinate reports) is a significant predictor of both role conflict and ambiguity.

Joyce (1986) specifically investigated the effects of implementing a matrix structure on role perceptions, concluding that the matrix structure increased the level of role ambiguity but did not significantly affect the level of role conflict. One explanation for this insignificant effect on role conflict is the complexity of the construct itself (Joyce 1986). There are four types of role conflict that may not all be affected by the implementation of a matrix structure. Specifically, person-role conflict and role overload should not have been affected in this situation. The introduction of a matrix structure should not create additional conflict between the behavioral standards of the person and the role (person-role conflict). In addition, role overload was purposely avoided by introducing the change at a time when project activity was slow to allow resources to concentrate on the structural changes (Joyce 1986).

During the 1980s, several studies were conducted to assimilate what had been learned about role ambiguity and role conflict (Fisher and Gitelson 1983; Jackson and Schuler 1985; Van Sell, Brief, and Schuler 1981). All three studies recognized organizational structure elements as antecedents to role conflict and role ambiguity. Recognition of this link is important because it implies a connection between multiple accountabilities (determined by organizational structure) and role strain. Van Sell, Brief, and Schuler (1981) determined that role ambiguity and role conflict are partially the result of a complex interaction of job content, leader behavior, and organizational structure. Fisher and Gitelson (1983) also identified elements of organizational structure as antecedents to role conflict and role ambiguity—boundary spanning for both ambiguity and conflict and participation in decision making for conflict. Jackson and Schuler (1985) studied four categories of variables, one of which was organizational context variables such as autonomy, feedback from others, leader consideration, formalization, organizational level, and participation in decision making. Consistent with the results found by Van Sell, Brief, and Schuler (1981), Jackson and Schuler (1985) found a high average correlation between many of the organizational context variables and both ambiguity and conflict.

Implications for the Organization

The previously discussed studies identified negative consequences for the organization resulting from role conflict and role ambiguity. Van Sell, Brief, and Schuler (1981) concluded that consequences of role ambiguity and conflict include lower productivity, tension, dissatisfaction, and psychological withdrawal from the work group. Fisher and Gitelson (1983) also identified decreased job involvement and increased dissatisfaction to be consequences of both role ambiguity and role conflict. Furthermore, they identified a negative relationship between both types of role strain and organizational commitment. Similarly, Jackson and Schuler (1985) found a negative relationship among the role stressors and job satisfaction, organizational commitment, and job involvement, as well as a weak relationship with performance. In addition, they discovered a positive relationship with absenteeism and a propensity to leave. In a recent study, Netemeyer, Burton, and Johnston (1995) aimed to clarify the causal relationships between role conflict and role ambiguity and their consequences. They concluded that role conflict directly affected tension, job satisfaction, and intention to leave, and indirectly affected organizational commitment and turnover. Role ambiguity had a direct effect on job satisfaction, organizational commitment, and turnover.

The negative consequences for the organization are clear. As role strain decreases job satisfaction, employees also feel less committed to their jobs. Employees are less motivated to work harder, because they are uncertain that their efforts will lead to recognized outcomes. As a result, productivity and performance suffer. If dissatisfaction and stress are at extremes, the employee's health may be negatively affected, resulting in absenteeism or a choice to leave the organization for a better situation. In this case, the organization is faced with the costs of recruiting, training, and developing a new employee.

The Old Paradigm

Multiple accountabilities have been constituent parts of organizational structures for decades. Research studies on the (negative) consequences of role strain have all concluded with a call for research on coping mechanisms (Fisher and Gitelson 1983; Jackson and Schuler 1985; Van Sell, Brief, and Schuler 1981), but this call has gone unheeded. Why is there a lack of research on effective strategies for managing multiple constituencies and a preoccupation with respect to the negative consequences of them? Indeed, why do workers and managers today continue to express frustrations in having to deal with multiple accountabilities? Why do they view them as deviations from the norm and as illegitimate practices?

We contend that the answer lies in an outdated management paradigm. Real organizational structures have been evolving over the twentieth century, but classic management principles have remained intact. Principles have not evolved along with organizational practices and designs. As we describe subsequently, both managers and managerial theorists still operate under the influence of the old principles of unity of command and span of control. The *unity of command principle* sets the expectation that the ideal managerial arrangement is a single reporting relationship in which a subordinate is responsible to one boss and one boss alone. This superior exerts exclusive control over the subordinate. The *span of control principle* is based on the assumption that there is a natural limit to the number of subordinates a superior can manage and supervise properly. Both principles are based on the core belief that authority is delegated downward; supervisors rule with command and control techniques, and each supervisor rules his or her own domain.

The principles of unity of command and span of control were used widely in military models of command for warfare. General Dwight D. Eisenhower is said to have limited his span of control to only three when serving as supreme commander of the Allied forces (Haimann and Scott 1970). These classic principles were applied in the scientific management movement in an attempt to develop effective administration (Fayol 1949; Taylor 1911). Indeed, these concepts have been in use as methods of managing large numbers of people at least since biblical times, as described in Exodus, where Moses is given counsel by his father-in-law:

> For this thing is too heavy for thee. Thou art not able to perform it thyself alone. . . . I will give thee counsel. . . . Thou shalt provide out of the people able men and place such over them, to be rulers of thousands, and rulers of fifties, and rulers of tens. And let them judge the people at all seasons; and it shall be that every great matter they shall bring unto thee, but every small matter they shall judge; so shall it be easier for thyself and they shall bear the burden with thee . . . (18:17–23)

Unity of Command

Vigorous and enthusiastic endorsements for the principle of unity of command can be found easily in both old and new management texts. Haimann and Scott (1970), for example, indicate that "[t]he main reason for the high regard in which the unity of command principle is held is that it is one of the major avenues for achieving coordination. . . . People are not confused by having two bosses" (p. 196). Unity of command, they argue, eliminates the possibility that contradictory orders will be issued because a subordinate is accountable only to the superior from whom he or she receives orders. Serving two masters, they say, causes confusion over which boss has seniority and which tasks take priority: "Ever since biblical times people have observed that it is difficult to serve two masters" (p. 196).

Throughout their description of the unity of command principle, Haimann and Scott (1970) use language such as "masters," "orders," "authority," and "violation." Their use of language captures the autocratic style of management based on classic management principles. For example, they describe organizational arrangements that create multiple accountabilities, such as functional authority, with strong negative language, such as "a violation of unity of command" (Haimann and Scott 1970, 232). In addition, the organizational diagram used to illustrate the problem of multiple accountabilities is drawn so that it accentuates a sense of confusion and chaos (Haimann and Scott 1970). The same organizational arrangements could have been depicted in a much less confusing manner.

Management texts such as those by Haimann and Scott (1970) indoctrinate the principle of unity of command in the minds of managers, students of management, and researchers as a cornerstone of good management practice. Since the late 1970s, many have perpetuated the principle with praise and recommendation. Sherman (1979, 438), for example, includes both unity of command and span of control in his list of basic principles of "organizing for strength." An organization should "emphasize unity of command," he claims, because overlapping authority is the number one cause of "organization shipwreck."

Sherman (1979, 438) also suggests that organizations should "watch span of control." That is, a member of management should have no more than seven people reporting to him or her. Many authors have supported the principle of unity of command by suggesting the application of military analogies for human resources management (Bettinger 1989; Cohen 1986; McCabe 1981). McCabe (1981) argues that the principle of unity of command is one of the primary methods for achieving cooperation and common goals. Both Cohen (1986) and Bettinger (1989) apply the use of unity of command to principles of marketing warfare. And, Finkelstein and D'Aveni (1994) extol the virtues of unity of command as an important concept in modern administrative theory.

Recent management textbooks, such as *Organizational Behavior* by Northcraft and Neale (1990), provide evidence that the principle of unity of command is alive and well today. Such textbooks preserve the classic principles and continue to teach the concepts both implicitly and explicitly. The righteous language praising the principle is no longer used (as in Haimann and Scott 1970), but we find the classic principle implicitly present in two sections of Northcraft and Neale's (1990) book. First, in the authors' treatment of the concept of span of control, they assume the principle of unity of command (see, e.g., the diagrams depicting span of control on p. 679 of their book). Second, in their discussion of organic structures, the authors describe the matrix as "the most complex and formal form of organic structure" (p. 682). However, in discussing the pros and cons of the matrix structure, the authors refer to a study by Duncan (1979) that cites as a weakness the "dual authority of the matrix manager and functional area manager" (Northcraft and Neale 1990, 684).

The old management principles are also embedded in the organizational charting programs of popular software packages. (Such programs can be viewed as "cultural artifacts" that reveal institutionalized assumptions, beliefs, and values.) For example, the standard organizational charting function in Microsoft's Powerpoint (version 7.0) is based on the classic management principles. The charting function does allow comanagers, but it is based primarily on the concepts of unity of command and span of control. None of the "hot buttons" included on the toolbar allows the creation of comanagers. The application of comanagers is not intuitively obvious. In addition to the obstacles in creating multiple accountabilities, it is quite difficult to create lateral relationships that span across levels. Instead, the program is designed for a scalar chain of command in which authority flows directly from one level to the next.

Span of Control

Span of control—the number of subordinates a superior can properly manage—is thought to be fixed by natural limits on human cognition and information-processing abilities. According to Sir Ian Hamilton (1921):

> The average human brain finds its effective scope in handling from three to six other brains. If a man divides the whole of his work into two branches and delegates his responsibility, freely and properly, to two experienced heads of branches he will not have enough to do. The occasions when they would have to refer to him would be too few to keep him fully occupied. If he delegates to three heads he will be kept fairly busy, whilst six heads of branches will give most bosses a ten-hour day . . . As to whether the groups are three, four, five, or six it is useful to bear in mind a by-law; the smaller the responsibility of the group member, the larger may be the number of the group— and vice versa . . . The nearer we approach the supreme head of the whole organization, the more we ought to work towards groups of three; the closer we get to the foot of the whole organization, the more we work towards groups of six. (Sir Ian Hamilton 1921, p. 229, quoted in Graicunas 1937)

Haimann and Scott (1970) fully endorse the concept of span of control, devoting an entire chapter to the principle in their book *Management in the Modern Organization.* The authors use references to Moses and General Dwight D. Eisenhower to create a moral imperative for the use of the "ageless concept" span of management. They note that the term *span of management* is synonymous with "span of control," "span of responsibility," and "span of supervision" (p. 242). The authors suggest that span of management is the reason for departmentalization and delegation of authority. If one individual could effectively manage one hundred reports, for example, there would be no need for departments. Limits on a manager's span of management dictate the number of executives required to run an organization and, ultimately, the size of the organization itself. Indeed, span of control is considered to be so fixed and immutable that it is possible to derive a precise mathematical model that calculates the optimal size of an organization and the required number of hierarchical levels (e.g., Graicunas 1937).

The "optimal" span of control persists as a research preoccupation. Based on a complicated mathematical model, Keren and Levhari (1979) determined that (1) the span of control increases from the top of the organization to the bottom, and (2) that when the cost of time is primary to wage costs, such as in the military, the spans are more constant. Chonko (1982) determined that a widened span of control increased both role conflict and role ambiguity for a group of sales representatives. Michlitsch and Gipson (1984) argue that a manager's span of control depends on his or her capacity to supervise. (A manager's capacity is directly related to a list of factors developed by the authors.) They conclude that the solution to many common management problems is to increase a manager's capacity, not reduce his or her span of control. Tarng and Chen (1988) confirmed the results of Keren and Levhari's (1979) study. They found that the optimal spans of control increase as one goes down the levels of the hierarchy. Katzner (1992) investigated the impact span of control can have on the level of profit realized by a company. And Gifford (1992) used economic theory to argue that a person's limited attention span limits a manager's span of control. Neuman (1978) argues, however, that advances in communications technology allow managers to increase their supervisory span of control from six (commonly believed to be the natural limit) to as many as sixteen.

Northcraft and Neale (1990) include span of control as one of four basic elements of organizational structure: job specialization, departmentalization, centralization, and span of control. Their prescriptions for good management in the 1990s rely on research conducted years ago. To teach modern organizational theory in 1990, they rely on studies from the 1970s; to describe the factors used to determine the proper span of control, the authors first refer to research conducted by Mintzberg (1979). Moreover, Northcraft and Neale (1990) rely on work done by Blau and

Schoenherr (1971) to conclude that a manager's span of control can be larger in organizations with routine technology. Given the great deal of organizational evolution toward lateral relationships and multiple accountabilities that took place in the 1970s and 1980s, organizational theory is still viewed through the lens of an outdated paradigm.

Ideas for Future Research

Despite shifts in organizational structure, people are still tied to the theoretical principles of unity of command and span of control. New managers are particularly susceptible to the old paradigm and often adopt a counterproductive autocratic style (Hill 1992). Greater congruence between principles and experience would improve both efficiency and effectiveness (Davis 1974). Bartlett and Ghoshal (1990, 140) call for a need to change "organizational psychology" ("the broad corporate beliefs and norms that shape managers' perceptions and actions") to precede a change in "organizational anatomy" (organizational elements such as communication and decision processes). They contend that companies successful in implementing a multidimensional organization have focused on organizational psychology and physiology before making the formal structural changes. Their observation underscores the importance of aligning managerial principles and organizational structure; one cannot be successful without the other. What is needed, we argue, is a radical shift in management paradigms.

Shifting Paradigms

First and foremost, there is an opportunity to resolve a clash between theory and practice. We identified the long-standing practice of organizational structures that create multiple accountabilities, and a recent trend toward an increasing number of accountabilities as organizations implement more fluid, complex, and dynamic structures, such as the network design (Baker 1992; Baker 1994, 115–22). Multiple accountabilities are viewed as problems, we argue, because managers and organizations are trapped by the outdated principles of unity of command and span of control. Thus, we begin by identifying alternative management principles that are more realistic and more positive, given the evolution of organizational structures and practices. After introducing these alternative principles, we then propose several specific research directions and methods.

Unity of Command → Multiplicity of Leadership

The first shift in principles takes us from unity of command to multiplicity of leadership. There are three important distinctions. First, a subordinate has multiple bosses, not a single boss. Each subordinate reports directly to two or more superiors, as well as indirectly to other superiors. Under unity of command, the organizational chart resembled a neat pyramid with clearly defined vertical relationships. With multiplicity of leadership, it may be difficult even to draw an organizational chart, because formal relationships are numerous and dynamic, depending on the needs of the business. Second, in addition to multiple bosses, employees are responsible for managing sideways, that is, building and managing multiple lateral relationships. These lateral relationships can include managing ties with customers, suppliers, and competitors as well as developing relationships with peers throughout the internal organization (Baker 1994). Third, with the creation of so many lateral relationships, a new philosophy of management is necessary—leadership. Replacing the term *command* with *leadership* denotes the elimination of an autocratic style of management that relied on formal authority. Instead, *leadership* signifies the need to utilize skills such as inspiration, persuasion, and creativity so that those who do not have direct authority can still positively influence employees. This aspect of the new management principle also emphasizes the fact that the subordinate needs to take some responsibility for managing the relationship. Baker (1994, 10) describes the main difference between the two old and new management philosophies as their ability to deal with what he terms the "dilemma of indirect management." Leadership and empowerment are more appropriate for managing multiple accountabilities than the old methods of command and control.

Span of Control → Span of Coordination

The second new principle is a shift from span of control to span of coordination. Building on the premise that there is a natural limit on the number of people one can manage, the old principle of span of control is based on three key assumptions. First, that the primary relationships in organizations are unidirectional and top-down. Second, that leadership is governed by the principles of command and control. And third, that at the organizational level, span of control dictates the size of the organization. The new principle differs in each of these three assumptions.

First, rather than thinking in terms of unidirectional top-down relationships, span of coordination incorporates omnidirectional relationships, including but not limited to vertical top-down relationships. "It's more productive," Baker (1994) says, "to think of span of coordination than span of control. The only way you can get your job done is to put much more emphasis on empowering others, much less on formal top-down authority and intrusive micromanagement" (p. 6). Coordination usually involves an exchange of ideas and a negotiation of terms in a formal or informal agreement. Coordination encourages integration across organizational boundaries. And integration is not restricted to internal boundaries; coordination takes place with external suppliers and customers as well.

Second, empowerment and leadership are more appropriate and effective management techniques than command and control. The new principle emphasizes initiating, building, and developing relationships as a method of motivating as opposed to giving orders. Third, the new principle eliminates the notion that optimal organizational size is dictated by some arithmetic formula. Span of coordination is flexible, allowing the size and shape of the organization to be driven by the external environment, strategy, and forces inside the organization (Baker 1992). Generally, organizations based on the new principles can be smaller ("leaner") than organizations based on the old ones. The Pooled Financial Services organization of General Electric Canada is a good example (Applegate and Cash 1989). This unit successfully transformed itself from a traditional hierarchy into a lean organization composed of self-managing teams, replacing old management principles with new ones in the process. The company was able to eliminate two complete organizational levels and 40 percent of its employees and yet increase productivity and quality.

Research Directions

1. *Developing practical strategies for applying the new management principles.* The new management principles and labels are a first step toward changing beliefs and behaviors concerning multiple accountabilities. Of course, it is easier to propose new management principles than to

put these into practice to solve problems of multiple accountabilities. For example, simply telling the people in the three cases we presented (see "Evidence of a Problem") that their multiple accountabilities should be viewed as normal and desirable practices would not help them or reduce their suffering. They (and their bosses) need effective strategies for operating with multiple accountabilities. However, organizational researchers have only just begun to explore this area (e.g., Tsui and Ashford 1994; Tsui et al. 1995). Therefore, an obvious research direction is to build on these pioneering studies. This would include investigating through in-depth interviews and ethnographic field studies the best practices for managing and handling multiple accountabilities. A wide range of practices should be considered, including informal strategies, formal programs, and training and education. The sampling frame should be broad enough to encompass a range of practices, including organizations of different size and form (functional, multidivisional, matrix, and network). It is possible, for example, that effective strategies for managing multiple accountabilities vary by organizational form.

2. *Measuring multiple accountabilities.* The opportunity to incorporate network theory, measures, and methods (Wasserman and Faust 1994) into research on multiple accountabilities is great. The "relationship" rather than the "individual" is the unit of analysis in network research, making this a natural method for measuring and understanding multiple accountabilities. Prior research on multiple accountabilities has focused on formal reporting relationships. Informal accountabilities, however, also exist, such as "dotted line" reporting relationships and those that are never openly acknowledged. Network methods allow for the measurement of the entire spectrum of formal and informal accountabilities, providing a fuller understanding of the extent of multiple accountabilities in an organization. For example: What is the mix of formal and informal accountabilities? Which type causes the most problems? Do multiple accountabilities, formal and informal, vary by organizational unit and level? Network methods would also permit the analysis of "third-order effects"—the effects of indirect accountabilities. Consider, for example, a person whose bosses also have multiple bosses versus another person whose bosses do not. Does the first person experience more problems than the second, due to the indirect effect of the bosses' accountabilities?

Network surveys that capture the whole network (everyone in the organization) would reveal the full extent of multiple accountabilities but are feasible only in an organization or organizational unit of less than about 150 people. For larger organizations, egocentric network measures, such as those used in Burt's (1992) social capital survey, are appropriate. It is also possible to combine egocentric network measures with large-scale surveys, using as a guide the topical module on Social Networks in the General Social Survey.

3. *Investigating the link between management principles and organizational structure.* There are many studies on the link between organizational structure and such variables as strategy, environment, and internal forces (e.g., Chandler 1962; Drucker 1995), but few studies on the connection between organizational structure and management principles (for an exception, see Gannon and Paine 1974). By examining the link between management principles and organizational structure, however, researchers can identify, diagnose, and perhaps remedy problems caused by the practice of multiple accountabilities.

The relationship between principles and structures can be described with a simple two-by-two typology that arrays the old and new management paradigms along the vertical axis, and traditional and modern (e.g., hierarchy and network) organizational structures along the horizontal axis (see Figure 2-1). The four cells represent matches and mismatches of principles and structures. Matches occur along the main diagonal (cells I and IV). The upper-left cell represents organizations operating with old principles and traditional structures whereas the lower-right cell represents organizations operating with new principles and new structures. Organizations in the minor diagonal (cells II and III) experience mismatches between principles and structures. The upper-right cell represents organizations trying to operate with old principles in new forms whereas the lower-left cell represents organizations trying to work with new principles in old forms.

This typology suggests three specific research questions. First, What is the numerical distribution of organizations across the four cells? This question is more than a mere accounting problem. The answer would document the extent of the problem of multiple accountabilities. The problem should be rare in cells I and IV, but for quite different reasons: In traditional organizations practicing classic management principles (cell I), multiple accountabilities seldom occur (Gannon and Paine 1974), and in network organizations practicing new management principles (cell IV), the numerous existing multiple accountabilities are accepted, understood,

Figure 2-1. A typology of management principles and organizational structure.

		Organizational structure	
		Traditional (hierarchy)	*Modern* (network)
Management Principles	*Old Principles* (span of control, unity of command)	**I** (match)	**II** (mismatch)
	New Principles (span of coordination, multiplicity of leadership)	**III** (mismatch)	**IV** (match)

and encouraged as good management practice (Baker 1992). This reasoning suggests that the problem of multiple accountabilities should occur primarily in cells II and III. However, the size (and, hence, the magnitude) of the problem is unknown.

Second, Does a match of management principles and organizational structure yield higher performance than a mismatch? Organizations that fall along the main diagonal experience "fit" or "congruence" between principles and structures, whereas those that fall along the minor diagonal do not. Generally, congruence leads to higher performance at both the individual and organizational levels (Nadler and Tushman 1977). Is this true for a match of management principles and organizational structures? This line of research would yield prescriptions for practice.

Third, What is the most successful path of organizational change? The history of organizational structures (reviewed previously) reveals a trend from hierarchical forms to network organizations, that is, from cell I to cell IV in the typology. Most network organizations are not created de novo (Baker 1992), but instead result from the transformation of old into new organizational forms (such as GE Canada). Transforming an

organization is difficult and risky; many try but few succeed (Beer, Eisenstat, and Spector 1990). The typology suggests three possible paths: (1)
from cell I directly to cell IV (changing principles and structures simultaneously), (2) from cell I to cell IV via cell II (changing structures first,
principles second), and (3) from cell I to cell IV via cell III (changing
principles first, structures second). Beer, Eisenstat, and Spector (1990)
argue that organizational change is more likely to be successful if structures are changed last (although the overwhelming temptation is to
change structures first). If so, then path 3 should be the best choice.
(However, this should be treated as a hypothesis to be tested.)

Answering these three specific questions calls for survey research of a
large number of organizations. Both the qualitative research used to discover effective strategies for managing multiple accountabilities and the
development of network measures of multiple accountabilities would help
determine valid measures for such a survey. The typology (Figure 2-1)
provides an appropriate sampling frame. This research would be a major
undertaking, especially if primary data had to be collected. It is possible,
however, that secondary data sources could be used (prior surveys of organizations).

Conclusion

Serving multiple masters is a time-honored practice that violates classic
principles of management. Judged by the principles of unity of command
and span of control, the practice of multiple accountabilities is a pressing
problem for individuals and organizations. Through interviews of practitioners, consultants, and researchers, we provided qualitative evidence
of the troubles experienced by those who have multiple accountabilities.
We then verified these problems by reviewing the research literature,
which emphasizes the negative consequences of multiple accountabilities
caused by role strain, role conflict, and role ambiguity. Old and new
management texts agree that the best prescription is to reduce or eliminate
the practice of multiple accountabilities, aligning organizational practices
with the classic management principles.

However, we disagree. Using the classic management principles of
unity of command and span of control to guide and judge organizational
practices today is a prescription for continued problems and even organizational disaster. Relying on old principles denies the reality of today's

organizations, where downsizing, teams, and new organizational forms create more and more multiple accountabilities. Of course, there are some cases in which the old principles still apply, as we described in our typology of principles and structures. Generally, however, the classic principles are increasingly out of place. Indeed, the old principles aggravate and contribute to the problems associated with multiple accountabilities because they label the practice as illegitimate and improper. The problems caused by mismatches of management principles and organization structures will continue to grow until practitioners, consultants, and researchers change perspective and develop effective strategies for handling multiple accountabilities.

This chapter supports and reinforces the basic premise of this book: the need for better alignment of theory and practice. The usual prescription is to align practice with theory, making current organizational practices conform to accepted theory. For multiple accountabilities, we recommend the reverse: aligning theory with practice. Theory should address multiple accountabilities as legitimate, desirable, and effective practices. Organizational forms have evolved in a way that makes multiple accountabilities the rule, not the exception, and the practice of serving multiple masters is now a critical component of optimal organizational design. Multiple accountabilities provide levels of coordination, integration, and communication that were not possible in the old organizational forms. Without multiple accountabilities, today's lean, fast, and flexible organizations could not function.

References

Applegate, L. M. and Cash, J. I. 1989. "GE Canada: Designing a New Organization." Harvard Business School Teaching Case #9-189-138. Boston: Harvard Business School Press.

Baker, W. E. 1992. "The Network Organization in Theory and Practice." In N. Nohria and R. G. Eccles (eds.), *Networks and Organizations: Structure, Form, and Action*. Boston: Harvard Business School Press.

———. 1994. *Networking Smart*. New York: McGraw-Hill.

Bartlett, C. A. and Ghoshal, S. 1990. "Matrix Management: Not a Structure, a Frame of Mind." *Harvard Business Review* 68(4), 138–45.

Beer, M., Eisenstat, R. A., and Spector, B. 1990. *The Critical Path to Corporate Renewal*. Boston: Harvard Business School Press.

Bettinger, C. 1989. "The Nine Principles of War." *Bank Marketing* 21(December), 32–34.

Biddle, B. J. and Thomas, E. J., eds. 1979. *Role Theory: Concepts and Research.* Huntington, NY: Robert E. Krieger Publishing.

Blau, P. M. and Schoenherr, R. A. 1971. *The Structure of Organizations.* New York: Basic Books.

Burt, R. 1992. *Structural Holes.* Cambridge, MA: Harvard University Press.

Chandler, A. D. 1962. *Strategy and Structure: Chapters in the History of the American Industrial Enterprise.* Cambridge, MA: MIT Press.

Chonko, L. B. 1982. "The Relationship of Span of Control to Sales Representatives' Experienced Role Conflict and Role Ambiguity." *Academy of Management Journal* 25, 452–56.

Cohen, W. A. 1986. "War in the Marketplace." *Business Horizons* 29(March–April), 10–20.

Davis, G. F., Dieckman, K., and Tinsley, C. 1994. "The Deinstitutionalization of the Conglomerate Firm." *American Sociological Review* 59, 547–70.

Davis, S. M. 1974. "Two Models of Organization: Unity of Command versus Balance of Power." *Sloan Management Review* 61(1), 29–40.

Davis, S. M. and Lawrence, P. R. 1978. "Problems of Matrix Organizations." *Harvard Business Review* 56(3), 131–42.

Drucker, P. F. 1995. *Managing in a Time of Great Change.* New York: St. Martin's Press, Inc.

Duncan, R. 1979. "What Is the Right Organizational Structure? Decision Tree Analysis Provides the Answer." *Organizational Dynamics* (winter), 59–80.

Eccles, R. G. and Crane, D. B. 1988. *Doing Deals: Investment Banks at Work.* Boston: Harvard Business School Press.

Fayol, H. 1949. *General and Industrial Management.* Translated from the original *Administration Industrielle et Generale* (1916) by C. Storrs. London: Pitman.

Finkelstein, S. and D'Aveni, R. A. 1994. "CEO Duality as a Double-Edged Sword: How Boards of Directors Balance Entrenchment and Unity of Command." *Academy of Management Journal* 37(5), 1079–1108.

Fisher, C. D. and Gitelson, R. 1983. "A Meta-Analysis of the Correlates of Role Conflict and Ambiguity." *Journal of Applied Psychology* 68, 320–33.

Fligstein, N. 1990. *The Transformation of Corporate Control.* Cambridge, MA: Harvard University Press.

Ford, R. C. and Randolph, W. A. 1992. "Cross-Functional Structures: A Review and Integration of Matrix Organization and Project Management." *Journal of Management* 18, 267–94.

Gannon, M. J. and Paine, F. T. 1974. "Unity of Command and Job Attitudes of Managers in a Bureaucratic Organization." *Journal of Applied Psychology* 59, 392–94.

Gifford, S. 1992. "Allocation of Entrepreneurial Attention." *Journal of Economic Behavior & Organization* 19(3), 265–84.

Graicunas, V. A. 1937. "Relationship in Organization." In L. Gulick and L. Urwick (eds.), *Papers on the Science of Administration.* New York: Institute of Public Administration.

Gross, N., McEachern, A. W., and Mason, W. S. 1958. "Role Conflict and Its Resolution." In J. B. Biddle and E. J. Thomas (eds.), *Role Theory: Concepts and Research.* Huntington, NY: Robert E. Krieger Publishing.

Haimann, T. and Scott, W. G. 1970. *Management in the Modern Organization.* Boston: Houghton Mifflin.

Hill, L. A. 1992. *Becoming a Manager.* Boston: Harvard Business School Press.

Jackson, S. E. and Schuler, R. S. 1985. "A Meta-Analysis and Conceptual Critique of Research on Role Ambiguity and Role Conflict in Work Settings." *Organizational Behavior and Human Decision Processes* 36, 16–78.

Joyce, W. F. 1986. "Matrix Organization: A Social Experiment." *Academy of Management Journal* 29, 536–61.

Kahn, R. L., Wolfe, D. M., Quinn, R. P., Snoek, J. D., and Rosenthal, R. A. 1964. *Organizational Stress: Studies in Role Conflict and Ambiguity.* New York: Wiley.

Katzner, D. W. 1992. "The Structure of Authority in the Firm." *Journal of Economic Behavior & Organization* 19(1), 41–67.

Keren, M. and Levhari, D. 1979. "The Optimum Span of Control in a Pure Hierarchy." *Management Science* 25(November), 1162–73.

Knight, K. 1976. "Matrix Organization: A Review." *Journal of Management Studies* 13(2), 111–30.

Linton, R. 1936. *The Study of Man.* New York: Appleton-Century.

McCabe, D. M. 1981. "Strategy and Tactics: Military Analogies for Human Resources Managers." *Personnel Journal* 60(December), 958–63.

Mercer, J. L. 1981. "Organizing for the '80s—What About Matrix Management?" *Business* 31(July–August), 25–33.

Merton, R. 1957. *Social Theory and Social Structure.* Glencoe, IL: Free Press.

Michlitsch, J. F. and Gipson, D. L. 1984. "Managing the Span of Control." *Supervisory Management* 29(6), 13–18.

Miles, R. E. and Snow, C. C. 1986. "Organizations: New Concepts for New Forms." *California Management Review* 28, 62–73.

Miles, R. E., Snow, C. C., Mathews, J. A., and Miles, G. 1997. "Managing in the Knowledge Age: Building the Cellular Organization." Working paper, Berkeley, CA: Haas School of Business, University of California.

Mintzberg, H. 1979. *The Structuring of Organizations.* Englewood Cliffs, NJ: Prentice Hall.

Morris, J. H., Steers, R. M., and Koch, J. L. 1979. "Influence of Organization Structure on Role Conflict and Ambiguity for Three Occupational Groupings." *Academy of Management Journal* 22, 58–71.

Nadler, D. A. and Tushman, M. L. 1977. "A General Diagnostic Model for

Organizational Behavior: Applying a Congruence Perspective." In J. R. Hackman, E. E. Lawler, and L. W. Porter (eds.), *Perspectives on Behavior in Organizations.* New York: McGraw-Hill.

Netemeyer, R. G., Burton, S., and Johnston, M. W. 1995. "A Nested Comparison of Four Models of the Consequences of Role Perception Variables." *Organizational Behavior and Human Decision Processes* 61, 77–93.

Neuman, P. 1978. "What Speed of Communication Is Doing to Span of Control." *Administrative Management* 39, 30–31, 46.

Nohria, N. 1991. "Note on Organization Structure." Harvard Business School teaching case #9-491-083. Boston: Harvard Business School Press.

Northcraft, G. B. and Neale, M. A. 1990. *Organizational Behavior: A Management Challenge.* Chicago: Dryden Press.

Platt, G. M. and Gordon, C., eds. 1994. *Self, Collective Behavior and Society: Essays Honoring the Contributions of Ralph Turner.* Greenwich, CT: JAI.

Sherman, C. 1979. "Organizing for Strength." *Personnel Journal* 58(July), 437–38.

Tarng, M. Y. and Chen, M. S. 1988. "Note on the Optimum Span of Control in a Pure Hierarchy." *European Journal of Operational Research* 33, 106–113.

Taylor, F. W. 1911. *The Principles of Scientific Management.* New York: Harper.

Tsui, A. S. and Ashford, S. J. 1994. "Adaptive Self-Regulation: A Process View of Managerial Effectiveness." *Journal of Management* 20, 93–121.

Tsui, A. S., Ashford, S. J., St. Clair, L., and Xin, K. R. 1995. "Dealing With Discrepant Expectations: Response Strategies and Managerial Effectiveness." *Academy of Management Journal* 38, 1515–43.

Van Sell, M., Brief, A. P., and Schuler, R. S. 1981. "Role Conflict and Role Ambiguity: Integration of the Literature and Directions for Future Research." *Human Relations* 34, 43–71.

Wasserman, S. and Faust, K. 1994. *Social Network Analysis.* Cambridge, MA: Harvard University Press.

Winship, C. and Mandel, M. 1983. "Roles and Positions: A Critique and Extension of the Blockmodeling Approach." In S. Leinhardt (ed.), *Sociological Methodology, 1983–1984.* San Francisco: Jossey-Bass.

Chapter 3

Running on Empty: Overworked People in Demanding Work Environments

Julia A. Welch, Rachel K. Ebert, *and* Gretchen M. Spreitzer

I n contemporary organizations, overwork is often viewed as a key problem inherent in today's demanding working environment. People at all organizational and socioeconomic levels note the growing expectation to routinely work evenings and weekends and the resulting conflict between personal and work life. A variety of factors have contributed to this growing tendency toward overwork that results in an imbalance between personal and work life. Increasing globalization requires employees to interact with colleagues around the world and, consequently, around the clock to connect across time zones. The plethora of corporate downsizings has resulted in fewer employees to accomplish the same amount of work. The increasing demand for employees to work more hours is exacerbated by the growing number of dual-career families and working mothers who have less time to manage household responsibilities.

Consequently, people are feeling more overworked than ever before, even to the point of burnout. In one study reported by *The Wall Street Journal,* half the employees surveyed reported having much more to do on the job than three years previously (Shellenbarger 1997b). Another study revealed that as much as one-fourth of the labor force is at risk of burnout (Shellenbarger 1997a). Recently, in a highly publicized case, a senior executive at Pepsi resigned because she suffered burnout from the intense time and travel demands required by her job and felt guilty that she could not spend more time with her young family (Shellenbarger 1997c). As conflicts between employees' personal and professional lives intensify and as the workforce becomes ever more fatigued, the public discourse surrounding overwork continues to grow.

The topic of overwork is of significant interest to practitioners and scholars alike. Practitioners realize that although the demand for more work from employees is not likely to diminish in the near future, the trend toward more working hours comes at a considerable cost. Longer workdays lead to stress and strain (Galambos and Walters 1992), which, in turn, can lead to higher accident levels, greater absenteeism, and reduced productivity (Ganster and Schaubroeck 1991). Stress-related workers compensation claims increased threefold during the early 1980s alone (Karasek and Theorell 1990). Organizations are also finding that some of their best people, fearing burnout, are choosing to give up their corporate career for jobs with more flexibility and fewer demands on their time (Fassel 1990). With the growing recognition of the costs of overwork, research on this topic is of utmost importance to organizations.

Similarly, the topic of overwork is also of interest to academics. Previous research has been less than clear on the appropriate conceptualization of the construct of overwork. A variety of interpretations have been applied to this construct, creating confusion about its meaning. Moreover, much of the research on overwork has been conducted on lower-level employees in manufacturing settings. As a result, the focus has been on dependent variables such as productivity, accident rates, job satisfaction, and turnover. We have less of an understanding of the nature of overwork for more professional employees and those working in service settings. Interesting dependent variables in these settings include customer satisfaction, responsiveness to change, and organizational commitment. Thus, the notion of overwork has the potential to expand the understanding of both research and practice.

Although the notions of work-family conflict, burnout, and loss of personal life balance are related to overwork, they have their own separate research streams and are thus beyond the scope of this chapter. Instead, we limit our focus to the specific issue of overwork, examining this phenomenon from both practical and theoretical perspectives. First, we review the current academic and popular literature on the issue of overwork. We then identify fruitful areas for research on the nature of overwork and levers that might reduce the negative consequences of overwork from a series of informal interviews with employees about the issue of overwork. And we offer ideas on a series of studies that, if executed, might advance our understanding of overwork.

Literature Review

Conceptualization of Overwork

The term *overwork* is more commonly used in the popular press than in the academic literature, although a few researchers refer to overwork specifically (Glass and Estes 1997; Schor 1992; Yogev 1982). Instead, the term *overload* is preferred by organizational scholars to describe the concept of excessive demands. Specifically, overload, or overwork, occurs when people do not have the resources (e.g., time, support staff) necessary to complete all that is required of them (Kahn and Quinn 1970; Katz and Kahn 1978).

Much confusion has surrounded overload since its conceptualization by Kahn. First, researchers have confused the concepts of role overload and interrole conflict so much over the last several decades that entire articles, and even dissertations, have been devoted to clarifying these constructs (Coverman 1989; Forti 1994). Although there is still disagreement over whether overload is a component of interrole conflict or a distinct concept, the general consensus is that overload results from having too many demands, whereas interrole conflict results from having demands in one role (e.g., work) that are incompatible with the demands in another (e.g., family).

Researchers have also disagreed over whether overwork is an objective or subjective concept. Some researchers view overwork as an objective evaluation of the number of hours worked (Glass and Estes 1997; Schor 1992). Others claim that overwork involves the perception of one's workload (Kennedy 1996; Schwartzberg and Dytell 1988). In other words, to the extent that an individual feels overworked, he or she is overworked, regardless of the actual number of hours he or she works. These researchers reason that it is difficult to determine whether a person is overworked based solely on hours worked because people have different coping strategies, and therefore some may be able to deal with the negative consequences of working long hours better than others. Still other researchers allow for both objective and subjective components in their conceptualization of overwork (Sutton and Kahn 1987; Yogev 1982).

As confusing as these conflicting interpretations are, at least these researchers acknowledged the possibility of other conceptualizations by stating the specific definition they chose to use. Most research on overwork either ignores this important distinction or defines overwork subjectively, only to operationalize it objectively (or vice versa). Although we allow for both the objective and subjective interpretations of overwork, in our agenda for future research, we focus primarily on subjective overwork, unless otherwise specified. We have chosen a subjective definition of overwork because we are concerned with the negative outcomes of overwork, and it is the perception of being overworked that leads to the negative outcomes, not necessarily the objective number of hours worked (Edwards 1992; Kahn et al. 1964).

Subjective overwork has been found to be related to many negative consequences, both mental and physical in nature. One study found that employed parents who felt overworked were more likely to suffer from mental strain such as distress and lack of calmness (Williams and Alliger 1994). Another study showed that public school teachers experiencing more overload were more likely to be dissatisfied with their job (Cooke and Rousseau 1984). This same study found overload to be related to physical strain, measured by such symptoms as tiredness, heart pounding, and sweating hands. Other negative outcomes of overwork include depression, nervousness, anxiety, and insomnia (Karasek 1979). As mentioned previously, these negative individual outcomes may lead to negative organizational outcomes such as higher accident levels, increased absenteeism, and reduced productivity (Ganster and Schaubroeck 1991; Hofmann and Stetzer 1996). Before turning to our agenda for future research, we next briefly discuss why we have seen such an increase in overwork in the past decade.

The Increase in Overwork

There are several reasons that work hours are increasing. Organizations are requiring employees to work more hours so that they can remain competitive in the global business environment (Loo 1996; Perlow 1997). Labor costs are significantly lower in other parts of the world, so organizations must get the most out of their employees in order to be cost-effective. There is a clear financial incentive for companies to squeeze as much time as they can out of salaried employees because they are not charged for the incremental hours these employees work. Even with hourly workers, companies prefer to pay overtime rather than hire additional workers because the fewer employees a company hires, the lower the company's expenses are for such things as benefits, recruiting, and training. Overtime is at its highest ever, an average of 4.7 hours per week (Hancock et al. 1995). The trend toward longer working hours is expected to continue according to a *Fortune* study, which reported that 75 percent of the CEO's interviewed said that they will have to work their managers harder because of increased global competition (Solo 1990).

Another factor that has led to the increase in the number of hours employees are expected to work is the organizational trend toward downsizing. Almost half of the companies in the United States have implemented some form of downsizing over the last decade (Hancock et al. 1995). Companies reduce their workforces and expect the "survivors" to carry the extra load (Mishra and Spreitzer 1998). Survivors are often told by management that they should feel grateful for not being laid off, compelling them to work even harder (Noer 1993). Furthermore, survivors suffer from job insecurity, which puts pressure on them to increase their workload so that they will not be laid off should another phase of downsizing occur (Kets de Vries and Balazs 1997; Scott 1995). In 1995, according to *Newsweek,* companies were asking 1 employee to do the job of 1.3 employees with no increase in pay and with fewer days off. In addition, average annual vacation and other paid leave had decreased by nearly four days over the last decade (Hancock et al. 1995).

Major demographic changes in the U.S. labor force have also contributed to the rise in overwork. In 1960, only 28.8 percent of married women between the ages of 25 and 34 participated in the workforce; in 1995, this percentage had increased to 72 percent. Moreover, in 1975, 36.7 percent of women with at least one child under the age of 6 worked outside the home, whereas in 1995 this group had increased to 63.5 percent (U.S. Department of Commerce 1996). As a result of the increase in dual-career families and working mothers, employees now have greater family demands on their time than when there was an at-home spouse who took care of the household needs. Many workers, both male and female, feel overworked because of the increased time demand to fulfill both family and job responsibilities.

In her book *The Time Bind,* Arlie Hochschild (1997) suggests that employees themselves may be responsible for their increased working hours. Many are not taking advantage of flextime and work-family programs. Whereas, some may be afraid that their participation in these programs will harm their chances for career advancement, others actually seek to work longer hours. In the dual-career household, work may be a retreat from family problems; at work, individuals may feel more in control and appreciated whereas at home their life may be more chaotic and less rewarding. Furthermore, Hochschild (1997) found that some employees are "overtime hounds," who sign up for more hours so that they can purchase the nonessential extras they desire for themselves and their families.

Finally, technology has brought about a growing sense of overwork. Even when employees are at home or on vacation, technologies such as beepers, e-mail, voice mail, laptops, and cellular phones make them always on call. In 1995, 5 million people owned cellular phones (Hancock et al. 1995), and by the year 2000, 60 million Americans will own pagers (Brophy 1996). Employees who are expected to use the available devices to access their work projects often feel tethered to their jobs twenty-four hours a day, seven days a week. Research has shown that employees who have computers to help them complete overtime work at home feel more overworked than employees who complete their overtime work at home without the use of a computer (Duxbury, Higgins, and Thomas 1996). Although technology has alleviated certain kinds of job pressures, it has created others, and with this new set of pressures comes the perception that one is never away from work.

In summary, our review of the literature makes evident the confusion about the conceptualization and operationalization of the construct of overwork. It also suggests that several trends ensure that overwork will continue to be a pressing problem for contemporary organizations.

Agenda for Future Research

Although the topic of overwork is clearly a key issue for organizations as they approach the new millennium, our review of the literature indicates that even more research is needed to understand truly the construct of overwork. In the next section, we outline an agenda for future research that addresses the nature of overwork as well as potential levers for reducing overwork.

What Is the Nature of Overwork?

We define overwork as a subjective phenomenon that is distinct from the objective number of hours worked. However, there is a limited understanding of how the number of hours worked influences the perception of overwork. By virtually all indicators, people feel more overworked today than perhaps ever before due to the effects of downsizing, technology, and globalization. Yet, although people are clearly feeling more overworked, opinions differ about whether individuals are actually working longer hours today than in previous decades. In research using the annual Current Population Survey, Schor (1992) found that employees were working an average of 163 more hours per year than in the 1960s. By contrast, Robinson and Godbey (1997), in research using a time diary methodology, claim that Americans are working approximately 140 fewer hours per year than in the 1960s. So why is it that people feel overworked, even when the amount of time they spend at their jobs may or may not be increasing? Clearly, other factors may also contribute to the feeling of being overworked. We identify some of the potential factors next.

Research Question #1: What factors contribute to feelings of overwork beyond the actual number of hours worked?

Robinson and Godbey (1997) suggest that workers feel overworked because their lives are less compartmentalized today. Now work and family domains are more integrated, partly due to the invasion of technology into our homes. Consequently, people do not feel as though they ever can really escape from work even when they may not be working more hours. Moreover, leisure time has become more fragmented, with most of it being available in short segments on weekdays instead of long periods on the weekends. Without longer stretches of leisure time, people may not feel as if they have had enough time to relax and replenish themselves.

Future research must seek to understand what contributes to the experience of overwork, beyond the number of hours worked. As a first step, researchers need to collect data on the actual number of hours worked as well as the subjective experience of overwork. This research must cut across a large number of organizations and across various levels within organizations so that a generalized model of overwork can be developed. In most cases, we would expect that more work hours would correlate with perceptions of overwork. However, researchers may learn the most from cases in which individuals work long hours but do not indicate that they feel overworked (or do not work long hours but do feel overworked). In these cases, researchers need to determine why long hours do not contribute to feelings of overwork (or the converse). They might look first at demographic factors. For example, employed women with young children may feel overworked no matter how many hours they work because of the intense time demands of the home and workplace. Researchers might also conduct interviews with individuals who feel overworked even though they are not working long hours to determine what other factors influence the perception of overwork. Perhaps different organizational structures and processes influence the experience of overwork. For example, some organizations may offer concierge services to help employees fulfill personal business needs while working thereby reducing feelings of overwork. Others may offer flextime so that workers can choose when they will work the required number of hours. These interviews can help researchers identify the range of variables that influence perceptions of overwork. Until systematic research is conducted, we will have a limited understanding of what influences the experience of overwork.

Levers for Reducing the Effects of Overwork

A second area for future research focuses on how to reduce the dysfunctional effects of overwork on employees. One obvious solution is to reduce the number of hours individuals work. Unfortunately, this solution by itself is improbable given the need to keep labor costs low in today's highly competitive global environment. Moreover, as indicated in our first research question, other factors influence the experience of overwork besides long hours. Hence, cutting back hours may have a limited effect on the actual experience of overwork. Consequently, researchers must discover more effective levers for reducing the effects of overwork.

In our informal interviews with people from different organizations and across different levels, we identified one potential lever for reducing the dysfunctions of overwork: employee empowerment. Because we have defined overwork in subjective terms, we draw on a subjective or psychological definition of empowerment. *Psychological empowerment* is defined as intrinsic task motivation manifested within the individual through four cognitive assessments regarding work: self-determination, meaning, impact, and competence (Thomas and Velthouse 1990). To be empowered, in this sense, means to be energized and motivated (Spreitzer 1995). We suggest that if employees experience one or more of the empowerment dimensions, they will feel more energized and perceptions of overwork may be lessened. Next, we briefly examine how each of the dimensions of empowerment may alleviate feelings of overwork.

Self-Determination

Self-determination reflects having a choice in initiating and regulating one's own actions (Deci, Connell, and Ryan 1989). Drawing on prior research (Karasek 1979; Rodin and Langer 1977), Sutton and Kahn (1987) suggest that having more control may reduce the stress and strain inherent in overwork. For example, employees working sixty hours a week who have a high level of control may experience less strain than employees working the same number of hours who have less control because the former may view it as their choice to work those hours. One study conducted at Baxter International, Inc., found that employees believed that having control over decisions helped them deal with heavy work demands (Hammonds 1997).

Our informal interviews concur with this finding. For example, one credit manager attested to the positive effects of having some flexibility and choice in his job. "Choice is powerful in relieving stress. If I'm allowed to juggle my time, I don't feel as overworked." Another financial services manager claimed that the flexibility she gained from telecommuting far outweighed the increase in job demands she received after a promotion. "I'm definitely less overworked now that I'm a sales manager and I telecommute. I have more control over my schedule even though I'm working harder and at a higher level." Therefore, giving employees more control over when (such as through flextime) and how (such as through telecommuting) they work is likely to enhance feelings of empowerment.

Some popular organizational interventions aimed at reducing the problem of overwork operate by increasing workers' choices about when and how they will work. Telecommuting allows employees the choice to work from home, thereby minimizing the time needed to commute to work and allowing them to take care of personal business more easily. Job sharing and part-time work allow employees the opportunity to work fewer hours but still remain connected to the organization. Charles Schwab and Co. chose to offer job-sharing and part-time work options instead of laying off workers, which helped overworked employees who were willing to take a cut in pay for more free time (Scott 1992). Finally, job sharing may be a legitimate way for overworked employees to reduce their workload without giving up challenging and stimulating work that they enjoy and are trained to do.

Meaning

Meaning refers to the intrinsic value of work (Thomas and Velthouse 1990). The personal meaning an individual derives from work may alleviate the work-family conflict caused by working long hours (Thompson and Bunderson 1997). When employees believe that their work is truly important, they may feel more energized (Quinn, O'Neill, and Debebe 1996) and less overworked, even when working long hours. Several of our interviewees agreed. As one bank president said, "It doesn't matter how many hours a day you work; if you're not working close to your conscience, you will feel overworked." Many entrepreneurs are willing to work incredibly long hours without feeling unduly overworked because of the excitement of starting their own business.

Impact

Impact reflects "making a difference" in terms of accomplishing the purpose of the task (Thomas and Velthouse 1990, 672). Empowered employees who feel that they have an impact on the system may feel less overworked because they know that the hours they are working are making a difference. By contrast, in some companies, "face time," or when an employee is at work even though he or she is not really making a difference, was more important than the actual impact of an employee's work. Our interviews indicated that in these organizations, employees felt quite overworked by the face time requirement. One automotive manager described this typical situation: "There are some areas of the company that are just notorious for working long hours with questionable value attached except for the fact that it's face time and it's expected." The employees who complied with the face time requirement felt more overworked, knowing that their time was having no productive impact. Consequently, companies such as Merck, Cigna, and Marriott International have begun to explore how they can reduce requirements for face time. Training managers to reward performance rather than time spent at work is critical to promoting a balanced lifestyle (Scott 1996). A senior executive at the Richardson Company argues that it is in the organization's best interest to discourage the wasteful practice of face time: "When you start to measure impact and not hours you find you have a tremendous boost in productivity" (Scott 1995, 40).

Competence

Competence reflects "the degree to which a person can perform task activities skillfully when he or she tries" (Thomas and Velthouse 1990, 672). A strong feeling of competence may also alleviate some of the pressures of overwork. For example, people who feel competent at their job may not take as long to complete their work, may not be as overwhelmed by their job requirements, and, consequently, may feel less overworked. If employees are highly competent at what they do, it may also be easier for them to cut back on their hours or find more efficient ways to do things. Finally, competence may give employees more credibility in the organization, which, in turn, can increase their options for dealing with overwork (e.g., more flexible work schedules, telecommuting).

While the foregoing discussion suggests that each of the four dimensions of empowerment may reduce feelings of overwork, no empirical research has been conducted on the relationship between empowerment and overwork. Future research should consider the following questions pertaining to this relationship.

Research Question #2: How does empowerment reduce overwork?

Consider a basic model in which objective overwork contributes to the subjective experience of overwork, which leads to individual outcomes (Katz and Kahn 1978; Sutton and Kahn 1987). The empowerment dimensions may influence this process at various points. For example, competence might reduce the actual number of hours worked while self-determination may help individuals feel less overworked. Meaning and impact may moderate whether individuals experience strain as a result of feeling overworked. If their work is meaningful and has impact, they may be willing to put up with feeling overworked. More research needs to be conducted in order to untangle the processes by which empowerment influences overwork.

To answer this research question, researchers should collect data on the actual number of hours worked and the subjective experience of over-work. They should also collect data on key individual outcomes of interest such as stress or productivity and the four dimensions of empowerment. Then, researchers can empirically test which of the four dimensions of empowerment mediate or moderate the relationships among objective overwork, subjective overwork, and individual outcomes. Regression or LISREL analyses should help flesh out empirically a path model linking these different constructs. Such research is critical for establishing the relationship between empowerment and overwork.

Research Question # 3: Under what conditions will empowerment alleviate or contribute to perceptions of overwork?

Future research should consider the factors that moderate the effect of empowerment on overwork. One factor that may facilitate empower-ment's effect on overwork is the kind of empowerment initiative the orga nization undertakes. According to Quinn and Spreitzer (1997), executives take two quite different approaches to the empowerment of their employ-ees. One approach views empowerment as a mechanistic process in which managers clarify the company's vision, delegate responsibility, provide workers with the necessary information and resources to do their specific tasks, and allow employees limited decision-making control. The other approach views empowerment as an organic process in which employees are encouraged to grow and take risks. Managers using this "organic ap-proach" understand the needs of their employees and create a trusting and supportive environment. We propose that the organic model of em-powerment will be more successful at alleviating overwork because it op-erates on an intrinsic level by influencing employees' perceptions and feelings. Through the organic approach, managers can ensure that em-ployees have more flexibility in how they do their work, design employees' work so that they find it more meaningful, resist organizational pressures to evaluate workers on face time rather than actual contributions, and invest in employee training so that workers feel more competent. Despite the complexities and difficulties, we believe that an organic approach to empowerment will increase the possibility that empowerment can allevi-ate overwork.

On the other hand, there are several conditions under which organi-zations' efforts at empowerment may actually contribute to feelings of overwork. First, in many organizations, empowerment is often implemented in conjunction with downsizing efforts. The organization rationalizes that the surviving employees are "empowered" because they are assigned the responsibilities formerly assigned to the victims of the downsizing. Invariably, employees feel overworked (Mishra, Spreitzer, and Mishra, 1998). Unless work is taken out of the organization through programs such as General Electric's much publicized "work-out" program, empowerment implemented in conjunction with downsizing is likely to lead to feelings of overwork.

Second, unless managers change the structure and processes of the organization to become more empowering, many of the organization's efforts at implementing empowerment will lead to feelings of overwork. All too often managers declare that employees are empowered, but do little to change the culture, structure, and processes necessary to make empowerment work (Quinn and Spreitzer 1997). Employees may begin to see the empowerment program as a farce designed to get people to work longer hours without more pay. In such cases, employees are likely to view empowerment as a burden instead of an opportunity and are likely to feel overworked.

To assess this research question, researchers should interview employees to determine what contextual factors exist surrounding the empowerment program. The following questions could be posed:

- ▲ Has the organization changed its structure and processes in order to facilitate empowerment?
- ▲ Does the organization take an organic approach to empowerment?
- ▲ Have work-out programs been developed to reduce the amount of unnecessary work?
- ▲ Has the organization implemented an empowerment program in conjunction with an organization downsizing?

Then researchers could look for themes regarding how organizational contextual factors shape the relationship between empowerment and overwork, for example, whether some of these contextual conditions are always associated with more empowerment and fewer feelings of overwork or whether others are frequently associated with less empowerment and more feelings of overwork.

Research Question # 4: Are some individuals more likely to feel overworked when empowered?

Some individuals may feel uncomfortable with notions of empowerment and, thus, feel overwhelmed instead of energized. Those with low "growth-need-strength" (Hackman and Oldham 1980) may not want enriched jobs but, rather, may want more narrow, precise jobs with little ambiguity. "Individuals with low needs for growth may not value empowerment or may even find it threatening and balk at being 'pushed' or stretched too far by their work" (p. 85). Such individuals may not be interested in having more choices in how they do their jobs. Thus, empowerment may feel more like a burden than an enriching opportunity. Similarly, individuals in other cultures may not desire empowerment. For example, in some Asian cultures, employees have been conditioned to believe in the importance of hierarchical control. In these cultures, employees are likely to work many hours without complaint. For instance, Japanese managers tend to work very long hours on a regular basis. Embracing empowerment would be quite difficult for such employees, and they may view empowerment as more of a burden than an opportunity.

Thus, future research must examine whether certain individual personality traits and cultural values are likely to result in empowered individuals feeling more overworked than revitalized. Researchers should collect data on individual empowerment and perceptions of overwork as described in our research questions. They should also collect data on relevant personality characteristics such as growth-need-strength. Then researchers could examine whether personality type moderates the relationship between empowerment and overwork. Similarly, researchers could collect data on empowerment and overwork from individuals in different cultures. Then, they could assess whether the magnitude and direction of the relationship between empowerment and overwork varies by culture.

While there are other possible levers for reducing overwork, we chose to emphasize empowerment for several reasons. First, unlike some solutions focused on reducing hours without reducing pay, implementing employee empowerment is a more practical and viable strategy for companies. Second, unlike more narrow work-family programs geared toward reducing overwork for employed parents, empowerment could conceivably reduce the potential for overwork for all employees, even those who do not have children. Single and married childless workers are beginning to resent all the money and energy that companies are investing in work-family programs. They also resent the greater flexibility working parents are granted and the underlying expectation that childless workers should pick up the slack for them (Madigan 1997). Because the potential benefits of empowerment would not favor workers with children over childless workers, empowerment may be a more desirable lever for alleviating the problems of overwork.

In summary, our four research questions identify some important areas for future research. They address some of the key issues pertaining to overwork from the perspective of both academics and practitioners.

Conclusion

Given the current business environment, overwork is an issue that will not diminish in the near future. Employees and employers will continue to be challenged by the need to do more work at a faster rate and with lower costs. An unfortunate consequence of this challenge is that employees are feeling more overworked than ever before. In the long run, this overwork is likely to have deleterious effects not only on employees in terms of work-life balance and family relations, but also on organizations in terms of productivity and burnout. As such, it is critical that organizations begin to identify levers for reducing the dysfunctional aspects of overwork. We suggest that empowerment may be one such lever; by giving employees choice and flexibility over when and how they work, by helping them infuse personal meaning into their work, by ensuring that their work has impact, and by enhancing their sense of competence, the dysfunctional aspects of overwork may be lessened. In addition to finding levers that may alleviate overwork, research in this area promises to inform the academic discussion on overload, stress, and even work-family conflict. The agenda for research presented in this chapter provides some important avenues for those interested in exploring the theoretical and practical issues related to overwork.

References

Brophy, B. 1996. "Fax Me a Bedtime Story: High-Tech Gadgets Are Turning Virtual Executives into Virtual Parents." *U.S. News and World Report* (December 2), 79.

Cooke, R. A. and Rousseau, D. M. 1984. "Stress and Strain from Family Roles and Work-Role Expectations." *Journal of Applied Psychology* 69, 252–60.

Coverman, S. 1989. "Role Overload, Role Conflict, and Stress: Addressing Consequences of Multiple Role Demands." *Social Forces* 67, 965–82.

Deci, E. L., Connell, J. P., and Ryan, R. M. 1989. "Self-Determination in a Work Organization." *Journal of Applied Psychology* 74, 580–90.

Duxbury, L. E., Higgins, C. A., and Thomas, D. R. 1996. "Work and Family Environments and the Adoption of Computer-Supported Supplemental Work-at-Home." *Journal of Vocational Behavior* 49, 1–23.

Edwards, J. R. 1992. "A Cybernetic Theory of Stress, Coping, and Well-Being in Organizations." *Academy of Management Review* 17, 238–74.

Fassel, D. 1990. *Working Ourselves to Death: The High Cost of Workaholism and the Rewards of Recovery.* New York: HarperCollins.

Forti, E. M. 1994. "Role Overload and Interrole Conflict in Work and Family Domains: Related but Distinct Concepts." *Dissertation Abstracts International: Section A: The Humanities and Social Sciences* 54(7-A), 2739.

Galambos, N. L. and Walters, B. J. 1992. "Work Hours, Schedule Inflexibility, and Stress in Dual-Earner Spouses." *Canadian Journal of Behavioural Science* 24, 290–302.

Ganster, D. C. and Schaubroeck, J. 1991. "Work Stress and Employee Health." *Journal of Management* 17, 235–71.

Glass, J. L. and Estes, S. B. 1997. "The Family Responsive Workplace." *Annual Review of Sociology* 23, 289–313.

Hackman, J. R. and Oldham, G. R. 1980. *Work Redesign.* Reading, MA: Addison-Wesley.

Hammonds, K. H. 1997. "Work and Family." *Business Week* (September 15), 96–99.

Hancock, L., with Rosenberg, D., Springen, K., King, P., Rogers, M. B., Kalb, C., Gegax, T. T., and bureau reports. 1995. "Breaking Point." *Newsweek* (March 6), 56–61.

Hochschild, A. R. 1997. *The Time Bind: When Work Becomes Home and Home Becomes Work.* New York: Metropolitan Books.

Hofmann, D. A. and Stetzer, A. 1996. "A Cross-Level Investigation of Factors Influencing Unsafe Behaviors and Accidents." *Personnel Psychology* 49, 307–39.

Kahn, R. L. and Quinn, R. P. 1970. "Role Stress: A Framework for Analysis." In A. McLean (ed.), *Occupational Mental Health.* New York: Rand McNally.

Kahn, R. L., Wolfe, D. M., Quinn, R. P., Snoek, J. D., and Rosenthal, R. A. 1964. *Organizational Stress: Studies in Role Conflict and Ambiguity.* New York: Wiley.

Karasek, R. A., Jr. and Theorell, T. 1990. *Healthy Work: Stress, Productivity and the Reconstruction of Working Life.* New York: Basic Books.

Karasek, R. A., Jr. 1979. "Job Demands, Job Decision Latitude, and Mental Strain: Implications for Job Redesign." *Administrative Science Quarterly* 24, 285–308.

Katz, D. and Kahn, R. L. 1978. *The Social Psychology of Organizations.* 2nd ed. New York: Wiley.

Kennedy, M. M. 1996. "When Does Work Become Overwork?" *Across the Board* 33, 53–54.

Kets de Vries, M. F. R. and Balazs, K. 1997. "The Downside of Downsizing." *Human Relations* 50, 11–50.

Loo, R. 1996. "Managing Workplace Stress: A Canadian Delphi Study Among Human Resource Managers." *Work and Stress* 10, 183–89.

Madigan, K. 1997. " 'Family' Doesn't Always Mean Children." *Business Week* (September 15), 104.

Mishra, A. and Spreitzer, G. M. 1998. "Explaining How Survivors Respond to Downsizing: The Role of Trust, Empowerment, Justice, and Job Design." *Academy of Management Review* 23(3), 567–88.

Mishra, K., Spreitzer, G. M., and Mishra, A. 1998. "Mitigating the Damage to Trust and Empowerment During Downsizing." *Sloan Management Review.* 39(2), 83–95.

Noer, D. M. 1993. *Healing the Wounds: Overcoming the Trauma of Layoffs and Revitalizing Downsized Organizations.* San Francisco: Jossey-Bass.

Perlow, L. 1997. *Finding Time: How the Corporation, Its Employees and Their Families Can Benefit From Changing the Way Time Is Used at Work.* Ithaca, NY: ILR Press.

Quinn, R. E. and Spreitzer, G. M. 1997. "The Road to Empowerment: Seven Questions Every Leader Should Consider." *Organizational Dynamics* 26, 37–49.

Quinn, R. E., O'Neill, R. M., and Debebe, G. 1996. "Confronting the Tensions in an Academic Career." In P. J. Frost and M. S. Taylor (eds.), *Rhythms of Academic Life: Personal Accounts of Careers in Academia.* Thousand Oaks, CA: Sage.

Robinson, J. P. and Godbey, G. 1997. *Time for Life: The Surprising Ways Americans Use Their Time.* University Park, PA: Pennsylvania State University Press.

Rodin, J. and Langer, J. 1997. "Long-Term Effects of a Control-Relevant Intervention With the Institutionalized Aged." *Journal of Personality and Social Psychology* 35, 897–902.

Schor, J. 1992. *The Overworked American: The Unexpected Decline of Leisure.* New York: Basic Books.

Schwartzberg, N. S. and Dytell, R. S. 1988. "Family Stress and Psychological Well-Being Among Employed and Nonemployed Mothers." *Journal of Social Behaviour and Personality* (special issue: Work and Family: Theory, Research, and Applications), 3(4), 175–90.

Scott, M. B. 1992. "Flexibility Can Be Strategic in Marketplace." *Employee Benefit Plan Review* 46(9), 16–20.

———. 1995. "Work/Family Programs: Their Role in the New Workplace." *Employee Benefit Plan Review* 50(3), 32–41.

———. 1996. "Work/Life Initiatives." *Employee Benefit Plan Review* 51(3), 26–37.

Shellenbarger, S. 1997a. "No, You're Not Too Tough to Suffer a Bout of Burnout." *Wall Street Journal* (June 25), B1.

———. 1997b. "People Are Working Harder—and Taking More Heat for It." *Wall Street Journal* (February 26), B1.

———. 1997c. "Woman's Resignation From Top Pepsi Post Rekindles Debates." *Wall Street Journal* (October 8), B1.

Solo, S. 1990. "Stop Whining and Get Back to Work." *Fortune* (March 12), 49.

Spreitzer, G. M. 1995. "Psychological Empowerment in the Workplace: Dimensions, Measurement, and Validation." *Academy of Management Journal* 38, 1442–65.

Sutton, R. I. and Kahn, R. L. 1987. "Prediction, Understanding, and Control as Antidotes to Organizational Stress." In J. W. Lorsch (ed.), *Handbook of Organizational Behavior.* Englewood Cliffs, NJ: Prentice-Hall.

Thomas, K. W. and Velthouse, B. A. 1990. "Cognitive Elements of Empowerment: An Interpretive Model of Intrinsic Task Motivation." *Academy of Management Review* 15, 666–81.

Thompson, J. A. and Bunderson, J. S. 1997. "Not Just a Matter of Time?: Transcending Temporal Determinants of Work/Nonwork Conflict." Paper presented at the 57th Annual Meeting of the Academy of Management, Boston, August.

U.S. Department of Commerce, Economics and Statistics Administration, Bureau of the Census. 1996. *Statistical Abstract of the United States 1996.* Washington, DC: U.S. Government Printing Office.

Williams, K. J. and Alliger, G. M. 1994. "Role Stressors, Mood Spillover, and Perceptions of Work-Family Conflict in Employed Parents." *Academy of Management Journal* 37, 837–68.

Yogev, S. 1982. "Are Professional Women Overworked? Objective Versus Subjective Perception of Role Loads." *Journal of Occupational Psychology* 55, 165–69.

Chapter 4

Underemployed Human Resources: Revealing the Secret Dilemma of Untapped Potential

Laura M. Morgan *and* Daniel C. Feldman

M any business leaders today feel that they employ too many people who are not contributing their full potential or adding sufficient value to the organization. From a managerial perspective, this problem of underemployment is typically attributed to a lack of motivation on the part of employees and is therefore addressed by modifying incentives and punishments for employees. When we asked administrators in various industries (including banking, medical care, and manufacturing) how they manage underemployed human resources in their organizations, they provided examples from the reward and disciplinary systems that they used to increase their employees' motivation. Thus, the problem of underemployed human resources is often considered synonymously with a lack of employee motivation and is addressed as such.

However, an alternative explanation exists for the prevalence of lack of employee contribution. These individuals could actually be suffering from an underutilization of their skills. That is, there may be large numbers of employees who are performing jobs that could be done by others with fewer skills, less experience, and lower levels of training (Feldman 1996). As a consequence, the employees are psychologically demotivated, which translates into lack of contribution to the organization.

Underemployed human resources often result from structural constraints within organizations that prevent employees from working at their full potential. In fact, many individuals find themselves in jobs that do not draw upon the full range of their skills and education or do not provide many opportunities for internal promotions. Under these conditions, underutilization results from the structure of the labor force, rather than from a lack of employee motivation. Thus, the motivation-based strategies for minimizing underutilization within the labor force are inappropriate in many cases. Moreover, under these circumstances, the discrepancy between what employees have to offer and what they contribute may be as detrimental to employees as it is to their managers.

In this chapter, we focus on underemployment, which results from these structural constraints within organizations. We define *underemployment* as an inferior, lesser, or lower quality type of employment relative to some standard, either to the employee's own past experience or to the experiences of others with the same education or work history (Feldman 1996). While underemployment has received considerable attention at the individual and societal levels of analysis, surprisingly little attention has been paid to underemployment as an organizational problem. Yet, underemployment is a pressing problem for organizations because of its direct and indirect consequences for company performance and employee morale.

We organize our discussion into four parts. First, we review the previous research on underemployment and show its relevance for understanding underemployment at the organizational level of analysis. Second, we discuss the direct and indirect consequences of underemployment on organization performance. Third, we identify the societal factors that affect an organization's propensity to have an underemployed workforce, as well as the organizational factors that affect an employee's propensity for becoming underemployed. Fourth, we present a series of research questions as a framework for advancing our understanding of underemployed human resources within organizations.

Present State of Research on Underemployment

It has been estimated that 25 percent of the workforce in the United States is currently underemployed (Henry 1994; Newman 1988). Moreover, other recent statistics project that underemployment will continue to be a problem in our society in the future. The Bureau of Labor Statistics estimated that one of five college graduates who entered the job market between 1984 and 1990 were either unemployed or underemployed in a job that did not require a college degree, and that 30 percent of college graduates would be underemployed by the year 2005.

While these statistics suggest that a significant proportion of working Americans experience underemployment, underemployment has been generally overlooked for many years as an important employment issue in need of research. The topic of underemployment has been underresearched until recently for a number of reasons. First, scholars have historically investigated issues of employment status only in terms of the employed versus the unemployed. A great deal of attention has been focused on the financial status and psychological well-being of unemployed workers, while it has been generally assumed that any individual who is gainfully employed is freed from the financial and psychological burdens of unemployment (Newman 1988). However, the discussion of unemployment fails to address the *quality* of employment experiences of workers reentering the workforce (Tipps and Gordon 1985). Furthermore, whereas unemployment may be temporary, underemployment may be a lifetime situation at work. The unemployment rate, by itself, is therefore an inadequate labor force indicator. Thus, it is critical that we consider underemployment in addition to unemployment in addressing issues of labor utilization (Sullivan 1978).

Second, a number of incorrect, but common, assumptions regarding the labor market have contributed to the dearth of scholarly study of underemployment. It has often been assumed (1) that those individuals who have employment problems lack the skills to qualify for existing vacancies; (2) that there is stability in employment patterns, such that individuals do not move frequently back and forth between employment and unemployment; and (3) that those individuals who are in the labor force rarely lose the motivation to work (Gordon 1972). These assumptions bias investigations of the labor market toward viewing employment as a dichotomous variable (unemployed versus employed workers), rather than focusing on underemployment as a third type of employment.

Third, scholars in various disciplines do not agree on the nature of underemployment. Different groups of researchers have defined the term differently and have examined nonoverlapping sets of dependent variables (Feldman 1996). For example, whereas economists and sociologists have investigated the objective dimension of underemployment as a discrepancy in skills required or compensation received from a job, psychologists and organizational behaviorists have studied the performance and emotional effects of such underemployment experiences.

Fortunately, the development of an integrated research agenda on experiences of underemployment recently has attracted more interest in academia. Despite differences in perspective, a recent review of the dimensions of underemployment revealed that across disciplines all definitions of underemployment share two elements: (1) an inferior, lesser, or lower quality type of employment that is (2) defined relative to some standard, either that of one's own past experience or to the experiences of others with the same education or work history (Feldman 1996). Feldman suggests that people can be underemployed in one or more of the following five basic ways:

1. Education—by working in a job that does not require the degree they have received for performance
2. Field of expertise—by working in a job that is not in their area of training
3. Field of interest—by being employed in a job that does not require the skills they prefer to use
4. Wages—by earning less than others who have comparable qualifications or by earning less than they earned at a previous job
5. Permanence of employment—by being employed for fewer hours than they desire to work

Within the underemployment literature to date, most of the research has focused on either the individual's emotional reactions to underemployment or on the macroeconomic causes and consequences of underemployment. Surprisingly, there has been little discussion of underemployment from the perspective of the employing organization. Despite the importance of considering the organizational context of underemployment, there are a number of reasons that the organizational perspective has been underrepresented in discussions of underemployment.

For example, in many organizations, more attention has been paid to workers as a force of opposition to change rather than as a potential source of increased productivity (Greenhalgh 1982). In addition, the increased technology that results from manufacturing and service delivery changes often forces people into less demanding jobs. Therefore, because the optimization of human capital is not considered one of the more important contributors to corporate profit, the problems associated with underemployment are not considered to be serious by many organizations.

Moreover, human productivity is hard to measure. It is difficult to assess whether managers are making optimum use of the human resources at their command and to assess the nature of the relationship between this optimization and productivity (Dunahee and Wangler 1974). The U.S. Government does not even have clear statistics on the national level of underemployment. Consequently, it is difficult to quantify the loss to specific organizations from underemployment.

Sometimes, too, even when executives recognize the existence of underemployment in their organizations, they do not view it as the company's responsibility or problem. Indeed, it may be considered more problematic to hire employees who are insufficiently skilled than to employ workers who are overqualified.

For a variety of reasons, then, the problems associated with underemployment for organizations have been largely neglected by scholars and executives alike, and have thus hindered the integration of theory and practice for organizations with underemployed human resources. As we discuss next, there are real costs to organizations experiencing widespread underemployment, and, accordingly, a real need for investigating the organization's role in and impact of underemployment.

Consequences of Underemployment for Organizations

Underemployment can both directly and indirectly affect corporate performance. It does so by negatively influencing employees' performance as well as attitudes.

First of all, underemployment negatively affects the stability of an organization's workforce. Research suggests that underemployment is positively related to intentions to turnover (Burris 1983; Feldman and Doerpinghaus 1992; Feldman, Doerpinghaus, and Turnley 1994; Tan, Leana, and Feldman 1994). In addition, because underemployed workers who are dissatisfied with their jobs are more likely to take "mental health days" (Breaugh 1981) or spend days job hunting, they may have increased levels of absenteeism as well.

Although different types of underemployment may affect productivity in different ways, qualitative data from Borgen, Amundson, and Harder (1988) suggest that underemployed workers are more fatalistic and see less point in trying to work hard. Glyde (1977) also suggests that underemployed workers experience more job dissatisfaction and alienation from work. Thus, although workers who experience different types of underemployment may respond in various ways to achieve equity (e.g., those who are underemployed in terms of wages may reduce the quantity of their work whereas those who are overqualified may reduce the quality), it can be expected that aggregate performance levels for the underemployed may be lower than those of the satisfactorily employed (Feldman 1996).

Underemployment may also negatively affect employees' attachment to their careers and their desires to advance through hard work. In many ways, underemployment represents a violation of the psychological contract between workers and organizations (Dunahee and Wangler 1974; Rousseau 1990). Underemployment appears to be a particular problem for employees who have been laid off or demoted. When workers are laid off and then forced to enter jobs in which they are underemployed, their levels of career investment or excitement about their careers most likely will have decreased. Underemployment represents a violation of expectations for recent graduates as well. When their expectations for challenging work are unfulfilled, graduates may respond to their disappointment by contributing less to their employers (Robinson, Kraatz, and Rousseau 1994). Similarly, underemployed contingent workers may experience a decrease in career attitudes, especially when their positions are not converted to permanent, full-time jobs (Feldman and Doerpinghaus 1992; Feldman, Doerpinghaus, and Turnley 1994). This decrease will likely translate into decreased effort by underemployed workers, thereby decreasing organizational effectiveness.

Indeed, underemployment might also adversely affect organizational climate by increasing the amount of careerist activity. Individuals who have difficulty finding satisfactory employment may become cynical about the relationship between hard work and employment success and begin to engage in nonperformance-based behaviors (such as networking and impression management) instead, to get better jobs in other organizations (Feldman 1996). Such careerist behaviors often include manipulative interpersonal and image management behaviors, which can change the organizational climate if many employees begin to adopt them. Thus, the state of underemployment appears to foster poor work attitudes and encourage self-limiting behaviors among employees.

Recent research suggests that many employees may respond to underemployment by performing fewer organizational citizenship behaviors (see Organ 1988; Van Dyne, Graham, and Dienesch 1994) or by infrequently contributing to their organizations above and beyond the call of duty (Feldman 1996). In support of this finding, Burris (1983) noted that underemployed workers frequently engaged in more activities outside of the workplace to fulfill their desires for challenge and excitement.

Although some theorists have argued that any form of employment provides "latent functions" (i.e., increased social interactions at work, greater sense of personal identity, and greater structure to the day) that are beneficial to workers and lead to more positive mental health (Jahoda 1982), recent empirical work suggests that underemployment can be as detrimental to overall mental health as unemployment (Feldman 1996; O'Brien and Feather 1990; Winefield et al. 1991). For example, difficulty in finding satisfactory employment and prolonged underemployment may lead to "learned helplessness" (Seligman 1975), which results in lower self-esteem, increased depression, and decreased feelings of self-control. The negative impact of decreased psychological well-being can also impede organizational effectiveness.

Antecedents of Underemployment

Just as there are several dimensions of underemployment, there are also many reasons for the existence of underemployment. However, while the antecedents of underemployment range from the societal level of the labor market to a microlevel of individual characteristics, most of the antecedents across levels are related, directly or indirectly, to experiences that are fostered by and occur within organizations. As we show subsequently, many of the factors that contribute to an underemployed workforce are the direct result of organizational conditions (e.g., downsizing) whereas others are due to the distribution of employees in terms of age, gender, race, or formal education. In this section, we explore which factors influence the amount of underemployment within an organization and which workers will become underemployed.

Many factors play a role in determining an organization's propensity to retain underemployed human resources. First, the profitability and growth potential of an organization may affect its propensity to invest in human resources. Companies that are prosperous may be more able and willing to create positions that require high-level skills, thereby increasing the likelihood that employees will secure jobs that utilize their skills. On the other hand, organizations that are in the process of downsizing may require some employees to assume lower-paying or lower-skilled positions.

Second, underemployment within organizations may exist due to the structure of the external labor market. Increasingly, government regulations on benefit payments and employers' lack of flexibility in terminating nonproductive employees make hiring permanent employees less attractive. Therefore, there are increased incentives to hire contingent workers. This trend has already emerged in organizations; statistics show that temporary jobs constituted 20 percent of the jobs created in the private sector after the 1991 recession. Such a decrease in hiring and training of permanent employees may lead to an increased percentage of underemployed human resources.

Third, the state of the overall economy may affect the level of underemployment within organizations. While government regulations may decrease organizational incentives to hire highly qualified workers on a full-time basis, economic recessions decrease an organization's ability to employ more workers. In fact, the most recent recession led to the loss of many white-collar jobs. Numerous white-collar workers were then forced to secure employment in jobs or fields outside of their areas of training and interest and in some cases were not fully compensated for their skills. As a result, the number of underemployed individuals increased. Thus, organizations that are most severely affected by a recession are most likely to experience underemployment within their labor force.

Fourth, increasingly employees are not being rewarded for improving their human capital through additional training and education. For instance, many organizations fail to reward employees for acquiring new skills (i.e., they do not utilize skill-based evaluations and compensation). Organizations that do not provide such rewards may be likely to have an underemployed labor force.

Similarly, research suggests that organizational factors such as job characteristics also affect workers' propensity for becoming underemployed. During organizational retrenchment, in particular, some employees are more susceptible to underemployment than others based on the relationship of their job's functional area to organizational profitability.

For example, during organizational decline, it is more likely that employees in marketing or research and development will be underemployed than those in finance, accounting, or law. This bias is due to the fact that organizations find it necessary to deal with creditors' demands and cut discretionary expenditures quickly during periods of decline (D'Aveni 1989; Feldman 1996). In addition, declining organizations are more likely to decrease their "administrative intensity" (the number of managers relative to the number of workers), which suggests that greater numbers of employees will retire early or enter lower-skilled, lower-paying jobs (Cameron, Whetton, and Kim 1987). Middle managers are especially likely to face this dilemma of underemployment during organizational decline, because their jobs entail neither front-line supervision nor strategic planning. Similarly, staff workers may be more vulnerable to layoffs and subsequent underemployment than line workers, because their job functions are viewed as less essential (D'Aveni 1989; Feldman 1996).

A number of individual-level characteristics increase workers' susceptibility to underemployment, too. In terms of employees' work history, research has shown that individuals who have been previously laid off from their jobs are more likely to experience underemployment (Feldman 1996; Kjos 1988; Tan, Leana, and Feldman 1994) because they may suffer from some stigma in the labor market. Furthermore, the length of time that individuals have been unemployed may affect their chances of accepting jobs that do adequately compensate them or utilize their skills (Winefield and Tiggemann 1989). Individuals who have been unemployed for a long period after graduation or a layoff may face stigmas in the marketplace or may become financially desperate and settle for temporary or contract employment (Feather and O'Brien 1986a, 1986b).

A similar phenomenon exists during periods of organizational retrenchment. Employees who have been career plateaued (i.e., they are unlikely to be further promoted or given positions of increased responsibility in their companies) are more prone to underemployment than their coworkers. Because career-plateaued employees are not necessarily critical to organizational performance, they are more susceptible to layoffs or termination and, consequently, may have to accept other jobs at lower wages and with fewer responsibilities.

Individuals' demographic characteristics, particularly gender, race, age, and education, may also increase susceptibility to underemployment. Because women have suffered more downward mobility in the United States than men (Newman 1988), are more vulnerable to being laid off from their jobs than men, and have more difficulties finding satisfactory reemployment than men (Marshall 1984; Nowak and Snyder 1983), they are more likely to experience underemployment. In addition, many women may be willing to settle for lower wages in order to balance family demands and work (Rosen 1987), or they may settle for jobs that require less education than they possess in order to support their children after a divorce (Weitzman 1985). For example, in 1985, women accounted for two-fifths of the permanent wage and salary positions, yet they comprised almost two-thirds of the temporary workforce (Henson 1996).

Although racial differences in terms of underemployment have been studied less thoroughly, the evidence suggests that racial minorities are more likely to become underemployed (Tipps and Gordon 1985). This evidence is largely based on career-history factors. In particular, since the national unemployment rate for racial minorities is consistently higher than that of Caucasian workers, regardless of industry, job classification, age, or gender (Ullah 1987), racial minorities sustain longer periods of unemployment following layoffs than do their Caucasian counterparts and fare worse in terms of gaining satisfactory reemployment (Leana and Feldman 1995; Newman 1988). In addition, racial minorities are disproportionately represented in the contingent workforce; African-Americans represented approximately 20 percent of the temporary workers—double their representation in the population as a whole (Henson 1996).

Age and education are also related to levels of underemployment, but their effects are mixed. For example, older workers, although they may be less vulnerable to layoffs because of seniority, may also have more difficulty finding reemployment after layoffs due to age discrimination (Dunn 1979; Kaufman 1982). In addition, more educated workers seem to be less vulnerable to layoffs and underemployment; however, they suffer greater absolute and relative losses of income during underemployment (Burris 1983; Leana and Feldman 1995; Newman 1988). Overall, then, underemployment can be expected to be positively correlated with age and negatively correlated with education (Feldman 1996).

In sum, many organizational factors and experiences affect both the frequency of underemployment within organizations and an individual's propensity to become underemployed. Furthermore, research has shown that underemployed human resources affect an individual's productivity and attitude and, consequently, company performance.

Extending the Agenda: Future Research Directions

Taking into account the organization's role in and experience of underemployment can further enhance research on underemployed human resources. The research agenda can be fruitfully extended by considering the organizational context more carefully in future investigations of the nature, antecedents, and consequences of underemployment.

An organizational level of analysis can contribute to our understanding of the definition of underemployment. For example, when a college professor is required to teach undergraduate courses rather than graduate courses, the professor may consider himself or herself underemployed whereas his or her colleagues may not because the professor's education level matches that required of the position. Therefore, it is important to investigate the relationship between the objective indicators and the subjective experiences of underemployment by considering questions related to psychological framing, mediating organizational factors, and employers' perceptions of underemployment.

1. *What is the importance of psychological framing as a filter for personal experiences of underemployment?* Because underemployment is an inferior, lesser, or lower quality of employment (Kaufman 1982) relative to one's previous work experiences or to the employment experiences of others with the same education and work history (e.g., Quinn and Mandilovitch 1975), increased use of relative deprivation theory is quite appropriate in informing our understanding of underemployment. Relative deprivation theory helps us understand how people psychologically frame their experience, define themselves as underemployed, and under what circumstances they experience the greatest sense of frustration (Feldman, Leana, and Turnley 1997). Most researchers agree that there are four basic preconditions for individuals to experience relative deprivation: wanting some outcome, feeling deserving of that outcome, not receiving that outcome, and perceiving that some "comparative other" receives the desired outcome or more of the desired outcome (Feldman, Leana, and Turnley 1997).

Relative deprivation theory is useful in understanding with whom underemployed individuals compare themselves and whom they choose as referent others, the degree to which employees experience underemployment, and the circumstances that increase or decrease the amount of relative deprivation individuals experience. The extent to which individuals can explain their predicament of underemployment in terms of external events affects their degree of relative deprivation too. Employees' sense of entitlement also affects the degree to which underemployed individuals report relative deprivation. For example, white-collar workers may experience more relative deprivation during underemployment than blue-collar workers because they have a greater sense of entitlement, as a result of their educational investment and career history (Feldman, Leana, and Turnley 1997).

In conjunction with relative deprivation theory, work centrality is another factor that may affect employees' interpretation of their underemployment experiences. Scholarly discussions of the psychological meaning of work have varied from Karl Marx's contention that "people's essential being is intimately bound up in their work" to Charles Reich's stance that "for most Americans, work is mindless, exhausting, boring, servile and hateful—something to be endured while 'life' is confined to 'time off' " (Campbell 1981, p. 42). For those employees who simply aim to earn money, work may not be as central to their satisfaction with life, and it may be less important for them to spend a large percentage of time at work utilizing their preferred skills on preferred tasks. Therefore, the fact that they are overqualified for a job may not be detrimental to their job performance or psychological well-being. However, other employees may have well-defined goals in their careers, developed over time through family expectations, formal education, and professional socialization. Consequently, they may seek to maximize their potential in their jobs and feel underutilized when their needs are thwarted.

2. *How do organizational factors mediate the cognitive processing of underemployment?* The organizational context in which underemployment occurs is critical in shaping psychological interpretations of underemployment experiences. For example, individuals in organizations that emphasize meritocracy and individual contributions may interpret underemployment as a more negative experience because the "credo of meritocracy" suggests that people who fail to obtain adequate employment must lack the necessary "confidence and determination" (Newman 1988). Consequently, these underemployed individuals may also be more suspect to the deleterious effects of underemployment on psychological well-

being, such as feelings of deprivation and inadequacy, as well as a decrease in social interaction (see Feldman 1996; Feldman, Leana, and Turnley 1997; Newman 1988). By contrast, individuals working in team-oriented environments may be more likely to assess their work in terms of team success and be less sensitive to individual-level feelings of underemployment.

3. *How do employers perceive underemployment and underemployed individuals within organizations?* The literature has not yet answered this question. For example, drawing on the previous discussion of job characteristics as antecedents of underemployment, we find that managers may be more troubled by underemployment (and, thus, more likely to identify underemployment as a problem) in departments that are considered critical to the attainment of organizational profit (e.g., finance and accounting). In addition, stereotypes regarding individuals based on demographic characteristics and group membership may also affect employers' expectations of workers' job performance. These expectations formed on the basis of age, gender, or racial stereotypes may influence how seriously organizations view the underemployment problem.

Without concrete means for organizations and supervisors to assess levels of underemployment within organizations, the problem is less likely to be identified or remedied quickly. Thus, in order to pursue further research in this field, it is also necessary that we develop mechanisms to measure underemployment accurately. Given the variable nature of underemployment experiences, a multivariate approach that relies on both subjective and objective indicators of underemployment is most appropriate for its operationalization (Clogg and Shockey 1984; Feldman 1996). In addition, it is important to develop measurement instruments that account for the five different types of underemployment (education, field of expertise, field of interest, wages, and permanence of employment) (Clogg 1979; Feldman 1996).

Furthermore, more research is needed to develop organizational strategies to help reduce the number of underemployed workers and alleviate some of the negative consequences of underemployment. To date, researchers of underemployment have identified some steps that individual employees can take to decrease the likelihood that they will become or remain underemployed. Such steps include altering job search strategies, since the longer individuals delay and the less intense their job searches are, the more likely it is that they will become underemployed in the future (Feldman 1996). Similarly, the extent to which one is willing to consider geographical relocation or retraining can also affect his or her ability to gain satisfactory employment. While there are a number of economic and psychological costs to relocating (Dunn 1979), such as moving expenses and leaving family and friends, research has shown that workers who are willing to relocate geographically appear to be more successful in avoiding underemployment, particularly in cases of widespread layoffs (Leana and Feldman 1995).

Organizations, too, can implement strategies to reduce both the frequency and negative consequences of underemployment. Organizations can reduce underemployment by realistically communicating the skills and responsibilities required for their jobs. Unrealistic job descriptions can contribute to underemployment by perpetuating a poor fit between employees and their positions. A lack of honest communication during the interview process regarding the actual day-to-day tasks required of each position can increase the likelihood that potential employees will assume positions for which they are ill-suited. Realistic job previews would decrease turnover as well as incidences of decreased performance resulting from employees' unmet expectations.

In addition, the utilization of skill-based evaluations within organizations may decrease the frequency of underemployment. If employees are rewarded on the basis of their level of skill, as opposed to the number of hours they have worked, workers who have obtained additional training and education can be compensated accordingly. Skill-based evaluations also benefit organizations because they encourage the development of an increasingly competent, and particularly more stable, labor force. The effectiveness of such organizational strategies should be experimentally investigated.

Organizations can also assist underemployed individuals. Executives can encourage supervisors to identify workers who would like to contribute to the organization at a greater level yet have skills that are not being utilized in their current positions. Additionally, mentorship programs can provide assistance to underemployed workers. For instance, Corzine, Buntzman, and Busch (1994) found that individuals with mentors were less likely to think they had reached a career plateau and more likely to enjoy job satisfaction, and that this relationship was not associated with salary. Thus, it can be reasonably expected that mentors can help underemployed individuals broaden their social networks to increase future job opportunities, and help them locate more challenging opportunities. The extent to which these tactics enable organizations to alleviate the severity and negative consequences of underemployment for workers should also be experimentally investigated.

The previous discussion highlighted several issues that should form the basis of an extended research agenda on underemployment. The consideration of such topics regarding psychological perceptions of underemployment, measurement of underemployment, and organizational strategies that can reduce underemployment will make a critical contribution to our understanding of underemployment. However, studies of underemployment must also be extended to include a variety of populations as well as methodologies in various organizational contexts in order to broaden our knowledge.

Many of the studies of underemployed individuals have focused on a particular set of workers: managers who have been laid off and then reemployed, college graduates, and the contingent workforce (part-time or temporary workers). These analyses are appropriate given that these classes of workers are quite likely to become underemployed (Feldman 1996). Yet, other populations of workers might also be constrained from contributing maximally to their organizations. Studies might compare experiences, perceptions, and effects of underemployment for lower versus higher status workers, women versus men, or ethnic minorities versus the majority population. Tipps and Gordon (1985) conducted a comparative study of the prevalence of underemployment among demographic groups, but based their findings on data from the 1980 Current Population Survey. Findings that are generated from more recent data may be dramatically different given the changes in our socioeconomic climate since 1980. Furthermore, a deeper analysis of the *meaning* of underemployment for different people within the organizational context still has yet to be examined.

Additionally, much of our knowledge of the effects of underemployment has been based on cross-sectional data. Longitudinal studies of underemployment could prove to be both interesting and revealing in regard to discovering the likelihood that entering employees will become underemployed during their working lives, the long-term effects of underemployment for individuals and employers, and the effectiveness of personal and organizational strategies to reduce underemployment.

Different organizational contexts may also yield interesting results regarding the effects of underemployment. For example, the likelihood and results of underemployment within work teams may be quite different from underemployment in traditional hierarchical relationship.

Finally, a variety of industries should be studied to enhance our knowledge of underemployment as it operates within corporate organizations as well as other professions. Such industries might include legal, medical, academia, and even athletics or entertainment, where career paths are less likely to be linear.

Conclusion

Underemployment has significant negative consequences for organizations as well as for employees. In this chapter we discussed societal and organizational factors that increase the likelihood of underemployment in the workplace. In framing our research agenda, we focused on issues of organizational context to expand our understanding of the nature, antecedents, and consequences of underemployment. The transformation of the research agenda for underemployed human resources to include the organizational perspective will increase both our understanding of the nature of underemployment within organizations and our ability to identify and manage underemployment within organizations. Equally important, more sophisticated investigations of underemployment will help organizations harness the untapped potential that exists within the human capital of each company.

References

Borgen, W. A., Amundson, N. E., and Harder, H. G. 1988. "The Experience of Underemployment." *Journal of Employment Counseling* 25, 149–59.

Breaugh, J. A. 1981. "Predicting Absenteeism From Prior Absenteeism and Work Attitudes." *Journal of Applied Psychology* 66, 555–60.

Burris, B. 1983. *No Room at the Top: Underemployment and Alienation in the Corporation.* New York: Praeger.

Cameron, K., Whetton, D., and Kim, M. 1987. "Organizational Dysfunctions of Decline." *Academy of Management Journal* 30, 126–38.

Campbell, A. 1981. *The Sense of Well-Being in America: Recent Patterns and Trends.* New York: McGraw-Hill.

Clogg, C. 1979. *Measuring Underemployment: Demographic Indicators for the United States.* New York: Academic.

Clogg, C. and Shockey, J. W. 1984. "Mismatch Between Occupation and Schooling: A Prevalence Measure, Recent Trends, and Demographic Analysis." *Demography* 21, 235–57.

Corzine, J., Buntzman, G., and Busch, E. 1994. "Mentoring, Downsizing, Gender and Career Outcomes." *Journal of Social Behavior and Personality* 9(3), 517–28.

D'Aveni, R. A. 1989. "The Aftermath of Organizational Decline: A Longitudinal Study of the Strategic and Managerial Characteristics of Declining Firms." *Academy of Management Journal* 32, 577–605.

Dunahee, M. H. and Wangler, L. A. 1974. "The Psychological Contract: A Conceptual Structure for Management/Employee Relations." *Personnel Journal* 53(7), 518–26.

Dunn, L. F. 1979. "Measuring the Value of Community." *Journal of Urban Economics* 6, 371–82.

Feather, N. T. and O'Brien, G. E. 1986a. "A Longitudinal Analysis of the Effects of Employment, Different Patterns of Employment, and Unemployment on School-Leavers." *British Journal of Psychology* 77, 459–79.

———. 1986b. "A Longitudinal Study of the Effects of Employment and Unemployment on School-Leavers." *Journal of Occupational Psychology* 59, 101–11.

Feldman, D. C. 1996. "The Nature, Antecedents and Consequences of Underemployment." *Journal of Management* 22(3), 385–407.

Feldman, D. C. and Doerpinghaus, H. I. 1992. "Patterns of Part-Time Employment." *Journal of Vocational Behavior* 41(3), 282–94.

Feldman, D. C., Doerpinghaus, H. I., and Turnley, W. H. 1994. "Managing Temporary Workers: A Permanent HRM Challenge." *Organizational Dynamics* 23, 49–63.

Feldman, D. C., Leana, C. R., and Turnley, W. 1997. "A Relative Deprivation Approach to Understanding Underemployment." *Trends in Organizational Behavior* 4, 43–60.

Glyde, G. P. 1977. "Underemployment: Definition and Causes." *Journal of Economic Issues* 11(2), 245–60.

Gordon, D. M. 1972. *Theories of Poverty and Underemployment: Orthodox, Radical and Dual Labor Market Perspectives.* Lexington, MA: Lexington Books.

Greenhalgh, L. 1982. "Maintaining Organizational Effectiveness During Organizational Retrenchment." *Journal of Applied Behavioral Science* 18(2), 155–70.

Henry, W. A., III. 1994. *In Defense of Elitism.* New York: Doubleday.

Henson, K. D. 1996. *Just a Temp.* Philadelphia: Temple University Press.

Jahoda, M. 1982. *Employment and Unemployment: A Social Psychological Analysis.* Cambridge, England: Cambridge University Press.

Kaufman, H. 1982. *Professionals in Search of Work.* New York: Wiley.

Kjos, D. 1988. "Job Search Activity Patterns of Successful and Unsuccessful Job Seekers." *Journal of Employment Counselling* 5, 4–6.

Leana, C. R. and Feldman, D. C. 1995. "Finding New Jobs After a Plant Closing: Antecedents and Outcomes of the Occurrence and Quality of Reemployment." *Human Relations* 48(12), 1381–1401.

Marshall, G. 1984. "On the Sociology of Women's Unemployment, Its Neglect, and Significance." *Sociological Review* 32, 234–59.

Newman, K. S. 1988. *Falling From Grace.* New York: Free Press.

Nowak, T. C. and Snyder, K. A. 1983. "Women's Struggle to Survive a Plant Shutdown." *Journal of Intergroup Relations* 11, 25–44.

O'Brien, G. E. and Feather, N. T. 1990. "The Relative Effects of Unemployment and Quality of Employment on the Affect, Work Values, and Personal Control of Adolescents." *Journal of Occupational Psychology* 63, 151–65.

Organ, D. W. 1988. *Organizational Citizenship Behavior: The "Good Soldier" Syndrome.* Lexington, MA: Lexington Books.

Quinn, R. P. and Mandilovitch, M. S. 1975. *Education and Job Satisfaction: A Questionable Payoff.* NIE Papers in Education and Work. Vol. 5. Washington, DC: National Institute of Education.

Robinson, S. L., Kraatz, M. S., and Rousseau, D. M. 1994. "Changing Obligations and the Psychological Contract: A Longitudinal Study." *Academy of Management Journal* 37, 137–52.

Rosen, E. I. 1987. "Job Displacement Among Men and Women: The Crisis of Underemployment." *International Journal of Sociology and Social Policy* 7, 31–42.

Rousseau, D. M. 1990. "New Hire Perceptions of Their Own and Their Employer's Obligations: A Study of Psychological Contracts." *Journal of Organizational Behavior* 11, 389–400.

Seligman, M. E. P. 1975. *Helplessness.* San Francisco: Freeman.

Sullivan, T. A. 1978. *Marginal Workers, Marginal Jobs.* Austin: University of Texas Press.

Tan, G. Y., Leana, C. R., and Feldman, D. C. 1994. "A Longitudinal Study of Predictors of Job Loss Coping Strategies." *Proceedings of the National Academy of Management* 68–72.

Tipps, H. C. and Gordon, H. A. 1985. "Inequality at Work: Race, Sex and Underemployment." *Social Indicators Research* 16, 35–49.

Ullah, P. 1987. "Unemployed Black Youths in a Northern City." In D. Fryer and P. Ullah (eds.), *Unemployed People.* Milton Keynes, UK: Open University Press.

Van Dyne, L., Graham, J. W., and Dienesch, R. M. 1994. "Organizational Citizenship Behavior: Construct Redefinition, Measurement, and Validation." *Academy of Management Journal* 37, 765–802.

Weitzman, L. 1985. *The Divorce Revolution: The Unexpected Social and Economic Consequences for Women and Children in America.* New York: Basic Books.

Winefield, A. H. and Tiggemann, M. 1989. "Job Loss Versus Failure to Find Work as Psychological Stressors in the Young Unemployed." *Journal of Occupational Psychology* 62, 79–85.

Winefield, A. H., Winefield, H. R., Tiggemann, M., and Goldney, R. D. 1991. "A Longitudinal Study of the Psychological Effects of Unemployment and Unsatisfactory Employment on Young Adults." *Journal of Applied Psychology* 76, 424–31.

Chapter 5

Cultural Misunderstanding: Effective Communication in Globally Diverse Organizations

PYRRA ALNOT *and* MARY YOKO BRANNEN

Increasing globalization has brought people from different national backgrounds together to do business at an unprecedented rate. Billion dollar international joint ventures (IJVs), subsidiaries created by foreign direct investment, and global organizations are increasingly common. People are more likely than ever before to find themselves working for foreign subsidiaries, receiving overseas assignments, working on cross-national teams, or conducting negotiations with representatives from foreign organizations.

The transformation of the business environment into a global playing field has created enormous potential for organizational growth and profitability. It has also, however, led to a dramatic increase in misunderstandings, communication problems, and interpersonal conflicts due to differences in language and cultural backgrounds. These changes provide exciting new opportunities for academic research. They also create a need among practitioners for guidance on how to manage in the new globally diverse organizations. Success in one foreign venture does not guarantee success in another. For example, Disney's entry into the Japanese theme

*The authors thank Regina O'Neill and Lynda St. Clair for their helpful comments on earlier drafts of this chapter.

park market was tremendously successful (Brannen and Wilson 1996). However, Disney was much less successful when it followed a similar strategy for building a theme park in France, losing $920 million in its first year of operation (Brannen and Wilson 1996).

Many organizations are now made up of members from a variety of national and ethnic cultural backgrounds. The purpose of this chapter is to examine the issue of misunderstandings in globally diverse organizations. First, we define and explain cultural misunderstanding, drawing on a model of negotiated culture (Brannen 1994). Second, we discuss the different ways in which executives, change agents, and academic researchers have approached the problem of miscommunications in these organizations. Finally, using the academic research related to these two different perspectives as a springboard, we propose an agenda for future research. In this agenda, we suggest questions that need to be asked and methods that should be used to help gain insight into the pressing problem of cultural misunderstanding in today's organizations.

Defining and Explaining Cultural Misunderstanding

The world's economy is becoming increasingly integrated, resulting in greater interaction of people from different nations on a more regular basis. One indication of this increase is the change in international trade. International trade accounts for more than a quarter of all economic trade in most western European nations (Limaye and Victor 1991). Foreign direct investment is also on the rise (Limaye and Victor 1991). Over the past decade, the increase in economic integration between the world's nations has been reflected in the rapid increases in foreign direct investment and imports and exports. Overseas business is now undeniably important to organizations worldwide. In fact, almost all organizations are international in that they market their products internationally, conduct operations abroad, or have members from a variety of national backgrounds. For many organizations, the ability to remain profitable depends on their ability to cope successfully with global diversity. Therefore, researchers urgently need to address questions of how organizations and their members can most effectively meet the challenge of communicating in globally diverse environments.

Although people from different national backgrounds are sometimes able to carry out business together without much difficulty, more often than not problems arise from differences in language or culture. The degree to which cultural misunderstanding is a problem in interactions among people from different national backgrounds varies widely. In addition, cultural misunderstanding can be quite frustrating and emotionally distressing for those involved.

The financial costs of failure in international business are high. A three-year overseas assignment costs about $1 million, and the average cost of moving an expatriate overseas is $60,000 (Burzzcsc 1996). Between 16 and 40 percent of U.S. expatriates return early from their assignments, and each early return costs approximately $100,000 (Black, Mendenhall, and Oddou 1991). Cultural misunderstandings are certainly not the only cause of failure in international business. However, communication difficulties can prevent potential joint ventures from being formed, may exacerbate existing problems within international organizations, and in extreme cases may be a major factor in the failure of an international organization (Lane and Beamish 1990). Because the costs of failed international business are so high, it is especially important for researchers and practitioners to search for solutions to the problem of cultural misunderstanding.

Cultural misunderstanding includes barriers to communication arising from differences in language, failures to communicate effectively due to different understandings of situations, and conflicting beliefs about appropriate responses to these situations. Cultural misunderstandings vary in depth, ranging from language difficulties and differences in business etiquette to deeper conflicts involving core assumptions and values. Because cultural misunderstandings are often breakdowns in effective communication, in this chapter we use both the terms *misunderstanding* and *miscommunication*. Cultural misunderstandings occur at individual, group, and organizational levels. Thus, interpersonal misunderstandings arising from differences in national background, conflicts among subcultural groups within an organization, and companywide mistrust can all be forms of cultural misunderstanding. Participants may or may not recognize cultural misunderstandings when they occur, although they often become aware of their consequences. In this chapter, we use the term *cultural misunderstanding* usually in reference to differences arising from national background. However, we do not assume that all people who share a national background are culturally homogeneous. Most countries are culturally diverse, and people adopt the dominant national culture in varying degrees.

When people from different national backgrounds experience communication problems within organizations, it is sometimes unclear whether these problems arise solely from differences in national culture. Misunderstandings can also arise from differences in organizational culture, race, gender, religion, as well as individual differences. These factors are confounded with national culture and can make it challenging for organizational participants to diagnose the source of miscommunication. Because globally diverse organizations are multilayered environments, in some cases organizational participants can directly trace misunderstandings to differences in national background, but in others it is impossible to determine whether misunderstandings arise from these differences or some other source. Furthermore, participants may incorrectly believe that communication problems are attributable to differences in national background.

Different Perspectives on Cultural Misunderstanding

Executives, change agents, and academic researchers are all grappling with communication problems that arise in globally diverse organizations. Their quite different vantage points lead to striking differences in the way these groups frame communication problems that stem from differences in national culture.

Executives

How executives experience problems with intercultural communication seems to vary greatly depending on their position in the company and the type of organization. Executives and managers at different organizational levels are likely to experience problems arising from global diversity differently. In some globally diverse companies, expatriate and foreign national employees may experience the bulk of cultural misunderstanding. Executives within these organizations may not actually interact with people from different national backgrounds on a frequent basis. Thus, they may not be aware of the existence of intercultural communication problems within their organization. For instance, one executive pointed to figures showing the many countries his company was involved in and insisted that the company's employees did not experience any difficulties related to intercultural communication, although in fact they had. More than likely he did not hear about the miscommunications because many of the difficulties had been resolved by middle managers. Middle managers may be more aware of the complexities and challenges of interaction with people from different national backgrounds because they are more frequently called on to intervene in situations in which intercultural communication becomes problematic (Selmer 1996).

In other types of organizations, more people have direct experience with cultural misunderstanding. For instance, in IJVs in which there are approximately equal numbers of people from two national backgrounds, individuals at all levels of the organization are likely to interact and therefore are likely to experience difficulties with intercultural communication.

Executives and managers tend to describe misunderstandings that arise from differences in national culture as a cognitive problem. Consequently, they generally attempt to solve the problem through selection or training. They believe that employees either have or need to gain the appropriate knowledge and skills to be competent in globally diverse environments. For example, for overseas assignments or for working closely with people from different national backgrounds, executives we interviewed have suggested choosing only people who are well-suited for these situations. Several executives at U.S. companies mentioned selecting first- or second-generation Americans to do international work because they believe that these individuals would have gained the appropriate skills to do international work from their personal experiences in internationally diverse environments.

Executives also emphasized the importance of training employees to work in globally diverse environments. They feel that training is especially important for individuals who will be working abroad, as opposed to in domestic IJVs. Typically, executives are aware of the need to teach employees about the culture in which they will be working and may even offer minimal language training. Often this training is provided by external firms that specialize in preparing employees to work abroad.

Executives recognize the need for preparing employees to work in globally diverse environments in varying degrees. There are still some U.S. executives who feel that their employees do not need to adapt to the cultures of the people with whom they do business. One executive said,

"Getting along has to be done by international people; Americans are set in their ways." This statement suggests that some executives in U.S. companies expect the foreign nationals they work with to adapt to American styles of communicating and methods of doing business. It may reflect an unwillingness to commit resources to train Americans in skills that could make their intercultural interactions more effective. This executive's remark may also reflect underlying attitudes about American superiority. Such attitudes may ultimately harm a company's ability to compete globally.

Change Agents

In contrast to executives, change agents' framing of the problem of cultural misunderstanding tends to emphasize the role of emotional affect in interacting with people from different national backgrounds. Change agents we interviewed talked about intercultural interaction as a felt, emotional experience. They described the difficulty they experience in getting managers to be receptive to the emotional side of interacting with people from different national backgrounds. Change agents are often called into situations that are particularly volatile and conflict laden; this may be one reason that they focus on the emotional side of intercultural interaction. Change agents also stress the importance of the emotional work they do with organizations in which they intervene before problems arise. Thus, change agents tend not to view the solution to intercultural communication problems as a purely cognitive one. Although change agents recognize the importance of learning about the cultures and communication styles of people with whom one interacts, they do not believe that simply acquiring knowledge about another culture and its language will lead to smooth intercultural interactions. Instead, change agents view learning to interact with people from different national backgrounds as a lifelong process in which the emotional challenges are at least as important as the cognitive ones. They spoke of starting people on "a journey" rather than transmitting skills or knowledge. They also emphasized that people need to have a great deal of self-awareness in order to be able to communicate effectively in globally diverse environments. As one change agent said, "Understanding your own reactions is very important in cross-cultural interactions."

There is a striking contrast in the ways that change agents and executives frame the problems that arise from global diversity. The executives' understanding of the problem as cognitive leads them to look for solutions in selection and training, whereas the change agents' understanding of the important role of emotions in intercultural interaction leads them to look for solutions in self-awareness and growth. Although these two approaches may seem incompatible, it appears essential that the strengths of both should be combined. If executives would recognize the importance of the emotional aspects of intercultural interaction, they could effect positive change within their organizations.

Academic Researchers

Globalization and the proliferation of globally diverse organizations provide exciting new research opportunities for academics. In the past, management research has been largely parochial; its theories have been generated and tested primarily in U.S. companies (Boyacigiller and Adler 1991). Many organizational theories are implicitly assumed to be universally applicable. Globally diverse organizations allow researchers to test the universality of their theories. Furthermore, because effective intercultural communication is now critical for so many organizations, researchers feel that work in this area has an important "real-world" impact. The opportunity for interpenetration of research and practice is tremendous.

The problem of cultural misunderstanding has been approached in a variety of ways by academic researchers. A comprehensive literature review is well beyond the scope of this chapter. Instead, we provide an overview of approaches that academic researchers have taken in the study of cultural misunderstanding. In the field of communication studies, there has been work on intercultural communication (e.g., Gudykunst and Ting-Toomey 1988; Miller 1995) and cross-cultural training (e.g., Goldman 1992; Pruegger and Rogers 1994; Ptak, Cooper, and Brislin 1995; Tolbert and Mclean 1995). These studies approach cultural misunderstanding and its prevention rather directly. Other studies that do not directly focus on cultural misunderstanding are also relevant. In management research, there have been a number of studies on people's willingness to take overseas assignments (e.g., Aryee, Chay, and Chew 1996) and expatriate adjustment (e.g., Black 1992; Black, Mendenhall, and Oddou 1991; Dunbar 1992; Parker and McEvoy 1993). Psychologists have studied acculturation during cross-cultural transitions (e.g., Rogers and Ward 1993; Ward and Kennedy 1994). Organizational scholars have also studied cross-cultural interactions in organizations (e.g., Driskill and Downs

1995; Janssens 1995; Kopper 1993; Watanabe and Yamaguchi 1995). These studies often investigate the interactions of two cultural groups in an IJV or other globally diverse organization (e.g., Selmer 1996). Relatively little research has been published on cultural misunderstanding in work teams. An exception is Saphiere's (1996) study of the productivity of global business teams. In corporate strategy, some studies have focused on how differences in national culture affect foreign entry (e.g., Barkema, Bell, and Pennings 1997) and turnover among the management of acquired companies (Krug and Hegarty 1997).

Conceptual Problems Common to the Perspectives

All of the previously described perspectives on cultural misunderstanding share several assumptions about culture that are problematic. First, they generally assume that national cultures are homogeneous. Second, although they may consider differences in either organizational or national culture, they do not provide an understanding of how these cultures interact. Finally, culture is often conceptualized as a static variable when, in fact, culture is dynamic and malleable. These assumptions limit our ability to understand cultural miscommunication.

Equating culture and nation is problematic because national culture is not internalized in the same way by all who live in a nation. Individuals within a given national culture may hold beliefs typical of their culture to varying degrees (Brannen 1994). The assumption that all people from one nation are culturally similar may lead us to overlook other causes of cultural misunderstanding. Furthermore, some individuals from different national backgrounds may be more similar to one another than to others of the same national background. People who are cultural hybrids may serve as brokers for cultural change in globally diverse organizations.

Organizational actors are influenced by both their organizational and national cultures. Therefore, cultural misunderstandings may arise from differences in organizational as well as national culture.

To understand cultural misunderstanding, we must realize that cultures can change over time. Although many researchers now agree that culture is a dynamic phenomenon, in the past, culture was generally conceived of as a static variable. When culture is thought of as static, theories about what happens when people from different national cultures interact are quite different from when culture is considered dynamic. Several researchers have pointed out the flaws in conceptualizing culture as static (e.g., Brannen 1994; Boyacigiller and Adler 1991).

A recent model of negotiated culture (put forth by Brannen 1994 and expanded in Brannen and Salk 1998) explains how different cultures may influence each other through interaction. The model of negotiated culture posits that cultures change one another reciprocally through interaction. According to the model, "national cultural traits [are] elements that, over time, can be recombined or modified through ongoing interactions" (Brannen and Salk 1998). Negotiated cultures are more like mutations than hybrids. Hybrid cultures consist of a combination of elements from both cultures but do not contain any elements not present in the original cultures. By contrast, mutated, or negotiated, cultures contain new elements not present in either of the original cultures as well as elements from the original cultures.

An important implication of the model of negotiated culture is that it can create awareness by allowing people to attempt to negotiate cultures that address and resolve cultural misunderstandings. One manager at a U.S. company that had recently been acquired by a Japanese company expressed a great deal of consciousness about the process of cultural negotiation in his organization. The CEO of the new firm talked to his employees "about needing to build a culture that [was] not entirely Japanese or American." The manager responded by creating a newsletter to help deal with miscommunications and misunderstandings arising from differences in national culture. He said, "If we are going to build a culture, why not pay attention to the process and build a positive one?"

Agenda for Future Research

There are many avenues for future research on communication problems arising in globally diverse environments. Our agenda outlines research that should be undertaken on the antecedents and solutions of cultural misunderstanding at the individual, group, and organizational levels. We explain the need for research on the cognitive and emotional perspectives on cultural misunderstanding and then argue that research on cultural misunderstanding should be contextualized. Because the study of cultural misunderstanding in globally diverse organizations is relatively new, qualitative methodologies are especially appropriate (Eisenhart 1991). It is essential that longitudinal research be conducted since cultures change over time.

Research at the Individual Level

Research on cultural misunderstanding at the individual level should strive to achieve a deeper understanding of the antecedents of cultural misunderstanding. In particular, it is essential that we gain a better understanding of the ways that multiple layers of global diversity lead to cultural misunderstanding. Issues that will be important to consider include individuals' stances toward their culture of origin, nationalism, stereotypes, race, and gender. Issues of gender and race have received relatively little attention in research on interaction among people from different national backgrounds. Different national cultures have different gender roles and norms, and when people from different backgrounds interact, the participant's underlying assumptions about the appropriate roles for men and women may be called into question. Different nations have different racial and ethnic groups, and there are often tensions among these group members. It will be important to answer the question, How is cultural misunderstanding affected by the gender and race of the participants? Individual-level research should begin with exploratory, qualitative analyses. Microanalysis of natural conversation (Miller 1995) and interviews are research methodologies that will be useful for understanding interpersonal misunderstandings.

Individuals vary in the degree to which they adopt interaction and communication styles typical of others in their national culture. It would be interesting to investigate whether there are variations in the way people with different orientations toward their own background cultures interact with people with different national backgrounds. Does the extent to which people have internalized their culture of origin affect the ease with which they can communicate with people from other national backgrounds? Culture sketches can reveal how individuals of one national background vary (Brannen and Salk 1998).

More research is also necessary on the solutions to cultural misunderstanding at the individual level. Training and selection are commonly used to prevent cultural misunderstanding. It is critical that organizations know how to most effectively train and select individuals who will work in globally diverse environments. In particular, it will be interesting to research the effectiveness of training methods that teach people that culture is a dynamic, negotiated phenomenon rather than a fixed one. Longitudinal training studies comparing the performance and intercultural communication competence of those receiving various types of training should be used to determine which training methods are most effective.

Research at the Group Level

Future research on cultural misunderstanding should further explore the antecedents of group-level cultural misunderstanding. It is essential that more research on the antecedents and consequences of misunderstanding in globally diverse work teams be undertaken. The following questions will be especially important to answer: (1) How serious are the effects of cultural misunderstanding on the performance of globally diverse work teams? and (2) What factors make cultural misunderstanding more or less likely for globally diverse work teams? Group-level studies should be longitudinal and use observation, interviews, and surveys as research methodologies, which will add to both knowledge about small groups and cultural misunderstanding. Solutions to cultural misunderstandings among groups must also be examined. Network analysis could also be used to gain a better understanding of misunderstandings at the group as well as organizational levels.

Research at the Organizational Level

At the organizational level, research on cultural misunderstanding should focus on antecedents and solutions. It will be important to consider the issues that make problems with cultural misunderstanding especially likely. For instance, research on governance, strategy, and policy making will all be important. It will also be interesting to consider the role that organizational identity and image play in cultural misunderstanding. Research on solutions should focus on how organizations can create cultures that minimize cultural misunderstanding.

Emotional and Cognitive Skills

There is tension between the emotional approach of change agents and the cognitive approach of executives to the problem of cultural misunderstanding. Academic researchers can illuminate the importance of the role of both cognitive and emotional skills in communicating and doing business with people from different backgrounds. The role of emotion in intercultural communication is particularly understudied. Like executives, researchers have paid more attention to cognitive skills than to emotional ones. It is important to consider metaskills that include both emotional and cognitive components. Specific metaskills that should be researched include self-awareness and adaptability, and a method of measuring these types of skills should be developed. In addition, the relationship between these metaskills and intercultural communication competence, performance, and turnover should be explored. By identifying which skills and competencies are crucial for successful interaction in globally diverse organizations, researchers can help both executives and change agents who are concerned with preparing their employees or clients to succeed.

Contextualization

Much of the organizational research on national culture has ignored the contexts in which organizations are embedded. By failing to consider the context in which intercultural interaction takes place, a vacuum is created that highlights factors internal to the organization. Given that intercultural miscommunications are, by definition, heavily influenced by factors external to the organization, it seems essential to consider these factors when investigating intercultural communication in organizations. Important factors to consider include the type of legal systems, political and economic structures, geography, history, strength of economy, political stability, and state of development of the nations being researched. To conduct contextualized research, researchers must acknowledge and consider the implications of the multilayered environments in which globally diverse organizations are embedded. It is essential that researchers focus more attention on contextual factors both in making claims of generalizability and in setting boundary conditions.

Studying Success Cases

It is true that global diversity is often problematic for organizations. However, researchers who want to develop theories about effective communication in globally diverse organizations may also find it fruitful to investigate the cases in which people meet the challenges associated with global diversity successfully. To gain insight into what works, we must study the times when intercultural communication is successful. By focusing on successful cases, researchers can discover general principles of effective communication in globally diverse environments. And by studying successes, researchers can identify factors that are common across successful globally diverse organizations.

Multidisciplinary Approaches

Future research on cultural misunderstanding in globally diverse organizations should be multidisciplinary. Because context is so important, researchers will have to conduct background research that is multidisciplinary, drawing on such disciplines as history, economics, and political science. Research on the emotional and cognitive skills that are important to intercultural communication will need to draw on communication and psychology.

Internationally Diverse Research Teams

Finally, it is especially important that researchers who address the problem of cultural miscommunication form internationally diverse research teams, because a variety of cultural perspectives increases the likelihood that a more elaborate understanding of cultural misunderstanding will be obtained.

Conclusion

The problem of cultural misunderstanding is critical to the future of all organizations. As globalization continues to increase contact between people of different national backgrounds, it will become even more important to understand cultural misunderstanding and the multilayered environments in which it occurs. Our research agenda has laid out several areas of inquiry that should be investigated. Cultural misunderstanding is an interesting and challenging area in which to link together theory and practice, and the possibilities for future research are rich.

References

Aryee, S., Chay, Y. W., and Chew, J. 1996. "An Investigation of the Willingness of Managerial Employees to Accept an Expatriate Assignment." *Journal of Organizational Behavior* 17, 267–83.

Barkema, H. G., Bell, J. H. J., and Pennings, J. M. 1997. "Foreign Entry, Cultural Barriers, and Learning." *Strategic Management Journal* 17, 151–66.

Black, J. S. 1992. "Socializing American Expatriate Managers Overseas: Tactics, Tenure, and Role Innovation." *Group & Organization Management* 17, 171–92.

Black, J. S., Mendenhall, M., and Oddou, G. 1991. "Toward a Comprehensive Model of International Adjustment: An Integration of Multiple Theoretical Perspectives." *Academy of Management Review* 16, 291–317.

Boyacigiller, N. A. and Adler, N. J. 1991. "The Parochial Dinosaur: Organizational Science in a Global Context." *Academy of Management Review* 16, 262–90.

Brannen, M. Y. 1994. "Your Next Boss Is Japanese: Negotiating Culture Change at a Western Massachusetts Paper Mill." Ph.D. diss., University of Massachusetts.

Brannen, M. Y. and Salk, J. E. 1998. "Partnering Across Borders: Negotiating Organizational Culture in a German-Japanese Joint-Venture." *Human Relations.* 52(9).

Brannen, M. Y. and Wilson, J. M. 1996. "Recontextualization and Internationalization: Lessons in Transcultural Materialism From the Walt Disney Company." *CEMS Business Review* 1, 97–110.

Burzzese, A. 1996. "Foreign Toil." *Human Resource Executive* 10(9), 54–55.

Driskill, G. W. and Downs, C. W. 1995. "Hidden Differences in Competent Communication: A Case Study of an Organization with Euro-Americans and First Generation Immigrants From India." *International Journal of Intercultural Relations* 19, 505–22.

Dunbar, E. 1992. "Adjustment and Satisfaction of Expatriate U.S. Personnel." *International Journal of Intercultural Relations* 16, 1–16.

Eisenhardt, K. M. 1991. "Better Stories and Better Constructs: The Case for Rigor and Comparative Logic." *Academy of Management Review,* 16(3), 620–28.

Goldman, A. 1992. "Intercultural Training of Japanese for U.S.-Japanese Interorganizational Communication." *International Journal of Intercultural Relations* 16, 195–215.

Gudykunst, W. B. and Ting-Toomey, S. 1988. *Culture and Interpersonal Communication. Vol. 8: Sage Series in Interpersonal Communication.* Newbury Park, CA: Sage.

Janssens, M. 1995. "Intercultural Interaction: A Burden on International Managers?" *Journal of Organizational Behavior* 16, 155–67.

Kopper, E. 1993. "Swiss and Germans: Similarities and Differences in Work-Related Values, Attitudes and Behavior." *International Journal of Intercultural Relations* 17, 167–84.

Krug, J. A. and Hegarty, W. H. 1997. "Postacquisition Turnover Among U.S. Top Management Teams: An Analysis of the Effects of Foreign vs. Domestic Acquisitions of U.S. Targets." *Strategic Management Journal* 18, 667–75.

Lane, H. W. and Beamish, P. W. 1990. "Cross-Cultural Cooperative Behavior in Joint Ventures in LCDs." *Management International Review* 30, 87–102.

Limaye, M. R. and Victor, D. A. 1991. "Cross-Cultural Business Communication Research: State of the Art and Hypotheses for the 1990s." *Journal of Business Communication* 28, 277–99.

Miller, L. 1995. "Two Aspects of Japanese and American Co-Worker Interaction: Giving Instructions and Creating Rapport." *Journal of Applied Behavioral Science* 31, 141–61.

Parker, B. and McEvoy, G. M. 1993. "Initial Examination of a Model of Intercultural Adjustment." *International Journal of Intercultural Relations* 17, 355–79.

Pruegger, V. J. and Rogers, T. B. 1994. "Cross-Cultural Training: Methods and Assessment." *International Journal of Intercultural Relations* 18, 369–87.

Ptak, C. L., Cooper, J., and Brislin, R. 1995. "Cross Cultural Training Programs: Advice and Insights From Experienced Trainers." *International Journal of Intercultural Relations* 19, 425–53.

Rogers, J. and Ward, C. 1993. "Expectation-Experience Discrepancies and Psychological Adjustment During Cross-Cultural Reentry." *International Journal of Intercultural Relations* 17, 185–96.

Saphiere, D. M. H. 1996. "Productive Behaviors of Global Business Teams." *International Journal of Intercultural Relations* 20(2), 227–59.

Selmer, J. 1996. "What Expatriate Managers Know About the Work Values of Their Subordinates: Swedish Executives in Thailand." *MIR* 36, 231–43.

Tolbert, A. S. and Mclean, G. N. 1995. "Venezuelan Culture Assimilator for Training United States Professionals Conducting Business in Venezuela." *International Journal of Intercultural Relations* 19, 111–25.

Ward, C. and Kennedy, A. 1994. "Acculturation Strategies, Psychological Adjustment, and Sociocultural Competence During Cross-Cultural Transitions." *International Journal of Intercultural Relations* 18, 329–43.

Watanabe, S. and Yamaguchi, R. 1995. "Intercultural Perceptions at the Workplace: The Case of the British Subsidiaries of Japanese Firms." *Human Relations* 48, 581–607.

Chapter 6

Chaotic Role Movement in Large Organizations: From Planning to Dynamic Management

Nancy Tennant Snyder *and* Deborah Duarte

T his chapter addresses the phenomenon termed *chaotic role movement,* defined as the rapid movement of professionals and managers into new roles within a company in which the number of roles exceed the number of qualified people available. *Role* refers to a broad range of dynamic assignments that represent the current work of the organization. The term *role* is meant to be broader than a job description and may evolve over time to reflect the current business situation.

We discuss the emergence of chaotic role movement, explore its prevalence in today's business environment, and argue that it is a pressing issue in most large and global companies. We investigate the possible impact of chaotic role movement at the organizational level, including negative effects such as the loss of organizational memory, lack of continuity in assignments, lack of follow-through on projects, and the continual relearning of best practices. We also consider the positive effects, including cross-fertilization of ideas, development of broad expertise, and rapid learning across functional and geographic boundaries. Finally, we present a set of ideas about future research on chaotic role movement. This research agenda includes gaining a more in-depth and fact-based understanding of the prevalence of the phenomenon, how to measure it, and how to assess its impact at the organizational level.

The Death of Traditional Career and Succession Planning

It is almost mundane to talk about the dynamic nature of today's business environment. However, the current turbulent environment may be related to the emergence of chaotic role movement. In the past thirty years we have seen hostile takeovers, industry consolidations, downsizing, flattening of hierarchy, reengineering, outsourcing, globalization, and the creation of large shared services centers. The workforce has expanded to include not only the baby boomers but the baby bust generation, as well as an increased number of women and minorities. Life inside today's organizations consists of a diverse, fast-paced, competitive, and rapidly changing environment where leverage, speed, and innovation are critical for success.

Although these environmental changes are well-documented, the concept of "career" from both the individual and organizational perspective is still changing. According to Stevens (1994), job rotations traditionally were seen as one intervention to achieve more organizational effectiveness. Traditional job rotations in the literature have been defined as lateral transfers of employees between jobs in an organization that do not involve a change in financial compensation (Campion, Cheraskin, and Stevens 1994). In the past, job rotations were utilized to reduce job boredom (Miller, Dhaliwal, and Magas 1973) or as orientation for new hires (Wexley and Baldwin 1986).

Career development and succession planning were portrayed as "*a deliberate and systematic effort*" by the organization to ensure continuity in key positions and encourage individual advancement" (Rothwell 1994, 6, emphasis added). The focus was on orderly planning with sufficient planning time to identify and develop people, create candidate slates, and implement moves. In the past, planning time for this process was generally two to five years. Planned job rotations were used as development tools, to broaden experience, to reduce boredom, or as an orientation for new employees (Miller, Dhaliwal, and Magas 1973; Wexley and Baldwin 1986).

Contemporary Trends

Most literature focusing on career development today points out that the traditional notion of a career is outdated. According to Arthur (1992), most of the literature on career theory was developed before the turbulent workforce and organizational changes occurred. The well-planned vertical move up an organization's hierarchy has been replaced with the concept of career pandemonium (Brousseau et al. 1996). The career has been substituted with different roles that people move in and out of to perform the work of the organization. The traditional job or position has been overcome by the work that needs to be done. Careers in most organizations appear to be a series of projects punctuated with some ongoing work in a functional area, not a well-planned and deliberate sequence of positions, experiences, and training.

Today the problem is particularly acute. The competitive forces now driving the redesign of organizations and roles, and the shift toward downsizing, make accommodating the individual in his or her career without regard to organizational forces unrealistic (Arthur 1992). Additionally, organizations that are trying to redefine loyalty need to find new ways of earning it to avoid the false promises of career pathing that they have traditionally made (Dalton 1989).

Deliberate career- and succession-planning systems have now given way to accountability for filling demand on a moments notice, with little information about new roles, assignments, or the people who may be available. The following experience of a director of career and management development for a Fortune 150 company who maintains accountability for the careers of its almost 30,000 employees and 6,000 managers worldwide is typical. The company he works for is downsizing 2,000 employees, repatriating 20 higher-management employees from expatriate assignments, creating a shared services center, and implementing an enterprisewide information technology solution that will require 250 new assignments and involve a major reorganization. Incredibly, these changes have not been integrated, coordinated, or "planned." The director has been given the task of implementing these moves with barely two months' notice and a window of less than six months for completion. As this example illustrates, it seems that succession planning has given way to solving specific problems in real time. According to Rothwell (1994), career planning has been replaced with a form of risk management. The bottom line is that companies now operate in an environment in which there is more work to do than qualified people to do it, and more change than the system was designed to handle.

The Prevalence of Chaotic Role Movement

The literature provides little information on the phenomenon of rapid job changes. Hall (1976, 1984) identified its existence and extensively discussed the demand side of job movement—the existence of more jobs than people available. Campion, Cheraskin, and Stevens (1994) found that a common complaint among executives is that employees rotate too rapidly. They reported that ripple effects of this movement include more openings than an organization can fill, perhaps saving labor dollars and developing employees through a wide range of opportunities. On the other hand, this rapid movement reduces accountability. Employees are put in situations in which they do not have to implement their own plans and departments in the organization have no real guidance about how to balance development of people with the need to get work done.

Pepsi has recently taken proactive steps to slow the rapid movement of executives. One of the most dominant features of the Pepsi environment over the past few years was high turnover in management positions. Few executives ever stayed in one place long enough to execute strategy. Accordingly, Pepsi has recently implemented a system in which clearance from the chief executive officer is necessary for any movement of an executive who has not held his or her position for three years. This new system was put into place in an effort to provide a stable environment for executives to operate with accountability for their own successes or failures (Deogun 1997).

To build further the understanding of how prevalent chaotic role movement is, we conducted interviews with career-planning professionals from five global companies: Johnson & Johnson, Nortel, Whirlpool, Time Life, and Merck. All agreed that the phenomenon was prevalent in their organization. In fact, data from other types of organizational diagnosis efforts at four of these companies showed that people who participated in both management and employee focus groups reported that rapid changes in assignments and too rapid job rotation of individual managers were some of the most critical organizational issues impacting performance. Focus group participants stated that changes were often so quick that there was not enough continuity to allow any reasonable chance of task accomplishment. In addition, they described the need to "reinvent the wheel" and revisit goals and objectives as people came in and out of positions as a major waste of time and energy as well as a drain on employee morale.

When we asked the companies whether they routinely tracked or measured turnover rate in roles, one employee replied, "We would never track that, it changes too often!" In fact, the literature contains only a modicum of data that tracks the average rate of internal role or job changes by professionals.

For us to gain an understanding of how companies measure chaotic role movement, we asked a succession-planning professional from one of the companies we interviewed to calculate her company's chaotic role movement. She did, but said it was not easy. She performed the task manually and had to estimate some data. She found that of the 570 top worldwide managers that the company closely tracked, roughly 330 had changed their role in the past six months. This equates to 0.58 moves per year per person! These data are consistent with Campion, Cheraskin, and Steven's (1994) study of a large pharmaceutical's lateral movement of finance professionals—about 0.44 moves per year per person. To determine how difficult it was to obtain the data, we asked the succession-planning professional to explain the company's method of gathering the information. She explained:

> We have a room where we have the organization charts of the top 140 leaders on the four magnetic white-board walls. Each incumbent is shown with a photograph and brief history on magnetic cards so we can move them on the walls as a visual image when the executive committee deliberates moves. I went down to the organization chart room and counted how many people were new in their job this year given my knowledge of which magnetic cards we had to change. To get the status on the other 430 top managers was much harder. These managers are located in regions and we do not have one personnel system to track them. I checked my human resource information system to get as much of the data as I could, then I called each region and asked assistants to the human resources vice president for that region to count how many of the top managers had changed jobs. (Linda Krager-Walker, personal communication, September 23, 1997)

The consequences of chaotic movement can be positive or negative. Organizational learning may be enhanced by the movement of employees from one position to another, transferring important information about culture, best practices, and lessons learned. Chaotic role movement may also be one answer for jump-starting important projects. However, implementation may be left to people who were not involved in the initial chartering of the project, which could lead to "reinventing the wheel" and rehashing of already established goals, objectives, and processes. On the other hand, chaotic role movement may negatively impact organizational memory because it may disrupt behavioral patterns and the type of intensive interaction that allows people to meaningfully share what they have learned. Chaotic role movement may also have negative implications for task performance. Table 6-1 summarizes potential benefits and negative impacts from chaotic role movement.

Literature Review

We review the literature related to chaotic role movement in four parts: open systems theory, organizational and individual approaches, disadvantages, and advantages. Finding specific contemporary literature on this topic proved to be difficult. As a result, we use open systems theory to bring a broad conceptual framework to the topic of chaotic role movement.

Open Systems Theory

Katz and Kahn (1978) describe organizations as open systems that maintain the following characteristics:

1. They take energy from the environment and perform a transformation process that results in output back into the environment. In organizations, the input may range from money to raw materials or ideas, and the output can, of course, be goods or services.

2. The transformation process consists of a cycle of events that we typically call work or manufacturing. These are enabled by integration and coordination of people, divisions, factories, business units, and other entities. As the organization grows and differentiates, the process of integration and coordination can become more difficult and complex.

3. Organizations survive, in part, by storing energy and other vital resources in excess of their need. In other words, at times organizations

Table 6-1. Categories of Chaotic Role Movement with Positive and Negative Impact

Category	Advantages	Disadvantages
Organizational learning	Cross-fertilization of ideas, lessons learned, best practices; transfer of culture between organizational units; increased networks for sharing learning.	Too rapid change leaves little time for deep understanding of issues; too rapid movement may disrupt learning patterns in departments.
Projects	Movement may jump-start projects.	May leave implementation "hanging"; people working under rotated manager may experience too rapid change in objectives and goals; smooth transition of management in and out of positions; lack of consistency in management styles.
Development of expertise to execute strategy	Job rotation addresses broadening of experience; increased organizational network may lead to better integration across units.	May not lead to development of deep expertise in functional areas; succession planning needs may not be met due to less intensive experience and training in some areas.

will need more money than they may have or more work performed than they have people to perform it. In these cases, money may be borrowed from the bank. People may be hired, borrowed from temp agencies, or, sometimes, people with the company work in multiple roles.

Viewed in the context of open systems theory, chaotic role movement is symptomatic of today's problems with coordination and integration of work.

Organizational and Individual Approaches

According to Arthur (1992), career theory is the study of simultaneously looking at the persons doing the work and the institution. This new school of thought considers the approach of using an individualistic model of careers in which the individuals are the agents of their own progress. Unfortunately, this model often neglects the structural constraints facing managers in the organization. Structural constraints include downsizing, organizational design, and politics. Arthur (1992) concedes that if organizations exposed the rules for advancement, we could better study the new approach. Unfortunately, the rules are often kept hidden.

Brousseau et al. (1996) suggest that in order for companies to stay ahead of chaotic role movement, they must create systems that allow employees to take control of their careers and prepare themselves for constant changes. Professionals must constantly update and reinvent themselves for new, unforeseen career opportunities. They also point out that organizations need to develop a group of employees who have a high tolerance for uncertainty and a good deal of self-confidence. Furthermore, organizations need to develop a pluralistic approach to career management and organizational coordination and integration. This strategy will help employees develop themselves while simultaneously helping the organization to maintain a diverse, skilled workforce to meet dynamic environmental demands in staffing.

Disadvantages of Chaotic Role Movement

There are other disadvantages of chaotic role movement than those we referenced previously. These range from perceptions of the work environment and task, decreased productivity, increased workload, and disenfranchisement of those not rotated.

In a study of the leaders' movement in the U.S. army, participants were tested at the beginning of a job cycle, and then again six to nine months later. The results showed that their perception of the work environment decreased with changes and that task-related behaviors were negatively affected (Bons and Fiedler 1976). Moreover, rapid rotation of employees may reduce productivity because of the time it takes the manager to train a new employee and the increased likelihood of errors when an employee first learns a new job (Cheraskin and Campion 1996).

Finally, there is evidence that there are costs in terms of satisfaction and motivation for the employees who are left behind as well as for the manager themselves (Bons and Fiedler 1976; Cheraskin and Campion 1996). Employees who are subject to the rapid movement of their managers report that they are less satisfied than people with a more stable environment. Bons and Fiedler (1976) also found that perceptions of the work environment decreased with the number of changes made. The more change, the less satisfied people were and the more the work was negatively affected.

Advantages of Chaotic Role Movement

There are positive aspects associated with rapid role movement. Role movement may be one way to get the job done quickly. It could serve the purpose of coordination and integration in an environment of scarce resources. Other advantages may include broader experience for individuals, increased learning, increased job satisfaction, and transfer of organizational culture.

Cheraskin and Campion (1996) asked executives in a financial function of a large organization what benefits the organization received from rapid job rotation. The executives reported benefits that facilitated integration and coordination, including broader perspectives on other business units, adaptability and flexibility, exposure of leaders to other management styles, the building of a network of contacts, and interpersonal skills.

Role movement may also aid integration and coordination by increasing learning and development. Mintzberg (1973) suggested that job rotations increase managerial learning and are a key executive development tool. Schein (1978) supports this notion by noting that job rotations improve growth and development at any point in a manager's career. Job rotation has also been a strategy for professionals whose careers have plateaued (Slocum et al. 1985).

Organizational learning and culture may benefit from job movement. There is evidence that professionals engage in sensemaking when entering new jobs so that they can interpret the new experiences (Louis 1982). Chaotic role movement could add to organizational learning in the area of knowledge acquisition. Campion, Cheraskin, and Stevens (1994) found that executive perceptions of job rotations included helping with culture transfer.

Campion, Cheraskin, and Stevens (1994) also found that two organizational benefits of rotation were career affect benefits such as employee commitment, and organization integration benefits such as increased networks.

The literature we have presented suggests emerging research on chaotic role movement. In the next section, we suggest a research agenda focused on this phenomenon.

A Research Agenda

Research on chaotic role movement can be approached from at least three perspectives: individual, work group, and organizational. Although there is most likely interesting and relevant work at the individual and work-group levels, we address a research agenda targeted at the organizational level. We propose three streams of research that build on one another:

1. Developing a standard method of measuring chaotic role movement and comparing the rate across organizations;
2. Documenting and describing the positive and negative impacts of chaotic role movement; and
3. Measuring the positive and negative impacts of chaotic role movement.

The next sections outline potential research strategies in each of these areas.

Measuring Chaotic Role Movement

Finding a standard measure of chaotic role movement will aid in promoting research that is generalizable and comparable across organizations. What should the standard measure be? How can it be applied across disparate companies? A standard measure should facilitate consistency in research methods and improve reliability of results. On the practical side, it should provide companies with a way of determining whether their chaotic role movement rate is high or low compared with similar organizations.

A first step in developing a common measure of chaotic role movement would be to select a cross section of companies from different industries. These organizations could also be sorted by factors such as size, revenue, product mix, industry type, and number and location of sites. This would allow comparisons among companies with similar demographics and may even ultimately lead to a set of chaotic role movement indicators that vary along a number of different variables.

It also may prove useful to target common organizational levels for analysis, such as managerial or directorial, that are likely to be similar across organizations. Another approach may be to target typical organizational positions for analysis. This might include positions in which an employee has subordinates who are at the lower levels of the organizational hierarchy or who perform a specific configuration of responsibilities. In any case, a common definition of the types of people being examined would be necessary to ensure that results are comparable.

Next, a definition of a role movement would need to be developed. This could be created with input from some of the people in target roles. A move may be defined as a temporary move to a new project or position, a promotion, a lateral move to a new function, or the dramatic reorganization of an existing role.

To develop a standard measure, each organization would need to provide information about the number of moves per year (or another period of time) that fit the definition of a role movement for each individual in the target population. An aggregate chaotic role movement rate could be established for each organization, industry, or company type as well as for organizational levels. Thus, chaotic role movement rates could be tracked to determine whether there are trends across organizations, industries, levels, and other variables.

Documenting and Describing the Impact of Chaotic Role Movement

The second stream of research builds on the first and begins to describe and categorize the positive and negative impacts of chaotic role movement: What are the advantages and disadvantages of chaotic role movement? This research could relate the factors associated with chaotic role movement, such as rate and patterns of movement in different industries or organizational levels to categories of positive or negative impact. This research could begin to build data with which hypotheses could be formed about the positive, negative, or neutral relationship among rate of chaotic role movement and constructs such as organizational learning, employee satisfaction, customer loyalty, cost or schedule issues regarding project implementation, or development of expertise and competency.

One way to structure this research may be to gather qualitative descriptions about impact from individuals targeted for analysis in the first research stream. These data could be analyzed and categorized to determine types of negative and positive impact. These categories could then be related to factors such as rate of chaotic role movement, chaotic role movement in different industries, or chaotic role movement in different managerial levels.

Data could be supplemented with interviews and focus groups from other individuals in the organization such as subordinates and managers of chaotic role movement managers, customers, and top management. This would provide different perspectives about the impact of chaotic role movement as well as corroborate and augment data gathered from chaotic role movement managers. Interview and focus group data could also be triangulated with information supplied by documents such as project plans and schedules, employee satisfaction or morale surveys, and organizational culture analysis and succession-planning documents.

After the primary themes from the qualitative data are established, questionnaires and other instruments could be developed and distributed to examine how rates of chaotic role movement in different contexts are associated with standard categories of positive and negative impact. These tools would allow the collection of large amounts of data over a number of different organizational contexts.

Measuring the Impact of Chaotic Role Movement

Finally, how fast is too fast in job movement? The third stream of research begins to actually measure the specific impact of chaotic role movement in different situations. The content of the investigation would, of course, depend on the results of the activity in the second stream of research; however, the general idea is to begin to quantify the actual impact of chaotic role movement. The rate of chaotic role movement could be correlated to data such as customer satisfaction or employee morale, project costs, schedule or quality data, turnover in target positions, or the number of unfilled top management positions or top positions filled from the outside.

These three streams of research, although preliminary, would prove valuable in beginning to facilitate an understanding about the existence of chaotic role movement and its potential impact. They could provide organizations and leaders with guidelines about the circumstances when chaotic role movement becomes disruptive and allow them to plan better the rate and type of movement to ameliorate negative impacts and facilitate positives ones.

Conclusion

In this chapter we have discussed the emergence and impact of chaotic role movement in organizations today. Although chaotic role movement has been identified as a pressing problem because of its negative consequences (e.g., loss of organizational memory, lack of continuity and follow-through on projects, and continual relearning of best practices), we have also identified some positive effects (e.g., cross-fertilization of ideas, development of broad expertise, and rapid learning across functional and geographic boundaries). For researchers and practitioners alike, the most critical first step in mitigating the problems and maximizing the benefits of chaotic role movement is to gather more concrete evidence about the phenomenon. Until we can adequately measure chaotic role movement, it will be difficult to assess its impact on organizations and their employees.

References

Arthur, M. B. 1992. "Career Theory in a Dynamic Context." In D. H. Montross and M. C. J. Shinkman (eds.), *Career Development: Theory and Practice.* Springfield, IL: Charles C Thomas.

Bons, P. M. and Fiedler, F. E. 1976. "Changes in Organizational Leadership and the Behavior of Relationship and Task Motivated Leaders." *Administrative Science Quarterly* 21(3), 453–73.

Brousseau, K. R., Driver, M. J., Eneroth, K., and Larsson, R. 1996. "Career Pandemonium: Realigning Organizations and Individuals." *Academy of Management Executive* 10(4), 52–66.

Campion, M. A., Cheraskin, L., and Stevens, M. J. 1994. "Career-Related Antecedents and Outcomes of Job Rotations." *Academy of Management Journal* 37(6), 1518–42.

Cheraskin, L. and Campion, M. A. 1996. "Study Clarifies Job-Rotation Benefits." *Personnel Journal* 75, 31–38.

Dalton, F. W. 1989. "Developmental Views of Careers in Organizations." In M. B. Arthur, D. T. Hall, and B. S. Lawrence (eds.), *Handbook of Career Theory.* New York: Cambridge University Press.

Deogun, N. 1997. "Pepsi Challenge: Can Company's Brass Mute Flashy Culture and Make Profits Fizz?" *Wall Street Journal* (August 8), A1.

Hall, D. T. 1976. *Careers in Organizations.* Pacific Palasades, CA: Goodyear.

———. 1984. "Human Resource Development and Organizational Effectiveness." In C. J. Fombrun, N. M. Tichy, and M. A. Devanna (eds.), *Strategic Human Resource Management.* New York: Wiley.

Katz, D. and Kahn, R. 1978. *The Social Psychology of Organizations.* New York: Wiley.

Louis, M. L. 1982. "Managing Career Transition: A Missing Link in Career Development." *Organizational Dynamics* 10(1), 68–77.

Miller, F. G., Dhaliwal, T. S., and Magas, L. J. 1973. "Job Rotation Raises Productivity." *Industrial Engineering* 5, 24–26.

Mintzberg, H. 1973. *The Nature of Managerial Work.* Englewood Cliffs, NJ: Prentice Hall.

Rothwell, W. J. 1994. *Effective Succession Planning: Ensuring Leadership Continuity and Building Talent From Within.* New York: American Management Association.

Schein, E. H. 1978. *Career Dynamics: Matching Individual and Organizational Needs.* Reading, MA: Addison-Wesley.

Slocum, J. W., Cron, W. L., Hansen, R. W., and Rawlings, S. 1985. "Business Strategy and the Management of Plateaued Employees." *Academy of Management Journal* 28, 133–54.

Stevens, M. 1994. "Career-Related Antecedents and Outcomes of Job Rotations." *Academy of Management Journal* 37(6), 1518–42.

Wexley, K. N. and Baldwin, T. T. 1986. "Posttraining Strategies for Facilitating Positive Transfer: An Empirical Exploration." *Academy of Management Journal* 29, 503–20.

PART 2

Process Problems

Chapter 7

Designing Agile Organizations: Organizational Learning at the Boundaries

Jeffrey A. Martin *and* Paul R. Carlile

Organizations have been spending millions of dollars to improve or change their processes to become more agile in responding to changes brought on by growing global competition. However, in spite of the enormous amount of money and effort expended, difficulties persist. More than 80 percent of change efforts directed at processes fail to achieve the results hoped for by management. (Champy 1994; Micklethwait and Woolridge 1996). Executives and managers continue to complain that ineffective internal processes are hindering their organizations' ability to respond to the changing demands of the internal and external environment. An overwhelming sense of urgency often leads these organizations to begin efforts to change processes without a rigorous understanding of the efficacy of the methods being utilized.

How can we overcome this situation? The purpose of this chapter is to suggest a way to bridge the gap between theories of organizational process and the actual processes in practice. Our goal is to help establish an agenda for future research that will advance our understanding of how to create agile organizations through the design and implementation of effective organizational processes.

In this chapter, we view the organization as a bundle of processes that create or support the creation of value for a customer (Denison 1997;

Porter 1979). Furthermore, we view agility as the capacity "to respond to changing conditions faster than the competition" (Pascale 1996, 113). Thus, agile organizations can be described as a bundle of processes performed and integrated in a way that strengthens the capacity for change within the organization.

We begin with a detailed description of the characteristics of agile organizations and processes. We then review the existing academic literature on change efforts directed at redesigning organizational processes, with a special emphasis on research from the sociotechnical systems perspective. Drawing on this earlier research, we develop a framework based on communities-of-practice and organizational learning that can be used to organize our thinking about process problems. We discuss why normative and rational ideologies, which have dominated management practice in the past, are no longer appropriate in today's turbulent business environment. Finally, we provide an agenda for future research on designing agile organizational processes relevant to both management practice and scholarly theory building.

Agile Organizations

Agile organizations are able to institutionalize the ability to purposefully change themselves or their processes in whole or in part across multiple dimensions based on their perceived strengths, weaknesses, threats, or opportunities. Agile organizations accomplish this by developing the capability of collectively linking together working, learning, and the capacity for change across inter- and intraorganizational boundaries. Agile organizations respond and adapt to internal and external changes, anticipate future realities, and redefine the organization's purpose, mission, products, services, and industry. These organizations are fast, flexible, lean, and constantly create and disseminate new knowledge (Pascale 1996; Roth 1996).

When organizations fail to adapt to changing conditions faster than their competitors, it is often due to problems within and between the organizational processes (Hammer 1996; Hammer and Champey 1993; Porter 1979, 1985). Process problems exist when the individuals and groups executing the processes fail to adapt appropriately to unexpected occurrences or when a change in strategy demands creation, change, or replacement of existing processes. Organizations usually do not experience process problems as the result of an inefficient design for the tasks that need to be accomplished. Rather, they experience process problems as a result of an inability to handle "exceptions" to the rule. Furthermore, process problems often manifest themselves at the boundaries within organizations that are delineated by the major process groupings (e.g., engineering and manufacturing) when individuals from different communities are unable to effectively exchange information or solve problems together.

Organizational theorists have primarily focused their analysis of problems related to agility at either the microlevel of how individuals and small groups make sense of and respond to their environment (Weick 1995) or at the macrolevel of industry analysis through studies of organizational ecology (Hannah and Freeman 1977) and institutional theory (Dimaggio and Powell 1991). However, the explicit (canonical) and tacit (noncanonical) knowledge required by individuals and groups to make sense of problems and construct new ways to solve them is embodied at a different level of analysis, that of communities-of-practice (Brown and Duguid 1991; Lave and Wenger 1990; Orr 1990). A community-of-practice can be demarcated by organizational process groupings such as sales, design engineering, or manufacturing. As a unit of analysis, a community-of-practice embraces and demarcates the social and practical (e.g., the material requirements of the task) dynamics of getting the work done. Consequently, a community-of-practice as a level of analysis focuses on the social and practical combination of organizational processes and the challenge of agility.

In this chapter, we propose that the dynamics of how communities-of-practice interact across their boundaries with other communities-of-practice affects the efficacy of the creation of organizational knowledge required for action and, thus, the agility of the organization. Communities-of-practice embody and bound the knowledge of the organization's processes and can potentially cloister that knowledge of practice from the rest of the organization (Brown and Duguid 1991). Agile organizations thus distinguish themselves by becoming proficient at communicating and applying the knowledge of practice contained within multiple communities-of-practice to solve complex organizational problems.

Significance of Process Problems

Less than 16 percent of the change efforts in business organizations achieve the results hoped for by management and more than 68 percent of these efforts encounter significant problems (Micklethwait and Woolridge 1996). Over the past ten years, most organizational change efforts have come under the rubric of total quality management, just-in-time, customer value management, or business process reengineering. Central to how these efforts are implemented is the redesign or design of new business processes, sometimes with the goal of achieving economic efficiencies by accomplishing the outcome with fewer people. However, when we interviewed executives and management consultants and surveyed the popular management literature, we found that most of these recommended approaches for dealing with change (process problems) came up short in practice. Furthermore, we found that the reasons for failure were fundamentally grounded in human issues of organizational dynamics, rather than in the use of technical business skills (e.g., finance, operations, or cost accounting). Table 7-1 summarizes the results of our interviews and survey of the popular management literature.

The reasons given for failed change efforts as summarized in Table 7-1 are valid observations (Champy 1994; Cook 1996; Hall, Rosenthal, and Wade 1994; Hammer 1996; Lancaster 1995; Micklethwait and Woolridge 1996; Mumford and Hendricks 1996). However, they are not the root causes; rather, they are the symptoms of deeper problems that are not recognized or addressed in most change methodologies. For example,

Table 7-1. Interview and Survey Summary of Process Problems

Category	How Executives/Consultants Experience Process Problems
Leadership	Lack of executive commitment and skills
Culture	Inability of the people to adapt to new ways of doing business
Capabilities and skills	Lack of relevant workforce or management skills required by new environments and competitive realities
Structure	Ineffectual organizational design and communication
Process	Processes that are not efficient, not integrated across business units, and not effective at delivering value to the customer
Systems	Lack of effective process enablers and information systems
Trust	Inability to overcome fear and anxiety in the organization

reengineering's lack of success[1] has caused even reengineering gurus such as Hammer, Champy, and Davenport and consulting giants such as Booz Allen and Hamilton, Andersen Consulting, Gemini Consulting, and CSC Index to rethink the viability of their reengineering practices (White 1996). Unfortunately, they seem to be moving on to the next management fad rather than analyzing what really went wrong with the promising ideas and methodologies they were pursuing (Micklethwait and Woolridge 1996). We suggest that the failure of popular change methodologies, such as reengineering, can be attributed in part to a lack of understanding of the knowledge creation and transfer dynamics that take place at the boundaries between an organization's communities-of-practice. A key role management theorists serve is to help managers become better consumers of management approaches by informing them through rigorous research and dialog of the efficacy of popular management rhetoric.

Diverse Perspectives on Organizational Agility

There is no one single body of academic literature that sufficiently addresses the design of agile organizations and their processes for dynamic competitive environments. Historically, Adam Smith began the discussion with his account of the pin factory (Smith [1776] 1910), and until recently the operations research community led most of the discussion of process design. This is probably owing in part to the concrete nature of the problems they were trying to solve: How do we make things more efficiently in order to reap the largest possible economic rents? More recently, the quality and systems design community has provided a great deal of literature on organizational change and process improvement (Hammer 1996; Hammer and Champy 1993; Womack, Jones, and Roos 1991). Processes have been, and continue to be, primarily studied with theoretical tools that examine them from the viewpoint of an operationalization of information and efficiency. In the remainder of this section, we briefly review the theories of coordination and sociotechnical systems as

---

[1]During the early to mid 1990s, many change efforts championed by consulting practitioners were labeled as reengineering or one of its variants. There is currently a transition by consulting practitioners away from the term *reengineering* to *organizational growth, learning,* or *agility* as terms to describe change efforts being offered by consulting firms. This transition is due largely to the recent bad press *reengineering* has received.

they relate to processes and then describe how practice theory and organizational learning theory can further inform our understanding of organizational processes in practice.

An Organizational Theory of Coordination and Process Problems

James Thompson (1967) developed a topology of organizations that consists of the coordination of two primary parts: a stable technical core that provides operating efficiencies, and a system of administrative buffers that connects the stable technical core to the business environment. Each of these parts contains multiple subunits (e.g., engineering, order fulfillment, operations), each with their own set of independent processes optimized for efficiency within the subunit.

This system of administrative buffers was intended to protect the operating core from the variability of the external environment. However, rather than functioning to preserve the efficiencies of the operating core, this set of buffers protected the inefficiencies present within the organization's processes by brokering the organization's response to the environment (Denison 1997). These buffers severely constrained opportunities for organizational learning by limiting the sensemaking and bridging opportunities available to organizational members. In effect, organizational members were deprived of the capability and capacity required to adapt the organizational processes and practices. This fact was realized in the 1970s and 1980s, when organizations set about to find ways to "debuffer" the internal core by breaking down the organizations' boundaries.

Sociotechnical Systems Bring the Human System Into Play

An alternative approach to coordination that emerged in the academic literature was the work on sociotechnical systems (STS), which lays out the basis of much of today's process-based thinking (Pasmore 1978, 1988; Trist 1981; Trist and Bramforth 1951). STS theory focuses on developing the concept of fit between the human and the technical system. STS theory assumes that process problems are due to the inefficiencies of labor and that the solution is primarily to redefine the work flows at the front lines and develop organizational structures and governance mechanisms to support these new work flows. However, although STS theory develops the basic principles of process-based thinking, it still focuses on an internal perspective of developing efficiencies and does not adequately take into account marketplace factors such as customer issues, competitive pressures, or industry reconfiguration. Many of the problems with STS theory are demonstrated in the evolution and demise of the reengineering approaches championed in publications such as *Reengineering the Corporation* (Hammer and Champy 1993).

Because STS theory does not fully take into consideration the external environment, the importance of necessary linkages across different processes in an organization and their respective relationship to the operational demands of the market is not realized. STS theory views processes from a very explicit perspective and assumes that what is written about work processes is what actually occurs. This view decontextualizes the work and, thus, ignores the tacit components (i.e., noncanonical) existing within the work. Thus, much of the "knowing how things are done around here" is lost in the analysis, as well as a realization that the individual will need to figure out new ways to do things as the workplace changes over time.

Practice Theory Frames the Dynamic Character of Processes in Organizations

As proposed at the beginning of this chapter, to understand process problems in organizations, one must be able to frame the nexus or the relationship between work practices and the knowledge that individuals create and utilize to carry out those work practices. Sociological theories of practice (Bourdieu 1977; Giddens 1984; Ortner 1989) provide insight because they examine the reproduction of practices and the knowledge that individuals create and use as they engage in those practices. One way to understand a practice theory approach is to use the analogy of a game to understand what occurs in organizations "in actual practice." The game analogy consists of five ideas. First, there is the practice itself or a game consisting of concrete settings and activities. Second, there is a community of players, individuals who share the circumstances of the game (e.g., a community-of-practice). Third, players or individuals have a feel for the game (e.g., past experience)—both a tacit and explicit sense of how it is played and what the next move might be. Fourth, there is the playing of the game—a struggle with requirements, deadlines, and consequences—

with expected but uncertain outcomes. And fifth, multiple games are simultaneously played—by the organization as a whole and by and between individual communities-of-practice. The games played between individual communities-of-practice represent the dynamic and necessary interdependencies of the organization, and their success greatly affects the game played by the organization as a whole.

It is this practice-based or gamelike character of "processes" that must be understood and then represented when confronting process problems in an organization. Processes are not just decontextualized algorithms, routines, or inputs and outputs; they are also frameworks within which practices exist. Thus, designing an agile organization demands a more robust conceptualization of what a process is in order to include an understanding of practice and the knowledge and inclinations of the individuals who animate that practice. This conceptualization also helps us see why agility (the capacity for change) is more than simply the ability to change procedures because it also involves understanding the content of and the boundary dynamics among communities-of-practice.

Organizational Knowledge Creation Requires That Communities-of-Practice Learn from Each Other

Organizational learning and agility is accomplished through linking the various communities-of-practice that make up the organization. Nonaka and Takeuchi (1995, 62–73) describe an organizational knowledge creation and transfer cycle that loops from the individual to the group and then to the organizational level, a process that kneads both tacit and explicit knowledge through processes that they label "internalization" and "externalization." From this perspective, innovation is best understood as the process by which an "organization creates and defines [process] problems and then actively develops new knowledge to solve them" (Nonaka 1994, 14).

Nonaka and Takeuchi's (1995) model is helpful in outlining the knowledge creation and transfer cycle as it moves across the individual, group, and organizational levels, pulling in both tacit and explicit knowledge in order to accomplish this. What this model lacks is a clearer explanation of what they call "communities of interaction," the key concept that drives this knowledge creation and transfer cycle. It also lacks an understanding of the practice-based constraints within each community and overlooks the inherent difficulties of getting these communities to interact. It is this challenge of interaction that lies at the heart of process problems in an organization, and we have more accurately outlined this challenge with our description of multiple communities-of-practice. Communities-of-practice provides the primary unit of analysis in driving the knowledge creation and transfer cycle (see Figure 7-1), linking knowledge created by individuals to individuals in other parts of the organization.

To extend Nonaka and Takeuchi's model and improve our understanding of dealing with process problems in an organization, we propose that:

1. Community-of-practice be viewed as the most important unit of analysis (Carlile 1997a).
2. Tacit and explicit knowledge should be seen not as two different kinds of knowledge, but as lying on a continuum in which tacit knowledge supports our ability to apply explicit knowledge well (Bijker 1990).
3. Knowledge is not a neutral commodity that can easily be shared or traded with others, but is invested in a current way of doing and being successful in a particular community-of-practice (Carlile 1997b). Therefore, knowledge in one community-of-practice often comes into conflict with the knowledge and way of doing things in another.

By using this modified model, we can reconceptualize knowledge as "knowledge-in-practice" (Carlile 1997b) and be clearer about the challenges inherent in creating and then transferring knowledge across communities-of-practice. Learning or knowledge transfer takes place as the problems shared by communities-of-practice are made more explicit to each other. Making problems more concrete makes it easier for each community to apply its knowledge (both tacit and explicit) to the problem, which drives the internalization and externalization processes outlined by Nonaka (1994). Making the problems faced by each community more manifest provides the practical means to facilitate learning and joint problem solving and render knowledge more negotiable among communities with different methods of doing things (Carlile 1997b).

Figure 7-1. The knowledge creation and transfer cycle. *Source:* Adapted from Carlile, P. R. (1997b).

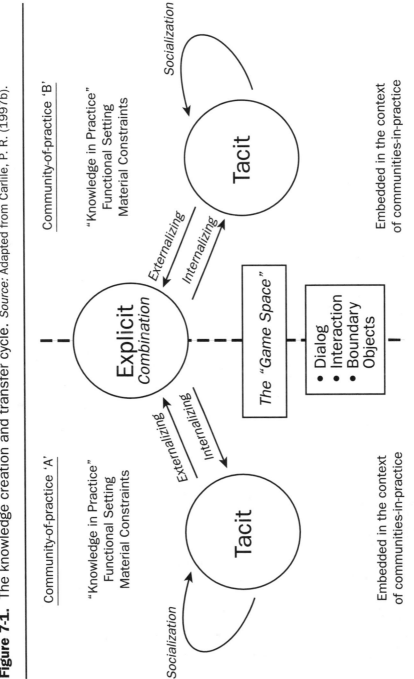

Creating an Organizational Learning "Game Space": Moving Knowledge across Boundaries

Learning and agility take place in organizations when knowledge is effectively created and transferred across *process boundaries*—the boundaries between different communities-of-practice. For this knowledge creation and transfer cycle to take place, as shown in Figure 7-1, both tacit and explicit knowledge in one community must be made more explicit at those boundaries. This is accomplished, in part, through dialog, interactions over time, and the utilization of various boundary objects (e.g., models or simulations, prototype parts, shared problem-solving methods), which render the knowledge from one community of-practice more accessible to another (Carlile 1997b). Furthermore, if this organizational learning is done well, knowledge can be created, applied, negotiated, and transformed as it moves across the process boundaries that demarcate the various communities-of-practice involved. However, the creation of this organizational learning "game space" and how it is played between communities-of-practice is mediated by explicit and implicit management ideologies used to coordinate and control them in the organization.

Normative and Rational Ideologies Have Dominated Management Practice

The need for more sophisticated management control began when Adam Smith observed the necessity and economic benefits of dividing up labor (tasks) (Smith [1776] 1910) to improve greatly the efficiency of production. Through this observation, he established the fundamental purpose of management as coordinating the division and reintegration of labor—what we call here the "game space"—which shapes how individuals live, work, and learn together. The realm of this game space has been defined by managers primarily through the application of rational and normative ideologies of control (Barley and Kunda 1992).

Rational ideologies of control encompass the principles of scientific management (Taylor [1911] 1967) and systems management, and include the mechanisms of work rules (constraints) and piece work or bonus incentives (markets) that are codified by management. Normative methods of control rely on a common set of values, beliefs, and norms of behavior (values) that allow subordinate discretion and are enculturated into all through a process of socialization. In practice, rational and normative mechanisms of control have dominated management methods since the 1870s and are used with varying levels of emphasis to reintegrate divided labor in the organization (Barley and Kunda 1992).

Competence: The Ideology of Competent Capable Action

As the complexity of organizations and the rate of change in the competitive environment have accelerated, it has become impossible for any one individual to apply primarily normative and rational methods and through them effectively control the entire organization. Individuals as well as teams have been increasingly compelled to make sense of their environment in a more dynamic fashion and take action based on their competence (e.g., knowledge workers). As a result, forward-thinking organizations are becoming much more concerned with leveraging competence and building capability into their organizations to deal with competitive demands (Hamel and Prahalad 1994; Ulrich 1997; Ulrich and Lake 1990).

The Game Space: Juxtaposition of Competence and Normative and Rational Ideologies

The juxtaposition of the ideologies of competence and normative and rational methods of management control provides us with an extended way to frame how we manage processes or a community-of-practice as a game space. This game space contains concrete activities and requirements and knowledgeable individuals who share those circumstances. This game space is circumscribed by various normative and rational controls that generate the measures or constraints that mediate the domain of a particular community-of-practice (see Figure 7-2) and its interface with other game spaces or communities-of-practice in the organization. By clarifying the mix of these managerial ideologies, we can visualize how they affect the interaction and execution of organizational processes.

Each community-of-practice demarcates a distinct game space. For example, Figure 7-2 represents three types of game spaces within a hypothetical organization: an assembly line, customer service department, and

Figure 7-2. The game space.

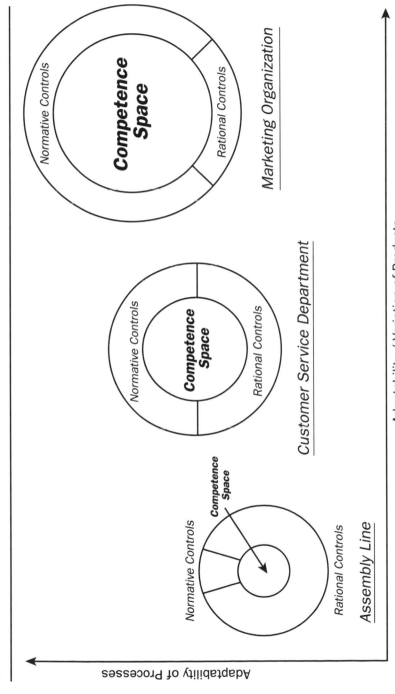

Normative Controls

**Competence
Space**

Rational Controls

Marketing Organization

Normative Controls

**Competence
Space**

Rational Controls

Customer Service Department

Normative Controls

**Competence
Space**

Rational Controls

Assembly Line

Adaptability / Variation of Products

Adaptability of Processes

marketing organization. Assembly line workers typically have the majority of their work defined by work rules (rational methods) and a much smaller area controlled by the more self-governing methods of values, beliefs, norms (normative methods), and individual craft skills (competence) (Hamper 1986; Womack, Jones, and Roos 1991). Furthermore, the magnitude of this game space is relatively small and highly structured by management. This is exemplified by the short training time required to prepare new assembly line workers, often measured in hours, to "play the game." This is a game space that focuses on efficiency, with low variation in the process execution and product produced.

The typical customer service department faces a more complex problem of management control. The product (service) and how it is delivered (process) has a much greater degree of variation, resulting from interactions with internal and external customers. Consequently, management must strongly rely on more self-governing methods of control, because the inability to anticipate every possible interaction precludes the explicit codification of how process steps should be performed in practice. Employees must learn how their tasks within the process interact with other tasks (e.g., billing and order entry), and are required to have a relatively moderate level of competence and capability to perform them. This game space is much greater in magnitude than that played on the assembly line, requiring a higher level of skill and greater level of socialization.

Marketing teams, in comparison to the two previous examples, demand a very large game space to accomplish the delivery of value to the organization effectively. As illustrated in Figure 7-2, there is a high degree of customization of the process and product delivered to the organization and the marketplace. Marketers are expected to bring significant and diverse creative, technical, and business skills to bear to elucidate the marketplace opportunities, construct marketing programs, and deliver measurable results (Kubr 1986). Marketers also act with a great deal of autonomy, with management relying primarily on self-governing methods of control (normative methods) of values, beliefs, and norms of behavior. Rational control methods are few, relying primarily on "market signals" (monetary incentives) and a few codified rules critical to maintaining a modicum of business discipline. The level of competence and the capability to deliver consistently effective marketing programs takes a much greater amount of training, socialization, and experience than required for the other two examples.

Designing a Learning Game Space: Creating Agility Through Learning at the Boundaries

An organization's agility is determined by how well it manages the interdependencies and intersections among the numerous game spaces that constitute the processes of the organization. For example, if the hypothetical company we previously illustrated wanted to shift from make-to-stock to make-to-order and provide accelerated delivery to customers, effective knowledge transfer and creation across the boundaries between communities-of-practice would be essential to realize the full potential of a process change of this magnitude. Otherwise, each community-of-practice would be left to optimize its own processes without the opportunity to change the inputs and outputs to achieve greater value and efficiency. This is where we come full circle and see the connections among communities-of-practice, game space, knowledge, and capability required to deal with process problems and, furthermore, to build agility or the capacity for change at the boundaries.

What underscores this capacity for change is the realization that organizations are colonized by numerous communities-of-practice, as illustrated in Figure 7-2, with their own competence space and rational and normative controls. The content of this competence space and how it is controlled or demarcated by the particular rational and normative constraints (e.g., output measures and working hours) must be open for negotiation and transformation in order for individuals to solve process problems as they occur at the boundaries. Otherwise, actors from different communities-of-practice will be unable or unwilling to make their knowledge fully accessible and to engage in problem solving with others because they are playing a different game. An overarching game space, which allows players from different communities-of-practice to participate fully, must be established. Organizational agility comes from a capacity for external adaptation, internal transformation, and learning across the processes that constitute the organization.

A New and Rich Agenda for Organizational Research: Agility

Being Willing to "Drop Our Tools" to Pursue Fruitful Research

Karl Weick (1996) used the allegory of a wildland fire-fighting crew of which most members failed to "drop the tools of their trade" and survive to sound an alarm to organizational scholarship. When Weick suggests that organizational scholars need to be willing to "drop their tools," he is drawing focus to the tools or "positions" of organizational scholarship "with which people identify and that in turn identify them" (p. 312) that each of us, to some extent, chooses. If organizational scholars wish to redefine the agenda for research and practice, we must be willing, from time to time, to drop our tools or, more appropriately, develop new tools to allow ourselves to integrate fresh observations and new theory into our research.

We suggest that practice theory and the empirical level of analysis of a community-of-practice are new tools that will greatly enhance our ability to frame process problems in organizations and the capacity to build organizational agility and learning. Practice theory emphasizes that to understand processes in an organization, one must adopt a concrete and practical understanding of the practice that constrains and enables individuals, paying particular attention to the activities, community, and knowledge with which they are engaged.

Weick (1996) stated that "scholars of organizations are in analogous threatened positions [to the wildland fire-fighters] and they too seem to be keeping their heavy tools and falling behind" (p. 301). This is particularly true of issues of process problems and organizational agility, in which the consultant-writers are currently leading the conversation. If we are to reclaim the practical ground in this conversation, we need to pursue research that can inform our understanding of actual practice in concrete ways.

Linking Macro- and Microlevels of the Analysis

There is no substitute for "deep description" (Geertz 1973) when looking at the contexts of various organizational interactions. In examining organizational processes, it is critical that we inform ourselves of the situated aspects of how processes are carried out and the concrete activities that guide them over time. By qualitatively studying communities-of-practice, we can begin to identify independent and dependent variables for a more generalized understanding of processes (McClintock, Brannon, and Maynard-Moody 1979). Furthermore, with our focus on individuals as engaged in practice, this unit of analysis provides an empirical connecting point between traditional splits between macro and microlevels of analysis.

Opportunities to study the interactions among communities-of-practice exist in which members of different communities-of-practice must link themselves together to learn or, in other words, to exchange and create knowledge to complete tasks. Many interesting types of organizations have been studied with the tools of the psychologist and sociologist that could be further understood by studying how they perform, adapt, and create processes in practice through the lens of practice theory. Examples of organizations that could be studied include cross-functional new-product development teams (Carlile 1997b), emergency room hospital teams (Osterlund and Carlile 1997), and aircraft carrier flight deck crews (Pfeiffer 1989). In contexts such as these, research opportunities exist in which new and richer explanations for organizational phenomena can be developed.

In addition to broadening the scope of our theoretical lenses, we must also strive to create better measures of processes that can be in turn linked to measures of performance that are salient to senior executives. This task is critical if we wish our research to inform practice in organizations. Most senior executives are trained in finance or have a financial background and look for what they call the "bottom line" of return on investment, return on assets, and net income, which creates a gap that needs to be bridged to softer organizational measures. For example, in the marketing literature there are good models of customer satisfaction, in which incremental improvements in the "soft" measures of customer satisfaction have been statistically linked to bottom-line performance, that could be adopted. Another model that may be helpful is the work done on the "balanced scorecard" (Kaplan and Norton 1996), which integrates soft and hard measures. It is our responsibility to create and collect measures that are accessible to practitioners and can be used by them to gain the support of executive management in applying methods based on our research in their intervention efforts.

Process Problems: The Research Questions

What research agenda will facilitate both management practice and scholarly theory building? What will improve how we design and perform processes in organizations and make organizations more agile and able to learn across their own boundaries? With these questions in mind, the research agenda that follows is organized around the categories that emerged from the interviews and review of the consultant-writer management literature (see Table 7-1). These categories are interrelated and focus on a larger or smaller portion of the process problems outlined in this chapter. We present them here as a loosely structured whole because we realize that investigating some of these concurrently will provide additional insight to unravel the relationships among variables as they occur at the level of practice.

Learning

How does learning occur across different communities-of-practice and what mechanisms or activities drive this learning? How is knowledge created and then leveraged when more than one firm is participating in the value chain? These questions are of great concern to organizations in which cross-functional innovation is paramount. For example, in terms of product development, How is the knowledge to produce a product transformed at various stages in the development process? What are the formal and informal processes involved? Here, observational data could be gathered on how the actual artifacts of the product are changed and how those changes take place, an example of organizational learning and how the design of formal and informal processes affects these changes.

Structure

What types of formal organizational structures facilitate organizational learning within and across communities-of-practice? How do these structures affect the evaluation and transformation of organizational processes? For example, one reason that multinationals exists is to enhance the pool of knowledge that can then be spread across the organization to deal with constantly evolving markets. In this case, what type of cross-functional team, matrix, or reporting structures facilitates these goals? Two multinationals with varying performance could be compared and their formal structures could be assessed to determine what structures generate the differences in learning and performance across the borders of a multinational.

Culture

What are the specific cultural attributes that exist in learning organizations whose internal and external boundaries are more permeable? For example, since dialog has been identified as critical in learning organizations (Schein 1993), how does it occur across internal and external boundaries? In the case of multinationals, another comparative case could be examined to assess beyond how a common culture has been nurtured to bridge across the national and cultural boundaries contained in a multinational. This could be accomplished through the use of broad survey instruments to identify and compare cultural attributes and correlate them to measures of organizational learning or operational and financial performance.

Capabilities

What bundle of capabilities does an organization need in order to be agile? How can we identify specific capabilities that a given community-of-practice needs to be successful? Are there certain basic capabilities that are essential for agility? For example, electronic commerce is impacting the banking industry, and in the case of the survivors and innovators, what has been the bundle of capabilities that has gotten them to this point? Since the impact and evolution of this change has been rather rapid, relatively short case studies could be collected examining how individuals (i.e., managers, team leaders) in each functional area observed, analyzed, and then acted in a boundary-spanning way to remake the capabilities in their banks to be successful in an electronic marketplace.

Infrastructure

What is the impact on the ability of different communities-of-practice to respond internally and externally to changes of different types of information systems utilized (e.g., integrated application suites, e-mail, video, information warehouses, databases) across the boundaries of different communities-of-practice? What type of human resource infrastructures (e.g., reward and promotion systems, training and hiring practices) not only facilitate learning at the boundaries, but also retain and develop employees who are important to such learning?

For the first question, various information system implementations could be studied longitudinally to examine any improvement on the speed of critical decision making, the movement of critical information and knowledge across boundaries, or the cycle time of implementing particular process changes. For the second question, large surveys could be conducted to examine the menu of human resource infrastructures and their histories (e.g., how long they have been implemented, level of acceptance and use). The results of these studies could then be correlated with various measures of learning such as the increase in innovations, the transfer of best practice across boundaries, and the familiarity of individuals with the work requirements and incentives of other communities-of-practice.

Leadership

What are the leadership/facilitator roles and styles that help or hinder organizational learning across communities-of-practice? What are the skills required to lead in a setting that requires learning across boundaries? Here, best-practice teams could be identified in an organization and their skills assessed in terms of what makes them the most productive. The careful concern here is that leadership might be examined both as an individual role and as a team role. These teams could be observed and the members could record the skills they utilize in day-to-day activities. For example, in the case of hospital emergency room teams in which the doctors are peers, how is leadership (ownership) of a patient's treatment determined and how does that role function? This kind of data, coupled with observation, could be used to generate leadership or skill repertoires required for all team members in cross-functional settings.

Trust

How does the way in which processes are designed, redesigned, discarded, and performed create perceptions of fairness? What creates perceptions of fairness when individuals are asked to work across organizational boundaries, where they are practicing outside their functional community-of-practice (e.g., in a cross-functional team)? How does this perception of fairness affect the willingness of individuals to make the knowledge from their community-of-practice accessible to other members of the cross-functional team?

The first question is rich with data, given all of the downsides now understood about much of the reengineering efforts over the last five years. An interesting case study could look at the differences in agility (capacity for change) in a company that has experienced a lot of fallout from its reengineering phase and compare that to a company that has chosen a less aggressive reengineering approach (e.g., AT&T as compared with US West).

The second and third questions, dealing with perceptions of fairness and its effects, continue to become more and more important as cross-functional teamwork becomes the mainstay of organizational decision making. Here, human resource practices—the combination of evaluation, reward, and promotion packages—could be examined (in terms of how they are structured and implemented, and in how they are experienced by the recipients) in organizations with best-practice reputations for working in cross-functional settings. A follow-up study could survey a large sample of organizations to explore the variables (human resources practices) that support rewards, promotions, and skills developed in a cross-functional setting, and these could be correlated to measures of learning and financial performance.

Conclusion

In spite of the vast quantities of money and human resources expended, more than 80 percent of organizational change efforts fail to achieve expected results. These change efforts always involve explicit or implicit changes in the organization's processes. Most of the approaches to understanding and designing processes have centered on the quality, information processing, or customer satisfaction frameworks, or their derivatives. This implies that the core process issues revolve around optimizing the processes of changing inputs into outputs while breaking down the boundaries between the organization and its customers and/or suppliers. However, what we have found is that while efficiency and customer focus are necessary attributes of effective processes, a failure in achieving these goals is not usually the reason that change efforts fail. We propose that it is also necessary to examine and integrate an understanding of work practices and how knowledge created and utilized by individuals in organizations constrains the design and execution of organizational processes.

Looking through the theoretical lens of practice, we have described how the core issues that determine the success of process design or redesign center on the interactions that occur between communities-of-practice at their boundaries, both inside and outside the organization. Not only does each community-of-practice occupy a game space, but also potentially interfaces through as a boundary game with various communities-of-practice. It is in this boundary game space where organizational learning can take place—where knowledge can be created, reflected on, and transferred across its internal and external boundaries. Organizations are not focusing enough attention in this "boundary game space," as well as the material, social, and political forces that constrain the performance of organizational processes and their integration. We suggest that practice theory and the level of analysis of communities-of-practice can provide a rich and robust way to examine processes and how individuals and organizations can create agility through the ways in which they live, work, and learn together.

References

Barley, S. R. and Kunda, G. 1992. "Design and Devotion: Surges of Rational and Normative Ideologies of Control in Managerial Discourse." *Administrative Science Quarterly* 37 (September), 363–99.

Bijker, W. 1990. "The Social Construction of Bakelite: Toward a Theory of Invention." In W. Bijker, T. Hughes, and T. Pinch (eds.), *The Social Construction of Technological Systems.* Cambridge, MA: MIT Press.

Bourdieu, P. 1977. *Outline of a Theory of Practice.* Cambridge, England: Cambridge University Press.

Brown, J. S. and Duguid, P. 1991. "Organizational Learning and Communities-of-Practice: Toward a Unified View of Working, Learning and Innovation." *Organizational Science* 2(1), 40–57.

Carlile, P. R. 1997a. "Routines Are Only Half the Story: The Case of Organizational Learning." Working paper, MIT Sloan School of Management, Cambridge, MA.

———. 1997b. "Understanding Knowledge Transformation in Product Development: Making Knowledge Manifest Through Boundary Objects." Ph.D. diss., University of Michigan, Ann Arbor.

Champy, J. A. 1994. *State of Reengineering Report.* Cambridge, MA: CSC Index.

Cook, E. G. 1996. "Seven Really Obvious Truths About Reengineering." *Journal of Business Strategy* 17(3), 14–16.

Denison, D. R. 1997. "Toward a Process-Based Theory of Organizational Design: Can Organizations Be Designed Around Value Chains and Networks?" In J. Walsh and A. Huff (eds.), *Advances in Strategic Management,* Vol. 14, 1–47. Greenwich, CT: JAI.

Dimaggio, P. and Powell, W. 1991. "Introduction." In W. Powell and P. Dimaggio (eds.), *The New Institutionalism.* Chicago: University of Chicago Press.

Geertz, C. 1973. *The Interpretation of Cultures.* New York: Basic Books.

Giddens, A. 1984. *The Constitution of Society.* Berkeley: University of California Press.

Hall, E. A., Rosenthal, J., and Wade, J. 1994. "How to Make Reengineering Really Work." *McKinsey Quarterly* (2), 107–28.

Hamel, G. and Prahalad, C. K. 1994. *Competing for the Future.* Boston: Harvard Business School Press.

Hammer, M. 1996. *Beyond Reengineering.* New York: Harper Business.

Hammer, M. and Champy, J. 1993. *Reengineering the Corporation.* New York: Harper Business.

Hamper, B. 1986. *Rivethead: Tales From the Assembly Line.* New York: Warner Books.

Hannah, M. and Freeman, J. 1977. "The Population Ecology of Organizations." *American Journal of Sociology* 82, 929–64.

Kaplan, R. S. and Norton, D. P. 1996. *Translating Strategy into Action: The Balanced Scorecard.* Boston: Harvard Business School Press.

Kubr, M. 1986. *Management Consulting: A Guide to the Profession.* Geneva: International Labour Organization.

Lancaster, H. 1995. "Re-engineering Authors Reconsider Re-engineering." *Wall Street Journal* (January 17 and 24; p. B1.

Lave, J. and Wenger, S. 1990. *Situated Learning.* Cambridge, England: Cambridge University Press.

McClintock, C. C., Brannon, D., and Maynard-Moody, S. 1979. "Applying the Logic of Sample Surveys to Qualitative Case Studies: The Case Cluster Method." *Administrative Science Quarterly* 24(4), 612–37.

Micklethwait, J. and Woolridge, A. 1996. *The Witch Doctors: Making Sense of the Management Gurus.* New York: Times Books.

Mumford, E. and Hendricks, R. 1996. "Business Process Reengineering RIP." *Personnel Management* 2, 22–26.

Nonaka, I. 1994. "A Dynamic Theory of Organizational Knowledge Creation." *Organization Science* 5(1), 14–37.

Nonaka, I. and Takeuchi, H. 1995. *The Knowledge-Creating Company.* New York: Oxford University Press.

Orr, J. 1990. "Talking About Machines: An Ethnography of a Modern Job." Ph.D. diss., Cornell University.

Ortner, S. 1989. *High Religion: A Cultural and Political History of Sherpa Buddhism.* Princeton, NJ: Princeton University Press.

Osterlund, C. and Carlile, P. R. 1997. "Creating and Maintaining Processes on the Fly in Hospital Emergency Rooms." Working paper, MIT, Sloan School of Management, Cambridge, MA.

Pascale, R. T. 1996. "Reflections on Honda." *California Management Review* 38(4), 112–17.

Pasmore, W. 1978. *Sociotechnical Systems: A Sourcebook.* San Diego: University Associates.

————. 1988. *Designing Effective Organizations: The Sociotechnical Systems Perspective.* New York: Wiley.

Pfeiffer, J. 1989. "The Secret of Life at the Limits: Cogs Become Big Wheels." *Smithsonian Magazine* 20(4), 38.

Porter, M. 1985. *Competitive Advantage: Creating and Sustaining Superior Performance.* New York: Free Press.

Porter, M. E. 1979. "How Competitive Forces Shape Strategy." *Harvard Business Review* 57(2), 137–45.

Roth, A. V. 1996. "Achieving Strategic Agility Through Economies of Knowledge." *Strategy and Leadership* 24(2), 30–37.

Schein, E. 1993. "On Dialogue, Culture, and Organizations." *Organizational Dynamics* 22 (autumn), 40–51.

Smith, A. [1776] 1910. *An Inquiry Into the Nature and Causes of the Wealth of Nations.* New York: Modern Library.

Taylor, F. W. [1911] 1967. *The Principles of Scientific Management.* New York and London: W. W. Norton.

Thompson, J. 1967. *Organizations in Action: Social Science Bases of Administrative Theory.* New York: McGraw-Hill.

Trist, E. 1981. *The Evolution of Socio-Technical Systems: A Conceptual Framework and an Action Research Program.* Toronto, Ontario: Ministry of Labour, Ontario Quality of Working Life Center.

Trist, E. and Bramforth, K. 1951. "Some Social Psychological Consequences of the Longwall Method of Coal-Getting." *Human Relations* 4, 3–38.

Ulrich, D. 1997. *Human Resource Champions: The Next Agenda for Adding Value and Delivering Results.* Boston: Harvard Business School Press.

Ulrich, D. and Lake, D. 1990. *Organizational Capability: Competing From the Inside Out.* New York: Wiley.

Weick, K. E. 1995. *Sensemaking in Organizations.* Thousand Oaks, CA: Sage.

————. 1996. "Drop Your Tools: An Allegory for Organizational Studies." *Administrative Science Quarterly* 41(June), 301–13.

White, J. B. 1996. " 'Next Big Thing': Re-Engineering Gurus Take Steps to Remodel Their Stalling Vehicles." *Wall Street Journal* (November 26), A1.

Womack, J. P., Jones, D. T., and Roos, D. 1991. *The Machine That Changed the World: The Story of Lean Production.* New York: HarperCollins.

Chapter 8

Overemphasis on Analysis: Decision-Making Dilemmas in the Age of Speed

Markus Vodosek *and* Kathleen M. Sutcliffe

I n recent years organizations have increased their reliance on measurement and data analysis to guide their strategies and control their operations. Contemporary management practices such as competitive analysis, total quality management (TQM), activity-based accounting, and process reengineering all require elaborate analyses of external and internal organizational factors. Consequently, many organizations emphasize measurement and data analysis.[1] As organizations strive to become more agile (see Chapter 7), however, they discover that too much emphasis on measurement and data analysis can deter them from responding quickly to changes in their competitive environment. Complaints about the resources spent on information analysis and the amount of time de-

---

The authors thank Lynda St. Clair and Regina O'Neill for useful comments on earlier drafts of this chapter. They are also grateful to the many executives who shared their experiences, and to Kathy Eisenhardt, Günter Müller-Stewens, Terry Brake, Hans Brechbühl, and Mary Craig for ideas and thoughtful comments.

[1]Before proceeding further, it is necessary to be clear about the use of the key terms *measurement, data, information,* and *analysis.* Although there are many fine-grained distinctions in the literature about what these terms constitute, in this chapter we are using them quite loosely. *Data* and *information* are often used interchangeably to mean facts or knowledge obtained from measurement, investigation, study, or instruction. *Measurement* loosely refers to the act or process of gathering data or information. *Analysis* refers to the process of interpreting or making sense of data or information. All these terms in effect constitute a process of information gathering and interpretation. The outputs of the process are the raw materials for organizational decisions and actions.

voted to collecting data and writing reports can be heard from people at all levels within the organization.

Conventional wisdom and current management practices suggest that more data and more analysis lead to better decisions. Yet, research on information and decision making indicates that more is not always better. This is especially true in high-velocity environments in which agility is critical to success (Eisenhardt and Tabrizi 1995). Thus, managers are caught in a double bind. If they follow conventional wisdom and conduct extensive analyses, they may lose precious time in implementing new strategies. On the other hand, if managers ignore conventional wisdom and abandon analytical rigor, they may place misinformed bets on emerging products or markets that can result in record write-offs (Courtney, Kirkland, and Viguerie 1997) and they may have to defend themselves against charges of mismanagement.

Academic researchers, in addition to managers, also have a vested interest in understanding more about overemphasis on analysis and its link with the decision-making process and its outcomes. Virtually all management texts discuss models of decision making, particularly "rational" decision-making models that emphasize data collection and analysis. Those models, however, have not been reevaluated pursuant to the enormous changes in competitive environments, organizational structures, and information technologies that affect decision makers on a daily basis.

This chapter addresses the issue of overemphasis on analysis in organizations in light of the rapidly increasing speed and complexity of the decision-making context. After providing evidence for this increasing speed and complexity of decision-making contexts, we examine why employees collect and analyze too much information and highlight the potential negative consequences of these behaviors for organizations. Next, we point out why overemphasis on analysis is a pressing problem for managers and consultants, and why it is an interesting topic for researchers. Then, we review the organizational literature to develop explanations for this overemphasis on data collection and analysis and summarize findings to date. Finally, we provide an agenda for future research, taking into account both the needs of practitioners and the interests of researchers.

Pinpointing the Problem

The Age of Speed

Global competition has forced companies in many industries to increase the speed with which they assess their competitive environment, develop new products, and bring them to market. In fact, the management press (e.g., Dimancescu and Dwenger 1996; Jones 1993; Meyer 1993; Stalk and Hout 1990; Vesey 1991) has identified the speed at which companies bring their products to market as one of the most critical issues for companies today. Empirical studies appear to support this contention. For example, Womack, Jones, and Roos (1990) have documented the importance of speed for competitiveness in the automobile industry. In addition, Eisenhardt and colleagues (Bourgeois and Eisenhardt 1988; Eisenhardt 1989; Eisenhardt and Tabrizi 1995; Schoonhoven, Eisenhardt, and Lyman 1990) have looked extensively at the effect of speed on the competitiveness of companies in high-velocity environments. They found that fast decision making by top decision makers based on rich real-time information (Bourgeois and Eisenhardt 1988; Eisenhardt 1989) and fast product innovation processes (Eisenhardt and Tabrizi 1995; Schoonhoven, Eisenhardt, and Lyman 1990) are closely linked to a company's performance. These studies support Huber (1984) and Huber and Daft's (1987) contention that postindustrial environments will require that organizations make decisions faster and more frequently. Arthur Martinez, the CEO of Sears, Roebuck & Co., attributes his success in turning around the faltering $32 billion retailer with 350,000 employees to the fast decisions that he, his chief financial officer, and his chief planning officer made within the first one hundred days of Martinez's tenure (Martinez 1997). These accounts provide evidence that today's organizations operate in an "age of speed," which requires organizations both to make decisions faster and to implement them more quickly.

Coping with Complexity

The need for speedy decision processes comes at a time when competitive environments are increasing in complexity (D'Aveni 1994). The problem with complexity is that it accentuates the perceived necessity of measurement and analysis. The logic goes something like this: As complexity increases, uncertainty increases because it becomes more difficult to understand cause-effect relationships in both internal and external decision environments. In addition to increasing uncertainty, the complexity arising from an increasingly diverse workforce, dispersed production locations, global markets, government regulation, legal constraints, conflicting customer demands, and technological changes also increases the number of factors that must be taken into account when making decisions. Increases in complexity, uncertainty, and in the number of decision factors are accompanied by a large increase in the amount of information available because of a continually increasing knowledge base and constant advances in information technology and measurement techniques (Huber 1984).

Overemphasis on Analysis

A Functional Response

Confronted with time pressures and increasingly more complex decision situations, decision makers respond with a number of behaviors that can be thought of as functional because they are intended as mechanisms to cope with speed and complexity. Although decision makers could respond to time pressures by collecting and analyzing less information, the opposite often occurs. As decision makers struggle to pay attention to all the variables relevant to particular decision situations, they are likely to feel pressure to gather and analyze increasing amounts of information.

In addition, the need for speed heightens the pressure to collect and analyze large amounts of data. Although collecting large amounts of data in the face of speed requirements may appear counterintuitive, this behavior makes more sense when we clarify its rationale: Although decision makers can often consider only a subset of decision variables when they are under time pressures, they cannot predict with certainty which variables are relevant to a given decision-making situation. Thus, to identify the correct subset of variables, it is common practice in many organizations to collect vast amounts of data and engage in extensive analyses and the write-up of reports with the expectation that the correct variables are captured somewhere in the data and analyses.

Also, analyses are often requested by superiors who underestimate the amount of resources it takes to do them. One reason for this phenomenon is that managers and employees tend to amass more data than actually necessary because they are held accountable for their actions and want to save face if their superiors ask for more details (Tetlock 1992).

Managers also tend to accumulate more data as a consequence of contemporary management practices such as TQM or process reengineering. For example, information and analysis is an important category in the Malcolm Baldrige National Quality Award. *Information and analysis* is the area concerned with the "scope, management, and use of data and information to maintain a customer focus, to drive quality excellence, and to improve . . . performance" (Dean and Bowen 1994, 406). The presumption is that decisions based on facts are better than decisions based on other criteria and that organizations that collect and analyze information will outperform those that do not (Dean and Evans 1994).

Furthermore, analyses may be an excuse for indecisiveness and lack of leadership. Extensive analyses may lengthen or delay decision processes until market or technological changes force a decision or a particular course of action for the analyst.

A Symbolic Response

Although it is true that information analysis is often critical to successful decision making, the functional or instrumental value of information analysis to decision makers may be superseded by its symbolic value. Analyses are often performed to create meaning and legitimacy for the people and organizations doing the analyses, rather than to provide information for decision making and action taking (Feldman and March 1981). Also, analyses are frequently sponsored by people to justify decisions that have already been made or actions that have already been taken (Weick 1979).

The Consequences of Too Much Data and Analysis

The people who actually perform analyses in organizations are commonly midlevel managers whose primary role is to focus on operations (Sutton 1988). Since attentional capacities and resources are limited, the more time and resources midlevel managers spend on data collection and analyses, the less time and fewer resources they have to spend on other pressing organizational problems. Furthermore, although the processing of vast amounts of information may be useful in decreasing uncertainty for decision makers, the opposite sometimes occurs (Daft, Sormunen, and Parks 1988; Sutcliffe 1991) because vast amounts of conflicting information may lead to disagreements and may increase hesitation to act.

There is another reason why spending time and resources on the collection and analysis of data might not necessarily be beneficial for the organization: Analyses are often flawed. Forecasts and competitive analyses, by their very nature, comprise an extrapolation of past and current socially constructed realities to predict future socially constructed realities (Starbuck and Milliken 1988). These forecasts and analyses are complicated by the fact that analysts' abilities to notice important connections between different data points and to interpret them correctly depend on their perceptual filters (Starbuck and Milliken 1988). In addition, tomorrow's realities might be influenced by variables that are unknown today. Thus, analyses often result in incorrect projections, leading to wrong decisions, and consequently to faulty actions (Mintzberg 1994). Furthermore, the core of an analysis is often derived from a comparison of past actions with their outcomes. Yet, feedback about the relationship between actions and outcomes may be misleading because the details of strategic decisions and their implementation are often forgotten, and because time delays between decision implementation and its effects on the system may lead to superstitious or erroneous understandings of cause-effect relationships (Sutcliffe 1997). In summary, the more emphasis an organization places on lengthy time-consuming analyses of historical information, the more likely that its decisions will be based on the wrong premises.

Why Overemphasis on Analysis Is a Pressing Problem for Managers and Consultants

Elaborate and time-consuming data analyses conflict with demands for speedy decision making and action taking, thus encouraging a trade-off of speed for presumed accuracy (i.e., reduction of uncertainty), which may undermine an organization's efforts to achieve the very goals it seeks. Although in some cases extensive analyses may lead to better decision making, it is also possible that the analysis of vast amounts of information can have deleterious consequences in that it consumes valuable time and resources, decreases the speed with which decisions can be made, and creates a sense of false security. The resulting waste of resources and the hindrance of speedy decision making are a pressing concern for managers and executives.

Analyses may create or exacerbate other untoward consequences for organizations. For example, the results of analyses often serve as inputs to strategic planning processes, which, in turn, lengthen the decision-making processes even further (Mintzberg 1994). Managers and executives, however, are increasingly concerned about the consequences of prolonged planning processes for their organizations' ability to act quickly. Consequently, successful companies, such as Robert Waterman's consulting company, have abandoned major analyses that tempt managers to develop strategic plans (see Waterman 1997).

Since overemphasis on analysis is such an immediate problem for managers and organizations, consultants and change agents who work for them need to be sensitive to the potential downsides of overanalyzing when diagnosing organizational problems and creating interventions.

Why Overemphasis of Analysis Is Theoretically Interesting for Researchers

As research on strategic decision making grows, there is more and more evidence to suggest that strategic decision effectiveness is shaped by both environmental factors and decision processes. Whereas, some scholars argue that environmental constraints determine choices and lessen the importance of choice processes (e.g., Pfeffer and Salancik 1978), other scholars argue that managers retain a substantial degree of control over strategic choices even in the context of constraints (e.g., Child 1972). The latter position is strengthened by the observation that "some managers make very poor strategic choices, with devastating consequences for their firms, while others in very similar circumstances make much better choices" (Dean and Sharfman 1996, 369). The collection of information relevant to the decision and reliance on analysis of this information in making the choice is central to effective decision processes (Dean and Sharfman 1993). Yet, currently there is limited scholarly understanding of how information analysis hinders or helps decision making in naturalistic settings in which decision speed is critical.

The analysis of data leads to information available in the organization. Availability of information, however, is completely decoupled from the issue of whether decision makers pay attention to it or not. Paying attention to information, in turn, is decoupled from the issue of whether this information becomes part of the decision-making process. What information managers pay attention to and what information they ignore and why is largely unknown. Furthermore, the mechanisms through which managers incorporate the information that they have focused on into their decisions have not been explored. If we had this information, we could better pinpoint the type of data that needs to be collected and the type of analyses that needs to be done. Organizations could then save large amounts of the time and resources currently spent on collecting and analyzing data that never enter the decision-making process.

The Organizational Literature and Overemphasis on Analysis

In the following sections, we discuss contributions of the organizational literature to the understanding of the current tension between the need for fast decision making and the desire for extensive data collection and analysis. First, we consider the different purposes of information analyses in organizations. Then, we continue with a discussion of the information acquisition and analyzing process, reflect on the role of the group in the process of data collection, analyzing, and decision making; and conclude with aspects of speed in this process.

Purposes of Information Analysis in Organizations

Few managers or scholars would argue with the idea that the collection and analysis of important information is a key to achieving control over decisions and their outcomes. Some scholars (e.g., Pfeffer and Salancik 1978, 14; Starbuck and Milliken 1988; Weick 1974: 117) argue that information gathering and processing are crucial to the success of the organization, even more crucial than strategic decision making itself. In addition to their instrumental value, the activities associated with the creation, collection, and analysis of information in organizations serve other purposes (Swanson 1978). Researchers have suggested that the creation, collection, and analysis of large amounts of information are ritualistic (Starbuck 1983), help organizational members make sense of their activities (Daft and Weick 1984; Weick and Daft 1983), or act as symbols and signals that create meaning or legitimacy (Feldman and March 1981; March and Sevón 1984). For example, for years the marketing department of a major appliance manufacturer constructed detailed five-year market projections for its products, including the features and colors of their washers, dryers, and refrigerators, even though the company was barely able to predict how its markets would behave two weeks in the future. In 1993 the company abandoned such detailed market projections because they did not seem to serve any other purpose than to provide meaning for the marketing department's activities.

The point is that information analysis serves both instrumental and symbolic purposes, and that more analysis does not ensure successful decision making. Most certainly, all things being equal, data collection and analysis may be important inputs to decision making (provided the correct data are collected and analyses are not flawed as discussed previously). On the other hand, information analysis may be largely symbolic, may be a consequence of history or inertial tendencies, and may consume scarce attentional capacities and resources that could be directed toward resolving other organization problems.

The Acquisition and Analysis of Information

Research indicates that the information acquisition process is often flawed. There is empirical evidence that formal reports are riddled with distortions and unintentional biases (Altheide and Johnson 1980; Hopwood 1972), and that organizations that rely on formal reports either get into trouble or perform ineffectively (Grinyer and Norburn 1975; Starbuck, Greve, and Hedberg, 1978). Thus, by engaging in data acquisition an organization not only may take resources away from operational processes that might increase its speed, but also may receive information that is useless or misleading.

Often, information collected in organizations is either too much, too little, or wrong. Evidence from laboratory studies suggests that individuals rarely acquire the right amount of information before they make decisions (Connolly 1988; Connolly and Gilani 1982; Connolly and Serre 1984). They acquire either too little information when decision stakes are large, or too much when stakes are low. Individuals are also not able to judge reliably the differential validity of information, nor do they consistently acquire information from the cheapest of available, equally valid sources.

Research in the area of organizational information processing shows that a myriad of factors affect the acquisition, analysis, and use of information in an organization, including individual difference variables and variables related to characteristics of the organization's information system, structure, and strategy (Sutcliffe, forthcoming). Organizational members' acquisition and use of information are not only influenced by appropriate normative factors, but also by several normatively irrelevant task characteristics. These findings indicate that large and costly departures from optimality may be frequently found in the acquisition and use of information in real-world settings.

In addition to the factors just cited, Sutcliffe (forthcoming) suggests that an organization's strategy, slack resources, and degree of inertia may be particularly important in affecting what information is collected and taken into account in making important decisions. For example, a company's strategic orientation is associated with differing assumptions regarding the external environment and the extent to which managers assume that the world is certain and therefore open to precise predictions about the future, or uncertain and therefore completely unpredictable (Courtney, Kirkland, and Viguerie 1997; Daft and Weick 1984). These assumptions may directly affect what and how much information managers collect and analyze.

The strong pursuit of a strategy can circumscribe attention and lead executives and other managers to focus on certain types of information and overlook other important information (Hambrick and Snow 1977). For example, managers in companies pursuing cost leadership strategies through quality improvement techniques (Sterman, Repenning, and Kofman 1997) often become singularly concerned with information related to efficiency and other issues related to streamlining internal processes. This may prove to be problematic for survival in the long run if managers become so focused on measuring and analyzing information related to internal improvements that they disregard information and analysis related to other aspects of their competitive environment. Sterman, Repenning, and Kofman (1997) recount the paradoxical case of Analog Devices. Analog Devices achieved serious improvements in quality as a consequence of focusing on measurement, control, and information analysis. Concurrent with realizing these productivity gains, however, its markets began to erode and demand began to fall. One simplistic explanation, consistent with research comparing failing companies and matched survivors (e.g., D'Aveni and MacMillan 1990), is that the decision makers at Analog Devices paid too much attention to analyzing internal information while failing to analyze important external information. A lesson to be learned is that decision makers who pay more attention to analyzing information related to the external rather than internal environment, and who analyze information related to the output side of the environment (e.g., decision makers who focus on customers and other general economic factors affecting demand) are more likely to survive in the long run than their counterparts who neglect to attend to these sectors.

Slack can influence information processing because it often promotes complacency or a decreased vigilance in searching for relevant information about environmental changes (Tushman and Romanelli 1985). On the other hand, slack may also be necessary, so that organizational members have the time to collect and analyze data. Finally, organizational inertia can affect information processes because inertia often leads organizational members to focus internally as search and decision-making processes atrophy (Boyd, Dess, and Rasheed 1993).

Group Processes and Information Analysis

Contemporary organizations rely increasingly on groups to make decisions. The collection and analysis of data in groups follows particular dynamics. Roberts (1977) and Gersick (1988) acknowledged that teams, at some point, need to move beyond analyzing the possibilities of a product to implementing product design and exploiting a chosen technology or market niche. Ancona and Caldwell (1992) found that in new-product teams in high-technology organizations, information-scanning and analyzing activities are negatively related to adherence to budgets and schedules, efficiency, and the quality of innovations. Evidently, the more teams engaged in scanning and information-gathering activities, the more likely they were to enter a cycle of complexity and negative performance. Ancona and Caldwell (1992) concluded that continuous exploration for new information brings a large amount of conflicting information into a team. To resolve the conflict, teams must engage in extensive and complex interactions. As the complexity grows, so does frustration with factors both internal and external to the group, which ultimately leads to more internal conflict, poor performance, and negative managerial ratings of performance.

Information Collection and Analysis in the Age of Speed

As noted previously, elaborate and time-consuming data analyses and planning processes conflict with current demands for speedy decision making and action taking. However, this does not mean that the most effective organizations forgo analysis of important information as a precursor to decision making. Recent studies suggest that organizations in high-velocity environments pay more attention to performance monitoring than to more traditional scanning activities. Organizational scanning provides information about the overall business environment. Scanning is critical for planning, strategy formulation, and long-term decision making. Performance monitoring, by contrast, provides more specific information about an organization's business situation and whether it is effective in fulfilling its goals and meeting the demands of stakeholders (Eisenhardt 1989; Huber 1991). Information about a company's performance relative to competitors, existing technologies, and product markets in which the company operates is useful for making operational and tactical decisions; is important for uncovering or discovering idiosyncratic threats, problems, or trends; and leads to more timely and accurate detection of problems and opportunities (D'Aveni 1994; Eisenhardt 1989). Decision makers in organizations in which performance is monitored continually through frequent, mandatory, intense, face-to-face operations meetings, or through other mechanisms such as frequent written reports detailing performance targets, sense the environment more quickly and accurately (Eisenhardt 1989). This enables them to initiate corrective actions before crises materialize (Eisenhardt 1989). In addition to its salutary effect on problem sensing, performance monitoring can positively influence performance indirectly through its effect on trust. Frequent interactions enable executives to develop norms of trust that permit quick and reliable responses when situations become difficult (Sutcliffe, forthcoming).

Other recent research examining differences between failing and surviving companies also highlights the pitfalls of extensive strategic planning, information gathering, and information analysis. For example, executives in failing and surviving companies appear to differ in the speed with which they update mental models (Barr, Stimpert, and Huff 1992; Hambrick and D'Aveni 1992). The performance differences can be explained by focusing on the possibility that surviving companies engage less in formalized scanning, strategic planning, and competitive analysis, and more in trial-and-error action. This enables better discernment of important trends, threats, and opportunities and facilitates second-order learning and changes in executives' mental models of key cause-effect relationships (Lyles and Mitroff 1980; Weick 1990).

What is important for the current analysis is that formal systems for learning about competitive environments (e.g., systems that emphasize long-term strategic planning and information analysis) are slow to operate and get bogged down in detail. Consequently, these systems often represent the environment as it was, not as it is. Moreover, opportunities for interaction and communication are often limited in these systems. Thus, decision makers in organizations with more formalized strategic planning or information systems are less likely to be aware of current environmental information than their counterparts in organizations without such systems. As Sutcliffe (forthcoming) argues,

> Action taking may be a better mechanism for generating data and for instantiating opportunities for dialogue, bargaining, negotiation, and persuasion that are essential for developing a good sense of what is going on and what to do about it. Further, action and cognition are mutually reinforcing. Actions allow for the assessment and reassessment of causal beliefs, which subsequently lead executives to undertake new actions to test the newly asserted relationships. Over time, as supporting evidence mounts, more significant changes in beliefs and actions evolve.

Action generates new information and increases opportunities for interaction that can help decision makers modify faulty understandings and update previously held inaccurate perceptions. In effect, action facilitates learning. Consequently, decision makers in more action-oriented organizations are likely to develop better representations of a current environment and to more quickly update existing environmental models than their counterparts in organizations that are less action-oriented (Sutcliffe, forthcoming). Furthermore, action-oriented organizations may adapt more quickly to future, changing environments than more sluggish organizations.

In summary, researchers have found that in contrast to their poorer performing counterparts successful companies:

1. Are more likely to collect and analyze information related to the external environment rather than the internal environment as well as information related to the output side of their environment rather than the input side of their environment (D'Aveni and MacMillan 1990);
2. Focus on analyzing real-time information instead of historical data and forecasts (Eisenhardt 1989);
3. Are more adept at building and updating maps of causal linkages; and

4. Learn more from their actions and the subsequent reactions of competitors than from analyses of historical data.

Agenda for Future Research

The purpose of this chapter was to consider information analysis in an age of speed. We began by highlighting an assumption embedded in conventional wisdom and magnified by contemporary management practices: that better decisions are a consequence of more extensive information collection and analysis. Moreover, we suggested that time-consuming data analyses might conflict with contextual demands for speedy decision making and action taking. In our subsequent discussion, we pointed out that there is little evidence to support the assumption embedded in conventional wisdom. Furthermore, results from studies of high-performing companies in high-velocity environments suggest that extensive analyses may be unnecessary to secure high performance. Our analysis reveals several areas that need to be extended in order to enhance current research in this domain.

Accuracy–Speed Trade-offs

We suggested that many organizations are under increasing pressure to make decisions more quickly. Research indicates that when decision makers are under pressure for speed, they are likely to search for evidence that confirms prior expectations (Fiske 1992, 884). By contrast, when decision makers are under pressure to be accurate, they are likely to be more thorough in their search and analysis activities. Although increased thoroughness may lengthen the analytical process, there is also evidence that it may encourage more innovative solutions. These trade-offs may have important implications for all organizations and especially for organizations pursuing innovation as a strategy. Future research should examine the trade-offs between accuracy and speed and answer questions such as the following:

▲ Under what conditions does accuracy or speed take precedence over the other in decision-making situations?
▲ What are the antecedents for accuracy or speed in decision making?

▲ Are accuracy and speed mutually exclusive approaches in decision making?

▲ What are the outcomes of decisions made quickly versus the outcomes of those made accurately?

Answers to these questions may help decision makers (and scholars) better understand the tensions between accuracy and speed in the dynamics of decision making.

Although the pursuit of information accuracy may have positive benefits such as contributing to more innovative decision solutions, it may also have some untoward effects in organizations. Specifically, as Weick, Sutcliffe, and Obstfeld (1997) suggest, the pursuit of accuracy may curtail intraorganizational interaction and communication because people may withhold judgments until they can demonstrate that their analysis is sound. In complex, partially understood environments, "norms that favor accuracy may silence the reporting of imprecise hunches about anomalies that could cumulate into crises" (Weick, Sutcliffe, and Obstfeld 1997, 36). A number of important questions in this area remain unanswered. For example, What factors influence the development of decision norms such as norms that favor information accuracy? or How do norms (e.g., accuracy versus speed) affect social interaction and communication processes and the outcomes of the decision process?

Accountability for Decisions and Its Influence on Analysis

Expectations of accountability are an implicit (and sometimes explicit) constraint on decision makers (Tetlock 1992, 337). As the complexity of decisions increases, so do accountability demands because decision makers often become accountable to more and different stakeholders (Tetlock 1985, 1992; Chapter 2 of this volume). Consequently, accountability pressures are likely to influence information search, use of information, and the extent of information analysis in an organization. Although there has been a dramatic rise in experimental studies examining accountability and its effects on information analysis and decision making, researchers have virtually ignored these processes in the field. Several questions remain to be answered. For example, how do social and organizational contexts affect accountability and how does accountability affect information analysis in the field?

Information Processes

In addition to research examining how accuracy–speed trade-offs and accountability demands affect the extent to which decision makers emphasize measurement and analysis, more work needs to be done in the areas of information acquisition and information processing. Specifically, research needs to focus on four areas. First, research is needed to better understand why important information is rejected, considered irrelevant, or unimportant, or why unimportant information (i.e., noise) is considered meaningful, relevant, and important (Vertzberger 1984). As noted previously, not all information in the decision environment is likely to be relevant for organizational success, and research suggests that attention to particular types of information may be crucial for survival (D'Aveni and MacMillan 1990). Studies examining how organizational members single out and give meaning to particular information still need to be conducted.

Second, research is needed on information flows within organizations, and particularly the extent to which information flows are symmetrical (Grunig 1990). Symmetrical information systems are those in which employees are provided with mechanisms for dialog with each other, supervisors, and top managers. Asymmetrical information systems, by contrast, lack mechanisms of dialog. Symmetrical information systems may enable employees to have a deeper understanding of their organization's goals, plans, and relationships with key actors in the environment than asymmetrical information systems. As a consequence, lower-level employees in symmetrical information systems may be better primed to recognize important information than employees in asymmetrical ones. Ultimately, this higher awareness of important information in symmetrical information systems may affect the quality of information analysis itself. Future research should test whether these speculations can be confirmed in the field.

Third, most research on information processes in organizations focuses either on top executives or organizations as the unit of analysis. This research includes work on the perception of managers (Boyd, Dess, and Rasheed 1993; Sutcliffe 1994, forthcoming), what managers pay attention to (D'Aveni and MacMillan 1990), environmental scanning (Eisenhardt 1989; Fahey and King 1977; Hambrick 1982; Sutcliffe 1994), and organizational information processing (Smith et al. 1991). Most of these studies assume that information is readily available for top executives to perceive, pay attention to, scan, or process. Traditionally, midlevel managers have been seen as suppliers of information to top managers (Thompson 1967; Westley 1990). Also, top managers have been found to receive information from external sources such as boards of other companies that they serve on, publications targeted to executives, and consultants (Mintzberg 1973). With the exception of the work by Dutton and Colleagues on how middle managers sell issues to top management (see Dutton and Ashford 1993; Dutton et al., 1997), there is little recent organizational research that examines exactly how information enters an organization or how information gets acquired, who acquires it, and in what form it reaches top decision makers. Consequently, this is an area of research that needs to be explored further.

Fourth, we need research on how information is interpreted within organizations. Specifically, little attention has been paid to examining how managerial and contextual characteristics affect decision makers' interpretations, although recent research (e.g., Milliken 1990; Milliken and Lant 1991) suggests there are several potential sources of influence. Three particularly important factors that are likely to affect how data and information are interpreted are decision makers' ideologies and beliefs, current organizational performance, and the changing nature of the context.

Conclusion

Anecdotal evidence suggests that organizations have increased their reliance on measurement and data analysis to guide their strategies and control their operations because it is assumed that more data and more analysis lead to better decisions. Yet research on information and decision making indicates that more is not always better, especially when agility is critical to organizational success. Thus, managers are caught in an apparent dilemma: how to make good decisions when there is little time to collect and analyze all the relevant information. We have argued that in some instances this seeming dilemma is just a chimera, since there is evidence that analyses are often flawed or do not serve the purpose for which they were intended (e.g., reduction of uncertainty). Nevertheless, in a significant number of cases, the dilemma may be a true one: so much information, so little time. We have analyzed this dilemma drawing from the organizational literature on information processing, attention giving, symbolic interactionism, and groups. We have proposed a number of avenues for future research and close with the hope that managers as well as consultants and other change agents have gained a better understanding of the decision dilemmas facing managers in an age of speed.

References

Altheide, D. L. and Johnson, J. M. 1980. *Bureaucratic Propaganda.* Boston: Allyn & Bacon.

Ancona, D. G. and Caldwell, D. F. 1992. "Bridging the Boundary: External Activity and Performance in Organizational Teams." *Administrative Science Quarterly* 37, 634–65.

Barr, P. S., Stimpert, J. L., and Huff, A. S. 1992. "Cognitive Change, Strategic Action, and Organizational Renewal." *Strategic Management Journal* 13, 15–36.

Bourgeois, L. J., III and Eisenhardt, K. M. 1988. "Strategic Decision Processes in High-Velocity Environments: Four Cases in the Microcomputer Industry." *Management Science* 34, 816–35.

Boyd, B. K., Dess, G. G., and Rasheed, A. M. A. 1993. "Divergence Between Archival and Perceptual Measures of the Environment: Causes and Consequences." *Academy of Management Review* 18, 204–26.

Child, J. 1972. "Organizational Structure, Environment, and Performance: The Role of Strategic Choice." *Sociology* 6, 2–22.

Connolly, T. 1988. "Studies of Information-Purchase Processes." In B. Brehmer and C. R. B. Joyce (eds.), *Human Judgment: The Social Judgment Theory View.* Amsterdam: Elsevier Science.

Connolly, T. and Gilani, N. 1982. "Information Search in Judgment Tasks: A Regression Model and Some Preliminary Findings." *Organizational Behavior and Human Performance* 30, 330–50.

Connolly, T. and Serre, P. 1984. "Information Search in Judgment Tasks: The Effects of Unequal Cue Validity and Cost." *Organizational Behavior and Human Performance* 34, 387–401.

Courtney, H., Kirkland, J., and Viguerie, P. 1997. "Strategy Under Uncertainty." *Harvard Business Review* 75(6), 66–79.

Daft, R. L., Sormunen, J., and Parks, D. 1988. "Chief Executive Scanning, Environmental Characteristics, and Company Performance: An Empirical Study." *Strategic Management Journal* 9, 123–39.

Daft, R. L. and Weick, K. E. 1984. "Toward a Model of Organizations as Interpretation Systems." *Academy of Management Review* 9, 284–95.

D'Aveni, R. A. 1994. *Hypercompetition: Managing the Dynamics of Strategic Maneuvering.* New York: Free Press.

D'Aveni, R. A. and MacMillan, I. C. 1990. "Crisis and the Content of Managerial Communications: A Study of the Focus of Attention of Top Managers in Surviving and Failing Firms." *Administrative Science Quarterly* 35, 634–57.

Dean, J. W., Jr. and Bowen, D. E. 1994. "Management Theory and Total Quality: Improving Research and Practice through Theory Development." *Academy of Management Review* 19, 392–418.

Dean, J. W., Jr. and Evans, J. R. 1994. *Total Quality Management, Organization, and Strategy.* New York: West.

Dean, J. W., Jr. and Sharfman, M. P. 1993. "Procedural Rationality in the Strategic Decision-Making Process." *Journal of Management Studies* 30, 587–610.

———. 1996. "Does Decision Process Matter? A Study of Strategic Decision-Making Effectiveness." *Academy of Management Journal* 39, 368–96.

Dimancescu, D. and Dwenger, K. 1996. *World-Class New Product Development: Benchmarking Best Practices of Agile Manufacturers.* New York: American Management Association.

Dutton, J. E. and Ashford, S. J. 1993. "Selling Issues to Top Management." *Academy of Management Review* 18, 397–428.

Dutton, J. E., Ashford, S. J., Wierba, E., O'Neill, R. M., and Hayes, E. 1997. "Reading the Wind: How Middle Managers Assess the Context for Selling Issues to Top Managers." *Strategic Management Journal* 18, 407–23.

Eisenhardt, K. M. 1989. "Making Fast Decisions in High-Velocity Environments." *Academy of Management Journal* 32, 543–76.

Eisenhardt, K. M. and Tabrizi, B. N. 1995. "Accelerating Adaptive Processes: Product Innovation in the Global Computer Industry." *Administrative Science Quarterly* 40, 84–110.

Fahey, L. and King, W. 1977. "Environmental Scanning for Corporate Planning." *Business Horizons* 20(4) 61–71.

Feldman, M. S. and March, J. G. 1981. "Information in Organizations as Signal and Symbol." *Administrative Science Quarterly* 26, 171–86.

Fiske, S. T. 1992. "Thinking Is for Doing: Portraits of Social Cognition From Daguerreotype to Laserphoto." *Journal of Personality and Social Psychology* 63, 877–89.

Gersick, C. J. G. 1988. "Time and Transition in Work Teams: Toward a New Model of Group Development." *Academy of Management Journal* 31, 9–41.

Grinyer, P. H. and Norburn, D. 1975. "Planning for Existing Markets: Perceptions of Executives and Financial Performance." *Journal of the Royal Statistical Society, Series A* 138, 70–97.

Grunig, J. E. 1990. "Theory and Practice of Interactive Media Relations." *Public Relations Quarterly* 35 (fall), 18–23.

Hambrick, D. C. 1982. "Environmental Scanning and Organizational Strategy." *Strategic Management Journal* 3, 159–74.

Hambrick, D. C. and D'Aveni, R. A. 1992. "Top Team Deterioration as Part of the Downward Spiral of Large Corporate Bankruptcies." *Management Science* 38, 1445–66.

Hambrick, D. C. and Snow, C. C. 1977. "A Contextual Model of Strategic Decision Making in Organizations." *Academy of Management Proceedings* 109–12.

Hopwood, A. G. 1972. "An Empirical Study of the Role of Accounting Data in Performance Evaluation." *Journal of Accounting Research: Empirical Research in Accounting: Selected Studies,* 10, 156–82.

Huber, G. P. 1984. "The Nature and Design of Post-Industrial Organizations." *Management Science* 30, 928–51.

————. 1991. "Organizational Learning: The Contributing Processes and the Literatures." *Organization Science* 2 (special issue), 88–115.

Huber, G. P. and Daft, R. L. 1987. "The information environments of organizations." In F. M. Jablin, L. L. Putnam, K. H. Roberts, and L. W. Porter (eds.), *Handbook of Organizational Communication: An Interdisciplinary Perspective.* Newbury Park, CA: Sage.

Jones, J. W. 1993. *High-Speed Management: Time-Based Strategies for Managers and Organizations.* San Francisco: Jossey-Bass.

Lyles, M. A. and Mitroff, I. I. 1980. "Organizational Problem Formulation: An Empirical Study." *Administrative Science Quarterly* 25, 102–19.

March, J. G. and Sevón, G. 1984. "Gossip, Information, and Decision Making." *Advances in Information Processing in Organizations* 1, 95–107.

Martinez, A. C. 1997. "Address by distinguished executive, Arthur, C. Martinez, CEO of Sears, Roebuck and Co." Presented at the meeting of the Academy of Management, Boston, August 10.

Meyer, C. 1993. *Fast Cycle Time: How to Align Purpose, Strategy, and Structure for Speed.* New York: Free Press.

Milliken, F. J. 1990. "Perceiving and Interpreting Environmental Change: An Examination of College Administrators' Interpretation of Changing Demographics." *Academy of Management Journal* 33, 42–63.

Milliken, F. J. and Lant, T. K. 1991. "The Effect of an Organization's Recent Performance History on Strategic Persistence and Change: The Role of Managerial Interpretations." *Advances in Strategic Management* 7, 129–56.

Mintzberg, H. 1973. *The Nature of Managerial Work.* New York: Harper & Row.

————. 1994. *The Rise and Fall of Strategic Planning: Reconceiving Roles for Planning, Plans, Planners.* New York: Free Press.

Pfeffer, J. and Salancik, G. R. 1978. *The External Control of Organizations: A Resource Dependence Perspective.* New York: Harper & Row.

Roberts, E. B. 1977. "Generating Effective Corporate Innovation." *Technology Review* 80, 27–33.

Schoonhoven, C. B., Eisenhardt, K. M., and Lyman, K. 1990. "Speeding Products to Market: Waiting Time to First Product Introduction in New Firms." *Administrative Science Quarterly* 35, 177–207.

Smith, K. G., Grimm, C. M., Gannon, M. J., and Chen, M. J. 1991. "Organizational Information Processing, Competitive Responses, and Performance in the U.S. Domestic Airline Industry." *Academy of Management Journal* 34, 60–85.

Stalk, G., Jr. and Hout, T. M. 1990. *Competing Against Time: How Time-Based Competition Is Reshaping Global Markets.* New York: Free Press.

Starbuck, W. H. 1983. "Organizations as Action Generators." *American Sociological Review* 48, 91–102.

Starbuck, W. H., Greve, A., and Hedberg, B. L. T. 1978. "Responding to Crises." *Journal of Business Administration* 9(2) 111–137.

Starbuck, W. H. and Milliken, F. J. 1988. "Executives' Perceptual Filters: What They Notice and How They Make Sense." In D. C. Hambrick (ed.), *The Executive Effect: Concepts and Methods for Studying Top Managers.* Greenwich, CT: JAI.

Sterman, J. D., Repenning, N. P., and Kofman, F. 1997. "Unanticipated Side Effects of Successful Quality Programs: Exploring a Paradox of Organizational Improvement." *Management Science* 43, 503–21.

Sutcliffe, K. M. 1991. "Determinants and Outcomes of Top Managers' Perceptions and Interpretations of the Environment." Ph.D. diss., University of Texas at Austin.

———. 1994. "What Executives Notice: Accurate Perceptions in Top Management Teams." *Academy of Management Journal* 35, 1360–78.

———. 1997. "Commentary on Strategic Sensemaking: Learning Through Scanning, Interpretation, Action, and Performance." In J. Walsh and A. Huff (eds.), *Advances in Strategic Management.* Greenwich, CT: JAI.

———. Forthcoming. "Organizational Environments and Organizational Information Processing." In F. Jablin and L. Putnam (eds.), *Handbook of Organizational Communication.* 2nd ed. Beverly Hills: Sage.

Sutton, H. 1988. *Competitive Intelligence.* New York: The Conference Board.

Swanson, E. B. 1978. "The Two Faces of Organizational Information." *Accounting, Organization and Society* 3, 237–46.

Tetlock, P. E. 1985. "Accountability: A Social Check on the Fundamental Attribution Error." *Social Psychology Quarterly* 48, 227–36.

———. 1992. "The Impact of Accountability on Judgment and Choice: Toward a Social Contingency Model." In M. P. Zanna (ed.), *Advances in Experimental and Social Psychology.* Vol. 25. New York: Academic.

Thompson, J. D. 1967. *Organizations in Action: Social Science Bases of Administrative Theory.* New York: McGraw-Hill.

Tushman, M. L. and Romanelli, E. 1985. "Organizational Evolution: A Metamorphosis Model of Convergence and Reorientation." In L. L. Cummings and B. M. Staw (eds.), *Research in Organizational Behavior.* Vol. 7. Greenwich, CT: JAI.

Vertzberger, Y. 1984. *Misperceptions in Foreign Policymaking: The Sino-Indian Conflict 1959–1962.* Boulder, CO: Westview.

Vesey, J. T. 1991. "The New Competitors: They Think in Terms of 'Speed-to-Market.' " *Academy of Management Executive* 5, 23–33.

Waterman, R. W. 1997. "Reflections on Excellence." In I. D. Colville (chair), *In Search of The Times: An Exercise in Sense Making.* Symposium conducted at the meeting of the Academy of Management, Boston, August 13.

Weick, K. E. 1974. "Review of the Book *The Nature of Managerial Work*." *Administrative Science Quarterly* 18, 111–18.

———. 1979. *The Social Psychology of Organizing.* 2nd ed. New York: Random House.

———. 1990. "Cartographic Myths in Organizations." In A. S. Huff (ed.), *Mapping Strategic Thought.* New York: Wiley.

Weick, K. E. and Daft, R. L. 1983. "Effectiveness of Interpretation Systems." In K. S. Cameron and D. A. Whetten (eds.), *Organizational Effectiveness: A Comparison of Multiple Models.* New York: Academic.

Weick, K. E., Sutcliffe, K. M., and Obstfeld, D. 1997. "Organizing for High Reliability: The Mindful Suppression of Inertia." Working paper #9710-25, University of Michigan Business School.

Westley, F. R. 1990. "Middle Managers and Strategy: Microdynamics of Inclusion." *Strategic Management Journal* 11, 337–51.

Womack, J. P., Jones, D. T., and Roos, D. 1990. *The Machine That Changed the World.* New York: Macmillan.

Chapter 9

Competitive External Pressures: Building Top Management Teams to Sustain Competitive Advantage in a Changing World

REBECCA S. WELLS *and* KAREN A. BANTEL

"I guess you could say we should have stuck to our knitting," remarked a retired executive of his former employer's unsuccessful diversification efforts. The gas and oil company he worked for had purchased several trucking companies, thus entering a business for which the top management turned out to be unprepared. Eventually, after incurring substantial losses, the company sold its trucking subsidiary, as well as other underperforming assets that did not relate to its core fuel business (personal communication, July 28, 1997).

A consultant was hired when a large mutual savings bank faced the prospect of deregulation. The consultant recommended that the bank privatize in order to take advantage of newly legalized opportunities, but the CEO declined, because "he didn't want to lose control" of the operation. By the time the bank did privatize, an irretrievable opportunity had gone by. In the fifteen years since then, a key competitor grew in assets at almost ten times the rate of this bank (personal communication, July 21, 1997).

The popular management literature is replete with parables of companies gone astray in their pursuit of competitive advantage. The stories

175

in the foregoing illustrate two of the most common strategic pitfalls: expansion into businesses that the acquiring top management does not adequately understand, and failure to capitalize on new opportunities (or respond to threats) when faced with environmental change. One is a failure of commission and the other a failure of omission. Easy enough to identify in hindsight, but how can these pitfalls be prevented?

At its essence, competitive advantage is manifested in a company's ability to earn sufficient rates of return on investment (ROI) to garner resources necessary to pursue the company's mission. These rates of return may be strictly financial or both social and financial, depending on the values of the company's stakeholders. However these yields are measured, for many U.S. companies, the competitive advantage essential to long-term viability is increasingly becoming ephemeral. Changes in information and manufacturing technologies have, in many cases, eliminated traditional economies of scale (Bernhardt 1994), and these technologies continue to evolve both rapidly and unpredictably (Bettis and Prahalad 1995). The saturated U.S. consumer goods market is open to global competitors (Barabba 1989), as market boundaries themselves shift with increasing speed (Prahalad and Hamel 1990). And U.S. companies cannot assume growth abroad: Global competition is intensifying as Third World production capabilities continue to rise (Berry 1997). At the same time, many of yesterday's innovations have become today's assumptions, as in the instance of total quality management, which has now become so widespread that it no longer offers a distinct source of competitive advantage (Bernhardt 1994).

Strategic Decision Making as a Source of Competitive Advantage

Two critical sources of competitive advantage are strategic decision making and implementation (Andrews 1987). Whereas, in practice decision making and implementation processes are highly iterative and integrated, the skills required to execute strategies are distinct from those required to formulate plans. The focus of this chapter is therefore limited to decision making. Specifically, the objective is to examine how the small group of executives with responsibility for company strategy, known as the top management team (Bourgeois 1980), develops the capacity to make optimal strategic decisions.

Decision-making competencies here refer to a top management team's ability to identify potentially relevant cues from the environment; subsequently develop plans based on syntheses of such cues; and, finally, select from the range of possible plans those that best utilize organizational capabilities to meet current and emerging environmental demands (Eisenhardt and Zbaracki 1992). Our concern is therefore with the ability of top management teams to effect optimal information processing throughout the strategic decision-making process.

Within strategic decision making, different competencies are critical to organizations in different contexts. Some companies may operate in predictable environments that require little adaptation. Others may sustain viable niches as nimble imitators and need reliable data about competitors and consumer preferences rather than the capacity to develop new products. For many companies, however, sustainable competitive advantage relies increasingly on both the quality and timeliness of original ideas. Murakami (1993, 20) asserts that, in increasingly global markets faced with continual improvements in production, companies must become adept at "concept creation," the continual development of new products, technologies, and systems. In a similar vein, Hamel (1993, 24) predicts that in the future, "competition will not be product vs. product; it will be corporation vs. corporation," as firms compete first and foremost for the intellectual leadership that will enable them to rewrite industry rules.

The remainder of this chapter addresses top management team capabilities to make strategic decisions in companies that depend upon both the quality and timeliness of original ideas. How can executives make more-creative and original decisions faster than competitors with access to similar information?

First, we identify the specific decision-making capabilities necessitated by complex, resource-scarce, and dynamic environments. Then we examine recent academic literature to assess current knowledge about elements of adaptive strategy. After identifying limitations in previous work, we suggest a framework for sustaining competitive advantage in complex, resource-scarce, and dynamic environments. We then draw upon both previous research and five new case studies to identify how top management teams may develop such a capacity. Finally, we make suggestions for future research as well as immediate implications for top management teams.

Environmental Implications for
Competitive Competencies

An organization's environment may be defined as the combination of all factors that executives must take into account when making strategic decisions (Duncan 1972). Factors affecting strategy may arise from either outside or inside the organization, as well as from current or potential customers, competitors, suppliers, or regulators. Three critical elements of these factors, taken as a whole, affect the nature of an organization's environment. The first is the complexity of the environment, which may be defined as the number and dissimilarity of environmental actors, as well as their degree of interconnection (Dess and Beard 1984). The second element is resource abundance, which determines an environment's ability to sustain organizational growth (Starbuck 1976). The third is dynamism, or the speed with which the environment changes (Dess and Beard 1984). Both complexity and dynamism increase the level of uncertainty faced by strategic decision makers, and, thus, the difficulty of their task (Bourgeois 1980), while resource scarcity decreases the margin for error.

To achieve superior returns, executives must go beyond merely reacting to the dynamic complexity that surrounds them and, instead, proactively turn these challenges into new sources of competitive advantage. Environmental complexity, resource scarcity, and dynamism each has critical implications for the capabilities required of strategic decision makers.

The first source, complexity, demands that companies pursue core strategies in multifaceted ways, such as through selling to many different markets or developing multiple approaches to existing markets (Nayyar and Bantel 1994). This competitive variety is necessary because the next source of competitive advantage arises from many different sources. Resource scarcity, the second source, requires innovation, as existing markets become saturated or shrink. Companies in resource-scarce contexts must be able to conceptualize distinctive bases of competitive advantage, or face decreasing returns due to relentless price competition. Finally, environmental dynamism necessitates that top management teams be flexible. Not only must they be able to generate ideas quickly but also to subsequently modify plans as environmental factors continue to change.

Capitalizing on Complex Change: Lessons from Current Literature

A review of strategic decision-making literature reveals two overarching prescriptive themes for managers who seek to capitalize on the complex change of their environments: the need for differentiation supporting openness to new ideas (Drucker 1992; Kanter 1996), and the need for integration among those ideas (Porter 1996; Prahalad and Hamel 1990). The need for differentiation, or ability to perceive and formulate an effective response to a wide range of disparate concepts, derives from both the variety and subtlety of environmental cues. Integration of differentiated activities is essential to the creation of sustainable competitive advantage.

Prahalad and Hamel (1990) define a company's core competence as "the collective learning in the organization, especially how to coordinate diverse production skills and integrate multiple streams of technologies" (p. 82). Integration is essential to the evolution of such a strategy, because it allows the company to replicate its activities without repeated high learning costs. Integration also allows companies to synthesize components into systems that cannot be successfully copied. Porter (1996) argues that competitive advantage stems from uniquely competent integration of activities, as well as from the strength of the activities themselves, because the business units themselves are too easily imitable.

It thus appears that company leaders are being advised to maintain a delicate equilibrium between differentiation and integration in their continual recalibration of strategy. Nonaka (1988) describes successful strategic development as "compressive," both generating new options from the bottom up and making connections from the top down. Bettis and Hitt (1995) suggest that "the significant dynamism in the new competitive landscape requires that firms concurrently unlearn and learn" (p. 14). Hedberg, Nystrum, and Starbuck (1976) recommend maintaining a balance between stabilizing and destabilizing influences, encouraging consensus and dissension simultaneously to maximize performance. None of these researchers, however, fully explicates how this might be achieved.

Research to date therefore indicates the broad attributes of adaptive strategy, but not the specific steps executives can take to build top management teams capable of developing such strategy. In the next section, we outline a conceptual model intended to address this gap.

Probing the Sources of Competitive Advantage: A Model for Combining Differentiation and Integration

How do top management teams incorporate both differentiation and integration into company strategy and, thus, maintain a "dynamic fit" (Itami 1987) with their changing environments? It appears that such a combination depends on something more than an uneasy coexistence between the two factors. Instead, an active, mutually supportive interchange between differentiation and integration can strengthen each one, while creating a synergy between them. This relationship has been described as an interpenetration, in which the potential of the whole is actualized through sustained tension between multiple necessary forces (Munch 1982). Interpenetration can be contrasted with less productive ways in which opposing factors within a system can relate. Such elements may also destroy each other or maintain mutual isolation, or else one element may dominate the other (Munch 1982), resulting in a failure of the system or at least greatly reduced output and potential.

Writing on the concept of interpenetration has drawn on Munch's (1982) analysis of the work of sociologist Talcott Parsons. Parsons postulated that adaptation, the imperative to act on new environmental realities, was in inherent tension with integration, the need to sustain cohesion among the elements of a system. In dysfunctional systems, either adaptation or integration can predominate, leading to dissipation of resources or stagnation. In functional systems, however, the adaptive forces dynamize the integrative elements, and, at the same time, the integrative forces restrain and, thus, stabilize the adaptive forces.

This perspective offers new insight into the two common strategic pitfalls illustrated at the beginning of this chapter. Companies that overreach, diversifying into areas for which they lack the managerial competence to extract competitive ROIs, may be said to suffer from excessive differentiation. The differentiating force of creativity, in the absence of adequate integration, leads to a dysfunctional form of competitive variety: companies expand their strategic repertoires beyond their capacity. Similar to this case is the company that innovates without adequate integration. The result may be a new product that other companies actually make better, because the innovating company has neglected its own competencies. On the other hand, companies that remain stolidly in place while newcomers leapfrog ahead of them may be described as excessively integrated. Lacking the dynamizing force of sufficient differentiation, these companies are unable to achieve adequate competitive speed.

Starting Within: Developing the Cognitively Complex Top Management Team

What type of top management team can sustain differentiation and integration simultaneously in company strategy? One approach to maintaining performance is to seek an alignment between managerial structure and environmental demands. Chandler (1990) and Prahalad and Bettis (1986) both observe that limited information-processing capabilities at the headquarters level can constrain the performance of multidivisional companies. This constraint can be addressed by reducing the requirements of top management. Alternatives include restricting ownership to units that the top management team is capable of overseeing or redefining the nature of top management's role relative to strategic planning for units.

Alternatively, executives can seek to increase the cognitive capacity of their top management team such that the team's internal complexity is sufficient relative to its environment (Ashby 1956). In fact, the definition of *cognitive complexity* entails the two elements identified thus far as key to adaptive strategy: differentiation, defined in cognitive terms as the ability to see multiple dimensions of situations; and integration, the capacity to make connections among those dimensions (Harvey, Hunt, and Schroder 1961).

Because of their divergent capabilities, cognitively complex individuals have been found to be creative (McGill, Johnson, and Bantel 1993). Higher cognitive complexity should therefore enhance capacity to recognize the relevance of seemingly unrelated cues from multiple aspects of the environment. Such creativity may yield two key advantages: the competitive variety necessary in complex environments, and the innovation essential in resource-scarce environments. In other words, not only should this cognitive capacity improve ability to plan for multiple strategic contingencies, but it should also foster development of the qualitatively new ideas necessary to achieve innovation.

In addition, because of their integrative capabilities, cognitively complex individuals have been found to process information more quickly and flexibly than others (Lee 1994). Thus, cognitive complexity at the team level as well should be associated with the ability to make connections among the disparate elements of the environment quickly. Such teams should be able to effect the swift changes in company strategy necessary in dynamic environments.

Although members of top management teams are likely to have relatively high levels of cognitive complexity as individuals, they are subject to inherent limits in information-processing capacity. Therefore, the key to sustaining adequate strategic decision-making capability in demanding environments may be to enhance the cognitive complexity of the top management team as a whole. Research to date has focused on two primary methods for enhancing the cognitive complexity of decision-making teams. First, the composition of the team may be expanded in order to broaden the group's access to relevant information. Second, the team may employ processes that facilitate the integration of these differentiated views.

The inclusion within a top management team of individuals with a diverse range of backgrounds should enhance the range of options perceived and, thus, an organization's innovative capacity (Cohen and Levinthal 1990; Dutton and Duncan 1987). Potential sources of cognitive diversity include demographic heterogeneity in factors such as age, length of service in an organization as well as specifically within a given team, functional experience, and academic major (Bantel and Jackson 1989). Diversity can have costs, however. For example, groups with the diverse membership conducive to strategic differentiation may experience greater difficulty communicating (Roberts and O'Reilly 1979) as well as have lower satisfaction and higher turnover (Pfeffer 1983).

It appears that teams may need integrating processes in order to capitalize on diverse compositions. Teams facing ambiguity seem to function better when leaders pay scrupulous attention to member input (Korsgaard, Schweiger, and Sapienza 1995), as well as when individuals listen carefully to each other (Weick and Roberts 1993). Therefore, top management teams may need some type of internal interpenetration of differentiation and integration in order to sustain both differentiation and integration in company strategy as a whole.

Case Studies of Success

In the preceding section, we outlined a model for how to develop top management teams capable of crafting adaptive strategies in complex, resource-scarce, and dynamic environments. In the following section, we present the stories of five companies to illustrate the principles discussed in the foregoing. Implications for research and practice follow.

The following five case studies represent companies from a range of industries that share the challenges of complexity, scarcity, and unpredictable change. Each is based on an interview with a senior executive who has worked in or with the company in question.

Each case illustrates how a top management team has achieved an internal interpenetration between differentiation and integration. The resulting team-level cognitive complexity is shown to yield three crucial sources of competitive advantage:

1. Competitive variety essential to sustained performance in complex environments;
2. Innovation crucial in resource-scarce environments; and
3. Competitive speed required in dynamic environments.

According to the model developed here, it is the creativity of cognitively complex top management teams that supports generation of the range of ideas necessary to achieve competitive variety as well as development of the qualitatively new concepts that will yield innovation. The flexibility of such cognitively complex top management teams is also posited to make competitive speed possible.

Case 1: Increasing Differentiation Enables WKBN Broadcasting and Sygnet Communications to Seize Complex New Opportunities

The evolution of WKBN Broadcasting and Sygnet Communications' leadership illustrates how a company can become more open in order to exploit complex new opportunities in a dynamic environment. In the early 1980s, Warren Williamson III was CEO of WKBN Broadcasting, a family radio and television business founded by his father in 1926. Among Williamson's professional activities was participation on a television trade association's engineering committee, whose function was to monitor TV bands to prevent their overuse. One day another member of the committee, an engineer working for Metro Media, was in a hurry to leave. As the engineer prepared to rush off, Williamson asked the reason for his haste. The engineer responded that he was leaving to file an application for a cellular telephone license.

Cellular telephones were the very competitors the engineering committee had been trying to fend off from their bands. By being open to seeing a nuisance in a new light, however, Williamson turned his colleague's comment into a remarkable opportunity. After doing some research on the subject, Williamson filed for a cellular telephone license himself. The new line of business was later spun off as Sygnet Communications, and since has become one of the top forty providers of cellular telephone service in the nation. In fact, as of mid-1997, the Williamson family was preparing to sell off its original broadcasting company while continuing to grow its telephone business.

Early business decisions at WKBN were made by a few prescient individuals—hence, the determination in the early 1950s to invest in an emerging source of entertainment called television. Three decades later, the critical source of environmental information was a colleague from a competing company. Consequently, engaging in professional activities such as serving on the committee monitoring TV bands increased the differentiation of strategic information at Williamson's disposal.

By this time, the board, although still family dominated, included three outsiders—a lawyer, a banker, and an accountant—whose participation in decisions gave Williamson additional specialized perspectives on a range of specific issues related to entry into a new market. WKBN's top management had thus also expanded the differentiation of expertise among its own members. By retaining a member of the founding family at the helm, the company was able to integrate this increased differentiation with a deep understanding of the company and its environment.

Today the board is no longer family dominated, and the CEO of Sygnet Communications is a nonfamily member (Williamson is now chairman). The top management team has expanded from the father–son collaboration that led the previous business to a group of four professionals (the CEO, and individuals with responsibilities in finance, technical matters, and operations, respectively) who actively confer with Williamson. It is this team that has recently financed the acquisition of a $250 million business, thereby more than doubling the size of Sygnet's cellular telephone enterprise. Williamson credits both the top management team and an active board for the company's continued success.

At critical junctures, Williamson has combined the insights of both internal and external sources with a clear understanding of his family's business goals. This interpenetration has enabled WKBN Broadcasting and Sygnet Communications to venture profitably into new markets while building on a central business competence that has evolved over seventy years (W. P. Williamson III, personal communication, July 16, 1997). By deliberately cultivating cognitive complexity, the top management sustained the creativity and flexibility necessary to turn environmental complexity and dynamism into new sources of competitive advantage.

Case 2: Outside Investors Create Product Focus and Integration for Microchip Technology

Lack of product and marketing focus, a symptom of excessive strategic differentiation, will often cause a company to founder. For example, Microchip Technology, a developer and maker of semiconductor memory devices, was a "dying chip operation" (Ristelhueber 1995, 63) when a group of venture capitalists bought it from parent company General Instrument Corp. The semiconductor industry is complex by virtue of the range of products that use these components. Semiconductor makers are also vulnerable to economic downturns that affect these products (Gianturco 1996). Finally, their competitive context is dynamic because of continuing technological change ("Hopping Code" 1996). Thus, complexity, scarcity, and dynamism all characterize the environment.

Recognizing that Microchip suffered from a lack of focus that left it weak in many of its market areas, the venture capitalists replaced Microchip's CEO and pushed the company to focus on one type of chip, the 8-bit embedded microcontroller, which had applications in a variety of markets. Between 1992 and 1997, Microchip jumped from fourteenth largest supplier in the world of this type of chip to fifth, with sales growing from $73 million to $334 million per year.

In this case, it took outsiders to force an underperforming company to build competitive advantage from an existing strength. Microchip had suffered from a failure to concentrate on the markets and products that could give it a competitive advantage, because the company's creative capacity was spread too thin. Microchip's potential was only realized when outside investors selected a strong CEO able to build an interpenetration between the company's technical differentiation and the integration needed to enhance focus. The result was innovation in a single product market, where Microchip now enjoys a notable competitive advantage.

Case 3: Kelly Services Sustains Differentiation through Customers

In the case of Kelly Services, systematically involving key customers enables executives to sustain a competitive advantage for this highly complex company. Kelly Services faces strategic challenges that derive largely from the company's own success. In the course of 1996, Kelly placed more than 800,000 people in flexible employment situations around the world. In the last few years, Kelly has been growing at an annual rate of more than 20 percent, mostly through internal growth rather than acquisitions, while maintaining high levels of earnings and assuming no debt. Thus, both high levels of complexity and substantial dynamism stem from Kelly's own strategy. Although best known as a provider of temporary clerical workers, Kelly Services is now the largest supplier of scientists and lawyers in the U.S. temporary employment market. In addition, Kelly operates in several countries in Europe, as well as Canada, Australia, and New Zealand.

The strategic-planning process at Kelly Services is thorough and systematic, and all major strategic decisions are made by a team that is diverse in both organizational tenure and function. What distinguishes Kelly's strategic processes from those of other companies, however, is not the general competence of its strategic review but, instead, the company's systematic inclusion of key customers in its planning. A team at Kelly works solely with several of the company's largest customers and meets with them frequently to discuss the customers' evolving needs. Members of this group include Johnson & Johnson, Allstate, Dow, Tenneco, and Kraft.

As Carl Camden, Kelly's executive vice president for marketing, sales, and public affairs, put it, input from these corporations provides a "huge driver" for Kelly's strategy. For example, Kelly Scientific Resources, which now provides highly qualified scientists to company's on a flexible basis, was the result of a request from one of Kelly's key clients, a pharmaceutical and consumer goods company (C. Camden, personal communication, July 25, 1997).

Communication with these companies effectively increases the cognitive complexity of Kelly's top management team by expanding its differentiated awareness of industry needs. This potential is realized because of the team's systematic integration of customer feedback into a clearly defined strategic-planning process. Members of the president's staff meet once a week to review progress toward closing strategic gaps, as well as twice a year to undertake more extensive review of company strategy.

Thus, Kelly sustains an interpenetration between differentiation and integration that enables the company to build on its existing strengths to meet evolving client needs. By drawing on a long-standing core of key customers, Kelly Services branches out opportunistically into new markets. Such creativity is supported by the fairly structured nature of Kelly's strategic-planning process, which ensures consideration of potentially relevant factors. Kelly therefore infuses its strategy with new ideas while maintaining integration in its core business in temporary-staffing services. The result is competitive variety that has supported growth in a highly competitive business.

Case 4: Differentiation through Employees at People's Bank

Another large organization that, like Kelly Services, has interpenetrated a differentiated range of environmental information with integrating supporting processes is People's Bank of Bridgeport, Connecticut. In this case, however, this balance has been sustained through the cultivation of strategically sensitive and aware employees (D. E. A. Carson, personal communication, July 21, 1997). Consumer banking, once a stable industry, has become highly complex and competitive as well as dynamic in the last two decades. This remarkable shift is attributable to changes in both regulation and technology, as previous restrictions on competition have been removed and computers have offered a viable alternative to personal banking (M. Nordlin, Andersen Consulting, personal communication, February 14, 1997). People's Bank, in existence since 1843, has thrived on these recent changes by drawing on talent from throughout the organization to build a cognitively complex strategic capacity no one individual could achieve.

Key continuing initiatives include encouragement of lateral as well as two-way vertical communication and timely updates sent to the entire staff to ensure that all employees are apprised of the organization's plans and performance. The bank provides in-service education for employees and also funds individuals to take courses at local universities. People's CEO then takes advantage of having well-informed employees by encouraging their input on ways to meet customer needs better.

By facilitating employee learning, People's Bank enhances the differentiation of available potentially relevant strategic information. By promoting communication within the organization, People's Bank achieves an interpenetration between this differentiated information base and an internal integration of ideas. Again, the result of such an interpenetration is a very high level of cognitive complexity at the top management team's disposal. In turn, this cognitive complexity yields both creativity and flexibility.

The result of this internal capacity has been the rapid deployment of innovative new services. In 1995 two midlevel employees from the bank's information services department worked with another employee in the product department to propose a banking interface for personal computers (PCs). This proposal was notable in part because it reflected active communication between two traditionally isolated departments. Top management gave the go-ahead, and the three employees proceeded to develop this service in ninety days. By 1997 approximately 40,000 of People's Bank's 300,000 checking customers used PC banking. This service was among the innovations responsible for a profit level that had reached $80 million in 1996.

Case 5: Allegheny Teledyne Inc. Makes the Most of a Merger by Sustaining Adequate Integration

Maintaining an interpenetration between new and continuing sources of leadership through a merger can enhance the strategic variety and speed of even corporate behemoths. Through the union of specialty metals maker Allegheny Ludlum Corp. and defense and industrial conglomerate Teledyne Inc., executives were able to create a stronger combined top management team that built on the existing strengths of both partners. The result was enhanced capacity in high-value-added specialty steel production ("Allegheny Ludlam" 1996), improved overall economies of scale in metal production, and a diversified corporate portfolio accompanied by management possessing relevant expertise ("Teledyne Spurns" 1996). Such a broad and flexible portfolio will be essential to sustaining competitive advantage through an era of unpredictable defense budget cuts.

According to a member of the company's board of directors, this achievement was the result of extensive planning and communication (P. S. Brentlinger, personal communication, July 15, 1997). Executives were able to build strong internal support for the merger by having open discussions about options and implications over an extended period of time.

The story of the Allegheny Teledyne merger is one of systematic and deliberate attention to integration during a period of major change. The top management team was therefore able to capitalize on the increased differentiation now available through its new members. The results of these efforts have been notable. Even after charges for costs of the merger, net income rose by 5 percent in the first year of combined operations ("Business Brief" 1997), and the company has won plaudits for excellence in customer service ("Jacobson Survey" 1997).

The cases we have outlined suggest a variety of ways through which top management teams may achieve cognitive complexity and, thus, maintain dynamic strategic adaptation. In the case of WKBN Broadcasting and later Sygnet Communications, a family business has broadened membership in its top management team as it has entered increasingly complex competitive territories. Microchip Technology needed help from outside investors to correct for a lack of focus that had left it weak in many areas: Being excessively open to opportunities left Microchip unable to create a competitive whole. Both Kelly Services and People's Bank expanded their top management team complexity through the systematic involvement of key groups of people in their strategic planning. Finally, executives at Allegheny Teledyne Inc. sustained enough integration through their merger to make unusual synergies possible.

Teams whose members have both diverse perspectives and common ground appear to be able to make new connections among seemingly disparate pieces of information. In turn, when a top management team's cognitive complexity is adequate for the complexity of the environment, the company may possess the capacity for continual reinvention necessary to sustain competitive advantage. Such a team may be as large as the entire staff, as in the case of People's Bank, whose members number 3,000.

Applications for Future Research and Practice

Evidence examined in this chapter suggests that future research examine both the consequences and antecedents of the top management team's cognitive complexity that may foster sustained competitive advantage in complex, resource-scarce, and dynamic environments. First, the central hypothesis that cognitively complex top management teams create and sustain competitive advantage in these types of environments merits empirical testing, for if this hypothesis proves false, all related inquiry is irrelevant. Before researchers can test the effects of team-level cognitive complexity, however, the construct itself needs to be operationalized in measurable ways.

One option would be to use cognitive mapping in order to depict team members' belief structures. This technique entails literally diagramming team members' concepts and their perceptions of the causal relationships among those concepts (Weick and Bougon 1986). To ascertain the cognitive complexity of a team, a researcher might develop a collective map for the group, and then examine both the variety of concepts within the map and the number and density of connections among those concepts. The more individuals reporting a given causal connection the denser that link would be. Another approach to measuring team level cognitive complexity would be laboratory studies involving teams in simulated problem-solving scenarios. Cognitive complexity might be inferred from the creativity and flexibility of a team's responses to study questions.

Once researchers have an acceptable operational definition of team-level cognitive complexity, they would ideally have actual top management teams participate in cognitive-mapping or decision-simulation exercises. Such tools could provide a measure of team cognitive complexity at an initial point in time. If these measurements are not feasible, it may be possible to use surveys whose questions address perceptions of team-level information processing.

Studies can then examine effects of cognitive complexity on company or business unit competitive behavior and outcomes. To assess competitive behavior, researchers may use existing instruments to measure both competitive variety and innovation, posited here to result from the greater creativity of cognitively complex top management teams (e.g., Dess and Davis 1984; West and Anderson 1996). Previously validated instruments may also be used to assess the competitive speed hypothesized to result from the flexibility of cognitively complex top management teams (e.g., Cho, Hambrick, and Chen 1994).

Researchers may also evaluate whether or not cognitively complex top management teams achieve improved company or unit outcomes in complex, resource-scarce, and dynamic environments. The challenge addressed in this chapter has been sustaining competitive advantage in environments requiring both creativity and flexibility. Although top management team cognitive complexity is expected to be useful in resource-scarce environments necessitating innovation, it is possible that this chapter's model will apply to environments that are not resource scarce. Thus, we expect cognitive complexity to yield competitive advantage in environments that are munificent as long as they are also characterized by both complexity and dynamism. In the absence of either complexity or dynamism, a simpler top management team, specializing in either speed or variety, is believed to be preferable (Nayyar and Bantel 1994).

Future research will also be strengthened by more specific examination of the intermediate outcomes of top management team cognitive complexity. For example, this chapter has focused on the capacity of top management teams to develop original ideas. However, it may also be possible that cognitively complex top management teams improve company performance because they communicate their vision more effectively to key stakeholders. And it may be that cognitively complex teams make just as many strategic errors as cognitively simpler top management teams but, because of their flexibility, are better able to adjust quickly when they take such missteps.

These examples suggest only two specific hypotheses about the value of cognitive complexity in improving strategic competence. An additional possibility is that cognitively complex teams may be better able to link vision to performance goals, thus supporting employees in achieving high-quality implementation. Such hypotheses are not necessarily mutually exclusive; instead, intermediate results of cognitive complexity may be cumulative and even synergistic. The more specifically research targets hypotheses about the effects of top management team complexity, the more useful the results promise to be.

As evidence accumulates that top management team cognitive complexity actually does predict superior performance, the next logical question is: What factors enable top management teams to achieve cognitive complexity? Research should seek to identify differentiating and integrating factors, as well as how top management teams maintain an interpenetration between the two.

Some research questions could be addressed through survey and archival data. For example, one question might be: Do top management teams need demographically diverse compositions to achieve cognitive complexity, or could demographically homogeneous teams be able to achieve this quality through other mechanisms for broadening their variety of information sources? Survey items could address team dynamics in order to learn what processes enable homogeneous top management teams to integrate information from beyond their boundaries. Surveys could also explore how diverse top management teams take advantage of the differentiated expertise and perspectives of their members.

Again, such investigation will benefit from a fine-grained approach that hones in on specific intermediate factors. With a few exceptions (e.g., Jackson, May, and Whitney 1995), little research has explored the mechanisms through which groups capitalize on the potential of diverse membership. Structured conflict techniques such as dialectical inquiry have been found to improve decision outcomes in laboratory settings (Priem, Harrison, and Muir 1995). However, even task-oriented conflict may have negative effects on member satisfaction and intent to stay (Jehn 1995). Given their already lower levels of social cohesion, demographically heterogeneous top management teams may find that the costs of additional conflict outweigh their benefits.

Such issues speak to the critical, and understudied, role of the leader in facilitating the work of the top management team. Such a role appears to entail encouraging participation from all members while finding ways to achieve closure despite possible continuing disagreement. Without such a facilitative role, cognitively complex top management teams may become quite dysfunctional. However, besides the study by Korsgaard, Schweiger, and Sapienza (1995) we previously cited, there has been little field work investigating the role of team leaders in facilitating effective decision making (Campion, Medsker, and Higgs 1993).

To gain insights into the dynamics we discuss here, researchers would need to utilize real-time investigations in addition to survey and archival data. Such research would ideally include observations of groups in action as well as informal interviews with participants (Van de Ven 1992).

For example, suppose predictive studies indicate that homogeneous teams that use consultants achieve higher cognitive complexity than similar teams that do not use consultants. Later descriptive research might probe to determine how top management teams could best achieve an interpenetration of this source of differentiation with integration within the team. Such qualitative approaches could later be supplemented by surveys whose content and timing of administration are based on a thorough familiarity of the processes at hand.

Longitudinal research may also yield insights about the life cycle of cognitive complexity within the top management team. How long does it take to develop this capacity in different circumstances? Once a team achieves a certain level of cognitive complexity, how long will it last? What interventions can sustain cognitive complexity, and how often are they needed? Do top management teams need the addition of new members in order to remain open to new ideas, or are other mechanisms equally or more effective?

The lesson for practitioners operating in complex, resource-scarce, and dynamic environments appears to be the importance of developing a mutually reinforcing balance between differentiation and integration within the top management team. The types of differentiation we examined here are compositional, focusing on ways to increase the heterogeneity of individuals involved in strategic decision making. However, there may also be processes that facilitate differentiation. Likewise, although the emphasis in this chapter is on integrating processes, there may also be ways to improve integration through composition. An example of this was seen in WKBN Broadcasting and Sygnet Communications, in which one individual has ensured continuity through a period of great change.

Conclusion

In this chapter, we asked how executives could make more creative and original decisions more rapidly than competitors with access to similar information. In our discussion, we examined one way to sustain this critical source of competitive advantage in complex, resource-scarce, and dynamic environments. By making more creative and flexible use of information, cognitively complex top management teams may be able to ensure the competitive variety, innovation, and speed necessary to thrive in these increasingly common contexts. The five cases we presented of organizations operating in such environments indicate a range of ways to develop cognitively complex top management teams. Finally, we made suggestions about how to test both the consequences and antecedents of cognitive complexity in top management teams. Such research may offer valuable insights into when cognitive complexity is useful and how to develop this quality at the team level.

Much more is not known than is known about how to build top management teams with the capacity to sustain competitive advantage. The research and cases examined in this chapter, however, suggest that top management teams that achieve cognitive complexity may be able to sustain competitive advantage despite—or perhaps even because of—the complexity that surrounds them.

References

"Allegheny Ludlum and Teledyne Agree to Merge." 1996. *Metal Center News* 36(6), 116.

Andrews, K. R. 1987. *The Concept of Corporate Strategy.* Homewood, IL: Irwin.

Ashby, W. R. 1956. *Introduction to Cybernetics.* London: Chapman & Hall.

Bantel, K. A. and Jackson, S. E. 1989. "Top Management and Innovations in Banking: Does the Composition of the Top Team Make a Difference?" *Strategic Management Journal* 10, 107–24.

Barabba, V. P. 1989. "The Enemy Within—Deep Within." In J. E. Prescott (ed.), *Advances in Competitive Intelligence.* Vienna, VA: Society of Competitor Intelligence Professionals.

Bernhardt, D. 1994. *Perfectly Legal Competitor Intelligence: How to Get It, Use It, and Profit From It.* London: Pitman.

Berry, J. M. 1997. "Increased Global Competition Helps Hold Down U.S. Inflation." *Washington Post* D1.

Bettis, R. A. and Hitt, M. A. 1995. "The New Competitive Landscape." *Strategic Management Journal* 16 (summer special issue), 7–19.

Bettis, R. A. and Prahalad, C. K. 1995. "The Dominant Logic: Retrospective and Extension." *Strategic Management Journal* 16(1), 5–14.

Bourgeois, L. J., III. 1980. "Strategy and Environment: A Conceptual Integration." *Academy of Management Review* 5(1), 25–39.

"Business Brief—Allegheny Teledyne Inc.: Profit Climbs 4.9%, Lifted by Synergies from Merger." 1997. *Wall Street Journal* B10.

Campion, M. A., Medsker, G. J., and Higgs, A. C. 1993. "Relations Between Work Group Characteristics and Effectiveness: Implications for Designing Effective Work Groups." *Personnel Psychology* 46, 823–50.

Chandler, A. D. 1990. *Scale and Scope: The Dynamics of Industrial Capitalism.* Cambridge, MA: Harvard University Press.

Cho, T. S., Hambrick, D. C., and Chen, M. J. 1994. "Effects of Top Management Team Characteristics on Competitive Behavior of Firms." *National Academy of Management Best Paper Proceedings* 12–16.

Cohen, W. M. and Levinthal, D. 1990. "Absorptive Capacity: A New Perspective on Learning and Innovation." *Administrative Science Quarterly* 35, 128–52.

Dess, G. G. and Beard, D. W. 1984. "Dimensions of Organizational Task Environments." *Administrative Science Quarterly* 29, 52–73.

Dess, G. G. and Davis, P. S. 1984. "Porter's (1980) Generic Strategies as Deter-
  minants of Strategic Group Membership and Organizational Performance."
  Academy of Management Journal 27, 467–88.
Drucker, P. F. 1992. "The New Society of Organizations." *Harvard Business
  Review* 70(September–October), 95–104.
Duncan, R. B. 1972. "Characteristics of Organizational Environments and Per-
  ceived Environmental Uncertainty." *Administrative Science Quarterly* 17,
  313–27.
Dutton, J. E. and Duncan, R. B. 1987. "The Influence of the Strategic Planning
  Process on Strategic Change." *Strategic Management Journal* 8, 103–16.
Eisenhardt, K. M. and Zbaracki, M. J. 1992. "Strategic Decision Making." *Stra-
  tegic Management Journal* 13, 17–37.
Gianturco, M. 1996. "Intel? No, Microchip." *Forbes* 157(5), 170.
Hamel, G. 1993. "Corporate Imagination and Expeditionary Marketing." In L.
  Brennan (ed.), *Challenging Conventional Thinking for Competitive Advan-
  tage.* Report No. 1021. New York: The Conference Board.
Harvey, O. J., Hunt, D. E., and Schroder, H. M. 1961. *Conceptual Systems and
  Personality Organization.* New York: Wiley.
Hedberg, B. L. T., Nystrum, P. C., and Starbuck, W. H. 1976. "Camping on
  Seesaws: Prescriptions for Self-Designing Organizations." *Administrative
  Science Quarterly* 21, 41–65.
"Hopping Code Technology Explained." 1996. *Security* 33(5), 24–26.
Itami, H. 1987. *Mobilizing Invisible Assets.* Cambridge, MA: Harvard University
  Press.
Jackson, S. E., May, K. E., and Whitney, K. 1995. "Understanding the Dynam-
  ics of Diversity in Decision-Making Teams." In R. A. Guzzo and E. Salas
  (eds.), *Team Effectiveness and Decision Making in Organizations.* San Fran-
  cisco: Jossey-Bass.
"Jacobson Survey Names Top Steel Suppliers." 1997. *Iron Age New Steel* 13(1),
  22.
Jehn, K. A. 1995. "A Multimethod Examination of the Benefits and Detriments
  of Intragroup Conflict." *Administrative Science Quarterly* 40, 256–82.
Kanter, R. M. 1996. "Power of Partnering." *Executive Excellence* 13(5), 7.
Korsgaard, M. A., Schweiger, D. M., and Sapienza, H. J. 1995. "Building Commitment, Attachment, and Trust in Strategic Decision-Making Teams: The
  Role of Procedural Justice." *Academy of Management Journal* 38(1), 60–84.
Lee, S. 1994. "Leadership: Revised and Redesigned for the Electronic Age." *Journal of Library Administration* 20(2), 17–28.
McGill, A. R., Johnson, M. D., and Bantel, K. A. 1993. "Cognitive Complexity
  and Conformity: The Effects on Performance in a Turbulent Environment." *National Academy of Management, Best Paper Proceedings* 379–83.
Munch, R. 1982. "Talcott Parsons and the Theory of Action II: The Integration
  and Development." *American Journal of Sociology* 87(4), 771–826.

Murakami, T. 1993. "Creating Creativity." In N. Brennan (ed.), *Challenging Conventional Thinking for Competitive Advantage.* New York: The Conference Board.

Nayyar, P. R. and Bantel, K. A. 1994. "Competitive Agility: A Source of Competitive Advantage Based on Speed and Variety." *Advances in Strategic Management* 10A, 193–222.

Nonaka, I. 1988. "Toward Middle-Up-Down Management: Accelerating Information Creation." *Sloan Management Review* 29(3), 9–18.

Pfeffer, J. 1983. "Organizational Demography." In L. L. Cummings and B. M. Staw (eds.), *Research in Organizational Behavior.* Greenwich, CT: JAI.

Porter, M. E. 1996. "What Is Strategy?" *Harvard Business Review* 74(November–December), 61–78.

Prahalad, C. K. and Bettis, R. A. 1986. "The Dominant Logic: A New Linkage Between Diversity and Performance." *Strategic Management Journal* 7, 485–501.

Prahalad, C. K. and Hamel, G. 1990. "The Core Competence of the Corporation." *Harvard Business Review* 68(3 May/June), 79–91.

Priem, R. L., Harrison, D. A., and Muir, N. K. 1995. "Structured Conflict and Consensus Outcomes in Group Decision Making." *Journal of Management* 21(4), 691–710.

Ristelhueber, R. 1995. "Revived Microchip Goes After MCU Giants." *Electronic Business Buyer* 21(8), 63–65.

Roberts, K. H. and O'Reilly, C. A., III. 1979. "Some Correlates of Communication Roles in Organizations." *Academy of Management Journal* 22, 42–57.

Starbuck, W. H. 1976. "Organizations and Their Environments." In M. Dunnette (ed.), *Handbook of Industrial and Organizational Psychology.* Chicago: Rand-McNally.

"Teledyne Spurns WHX to Merge with Allegheny Ludlum." 1996. *Iron Age New Steel* 12(5), 8–9.

Van de Ven, A. H. 1992. "Suggestions for Studying Strategy Process: A Research Note." *Strategic Management Journal* 13, 169–88.

Weick, K. E. and Bougon, M. G. 1986. "Organizations as Cognitive Maps." In H. P. Sims and D. A. Gioia (eds.), *The Thinking Organization.* San Francisco: Jossey-Bass.

Weick, K. E. and Roberts, K. H. 1993. "Collective Mind in Organizations: Heedful Interrelating on Flight Decks." *Administrative Science Quarterly* 38, 357–81.

West, M. A. and Anderson, N. R. 1996. "Innovation in Top Management Teams." *Journal of Applied Psychology* 81, 680–93.

Chapter 10

Poor Financial Performance: Causes, Consequences, and Measurement Issues

Jeffrey M. Bacidore *and* Anjan V. Thakor

anagers are custodians of the capital provided to a company by its financiers: shareholders, bondholders and banks, and other private lenders. Managers are therefore typically judged on how well they manage this capital. Poor performance in managing capital often results in diminished compensation and prestige for managers and may lead to the dismissal of upper management, as was the case for Apple Computer. From an organizational standpoint, poor financial performance can lead to major structural changes, such as divestitures, restructurings, and layoffs.[1] In extreme cases, poor performers can become targets of hostile takeover attempts, as was the case for ITT.[2]

But how is the financial performance of a company in managing its capital judged? What is the appropriate "scorecard"? One can take either an external or an internal perspective. The external perspective relies on capital market data, and perhaps the most celebrated external measure is total shareholder returns (TSR). TSR is defined as the stock price appreci-

---

[1]Examples of such restructurings include General Dynamics, Kodak, and Whirlpool Corporation.

[2]CEO ouster and takeover attempts are fairly extreme outcomes. It is estimated that about one-third of shareholder value is lost on average before there is a change in corporate control. See Jensen (1991).

ation over a chosen period (typically one year) plus dividends paid over that period expressed as a fraction of the stock price at the beginning of the period. It represents the return a shareholder would have earned by buying the company's stock at the beginning of the period and selling it at the end.

Internal measures focus on the drivers of shareholder value that can be managed by the company to impact the returns shareholders earn. For example, the Kaplan and Norton (1992) "balanced scorecard" approach emphasizes the importance of employees, customers, and business processes as drivers of shareholder value. Although many of the internal measures are nonfinancial, they are viewed as being positively correlated with "bottom-line" financial performance as reflected in TSR. Most companies, particularly those listed on U.S. stock exchanges, state their corporate goal as the creation of significant shareholder value. Thus, even though a variety of financial and nonfinancial measures are used internally to assess the performance of managers and to compensate them, TSR, an external measure, is the key metric for judging financial performance.

Although TSR is the ultimate metric for judging a company's financial performance, it is problematic to use it for assessing the realized performance of managers and for compensating them. The reason is that TSR depends in part on comparing stock prices at two points in time, and since prices are forward looking, TSR is strongly influenced by how the market's expectations about the company's future performance have changed. Clearly, past performance affects perceptions of future performance, but the latter is also driven by exogenous factors such as changes in the outlook for the overall economy, interest rates, exchange rates, and inflation expectations. This means that if we used TSR as a measure by which to judge managerial performance in every period and compensate the manager accordingly, we would be rewarding and punishing managers for things well beyond their control. For this reason, when it comes to judging managerial financial performance in corporations, TSR should be used only as a long-run measure of financial performance, rather than as a period-by-period measure for performance assessment and compensation. For example, *Fortune* magazine recently reported that Nike has delivered an average annualized TSR of 47 percent since 1986 (see Hamel 1997). Although it is useful to recognize that Nike's financial performance was outstanding over the last decade, that does not mean that Nike's TSR in a given quarter or year should be used to compensate its managers.

What is needed are measures that rely on realized performance and yet correlate highly with TSR. The search for such measures has been the Holy Grail for corporate finance researchers and consultants. Perhaps the most celebrated of these measures is Economic Value Added (EVA). In this chapter, in addition to critically analyzing EVA and suggesting a superior measure, we provide data on the actual financial performance of corporations on the basis of EVA and TSR. As we subsequently discuss, a large number of companies have exhibited inadequate financial performance.

A question of great theoretical and practical interest is, Why do firms perform poorly? We take up this issue and discuss five main organizational reasons for poor financial performance. Next we examine the research findings on the consequences of poor financial performance. Then we discuss how financial performance should be measured. Finally, we conclude with thoughts on an agenda for future research.

Causes of Poor Financial Performance

Many large, well-respected corporations experience poor financial performance. In fact, as we discuss subsequently in more detail, the majority of the companies in the Stern Stewart Top 1000[3] had negative average EVAs in recent years, suggesting that most companies actually destroyed shareholder value. What accounts for such poor financial performance? In this section, we discuss the main organizational reasons.

Poor Capital Allocation

Perhaps the simplest explanation for poor financial performance is that the corporation allocated capital to value-destroying projects. In such cases, even the best execution may not generate satisfactory financial performance of the project. Such a predicament may not be the result of poor judgment on the part of decision makers. It could quite simply be due to a poor realization of nature (e.g., bad luck). We should expect that some projects do worse than expected, which is exactly what *risk* means. However, in some cases, corporations systematically invest in poor projects. In fact, Deming (1990) argues that failures in most organizations are

---

[3]This is a list of the top 1,000 companies in terms of shareholder value creation compiled by Stern Stewart, a consulting firm, and published by *Fortune* magazine.

caused by systemic failures as opposed to individual error. This suggests that, even in corporations in which capital allocation is not driven by the self-interested behavior of managers, poor capital allocation could be due to the fact that the corporation does not have a well-designed capital allocation system in place that would allow value-maximizing managers to optimize shareholder value.

So what are some of the common impediments to maximizing the value of capital allocation? Boquist, Milbourn, and Thakor (1998) provide a thorough discussion of such impediments, which include the following:

1. *Lack of Appropriate Dynamic Structure.* Quite often, financial analysts view capital budgeting as a static situation, in which the net present value (NPV) of the project depends strictly on the expected cash flows of the project itself. However, in many instances, options are embedded in a project. For example, a corporation may be able to invest in capital in stages as opposed to all at once. Such staged investment allows the company to reevaluate the project at different points in time, terminating the project at any point if it appears to be no longer profitable. By doing so, the company is able to abandon a project before all the capital is invested. This option to abandon can often be extremely valuable, especially if a project requires a large initial investment. By ignoring these options, the corporation runs the risk of investing huge amounts of capital in a project only to find that the project will not succeed.

2. *Deficiencies in Analytical Techniques and Inconsistency in Their Application.* Some examples of this include poor identification of the base case, improper treatment of competitive entry and cannibalization issues, inadequate treatment of risk, and nonuniform assumptions and lack of consistency. Each of these will result in analysis that fails to measure truly the impact the project will have on shareholder value. To understand why, consider the following scenario, which highlights the importance of properly treating competitive entry and correctly identifying the base case. Let us say that you are planning to invest in a new technology that will allow you to cut the costs of your product. It is tempting to assume that the entire savings will accrue to shareholders. However, if this technology is readily available to your competitors, they may follow by cutting their costs, and, in a competitive marketplace, this will ultimately lead to reduced prices. Consequently, the real benefits of this project will accrue to

your customers instead of your shareholders. This may cause you to wonder, Why would a company ever invest in such cost-cutting projects if all the gains go to the customers? The key to understanding this question is to think about the base case, or what would happen if you did not undertake the project. It could be that your competitors will undertake the project, allowing them to undercut your price, which in turn will lead to decreased volume and profits for your company. In this case, it may be profitable to undertake the project because not undertaking the project is even more costly.

3. *Finance Function Not Viewed as a Strategic Partner.* In many corporations, the finance function is viewed as the "capital police" as opposed to strategic partners. Financial analysts merely enter near the end of the capital-budgeting process to vote up or down on whether the project is acceptable. In many cases, the financial analyst will send a project back to the project team noting that the project cannot be approved unless its rate of return is higher. This often results in the project team fudging the numbers to get a project approved. If the financial analyst is not involved in the process at the outset, it is much more difficult for the corporation to determine which projects are truly acceptable and which have had their numbers "massaged" simply to get through the approval process.

4. *Lack of Integration Across Capital and Expense Budgets.* In many organizations, the capital-budgeting procedure is disjoint from expense budgeting. To understand how this can cause distortions, consider a project involving the introduction of a new product line. Suppose the strategy implicit in the project is to flood the market with advertising and promotions in order to promote product awareness and, ultimately, to increase sales. If the expense budget is not coordinated with the capital budget, however, the amount of resources ultimately allocated in the expense budget may be significantly less than what was specified in the capital budget. This could compromise the project since the profitability estimates that led to project approval were conditional on a higher level of advertising and promotion.

5. *Inadequate Post-Auditing Procedures.* Quite often, a corporation does not track project performance throughout the life of the project in order to determine whether the estimated benefits are ultimately realized. By not monitoring the projects on an ongoing basis, the corporation may fail to detect poor performance on a timely basis, thereby delaying correc-

tive measures. Investigating project performance after investment is called *post-auditing*, and it should be an integral component of a well-designed capital-budgeting system. Post-auditing provides a great deal of information regarding the market environment, appropriateness of key assumptions, and so on. By not effectively post-auditing projects, corporations not only delay corrective action but miss valuable learning opportunities as well.

Although this list is by no means exhaustive, it is clear that regardless of the cause of poor capital allocation, it leads to poor corporate performance as these projects mature and are integrated into the business. It is important to keep in mind that the corporation is essentially a portfolio of earlier investments. If the mechanisms used to select these investments are flawed, the organization must ultimately correct these mistakes in the future, for example, via restructuring of operations or divestiture, which can place severe strain on the organization.

Failure to Communicate Strategy

Poor financial performance can also result from a failure to communicate effectively the company's strategy throughout the organization. A company's strategy is essentially the road map for the corporation, and unless the entire organization is focused on the same set of goals, it is difficult to achieve financial success. For example, suppose the company has decided to expand operations abroad to become a truly global player. If the entire organization is not made aware of the operational and behavioral consequences of this structural shift, managers with control of key resources—capital, information technology, and human resources—may not direct the resources necessary to implement the strategy effectively. Poor financial performance would follow, and the subsequent soul-searching would mistakenly place the blame on the globalization strategy, when the real culprit was the failure to communicate the strategy effectively.

Multiple Financial Measures

To assess the performance of a company, it is important for the key decision makers to agree on what constitutes success. Defining what is meant by financial success hinges on identifying the key financial performance measures that will be used in making such assessments. However, corporations often focus on a multiplicity of financial measures instead of a single, unifying measure that will be applied consistently and objectively. In many cases, managers choose these financial measures *ex post* in order to justify the initiation or continuation of pet projects or initiatives. Some companies have tried to avoid such abuse by creating a "point-rating" system, which attempts to unify financial measures such as NPV, internal rate of return (IRR), and payback, and nonfinancial measures such as customer satisfaction and product quality, into a single number by giving a predetermined weight to each measure. By explicitly assigning the weights *ex ante,* it is hoped that this sort of gaming behavior can be avoided. However, note that point-rating systems are quite ad hoc and do not guarantee that projects earning "high points" will maximize shareholder value.

This point is reminiscent of the Heisenberg Uncertainty Principle in quantum mechanics that argues that how an outcome is measured affects the outcome itself. This elevates the importance of performance measures and highlights the need to adopt a performance measure that has the desired behavioral implications and correlates highly with shareholder value creation.

Lack of Ownership

In a sole proprietorship, there is no separation of ownership and control, so the owner/manager can be naturally expected to maximize shareholder wealth. However, as described in the seminal work by Jensen and Meckling (1976), a manager who has only partial ownership of the corporation may engage in behavior that maximizes the manager's own utility but sacrifices shareholder value. To understand why, consider the following example. Suppose a given manager has a 1 percent equity stake in the company, (i.e., he or she owns 1 percent of the stock, while outside investors own the remaining 99 percent) and that the company is considering the takeover of another company. Assume that the manager will derive greater personal utility from managing a larger capital base (see, e.g. Harris and Raviv 1996). Furthermore, assume that if the takeover is completed, it will destroy $10,000 of shareholder value for the acquiring company. Since the manager has a 1 percent stake in the company, his or her share of the value loss will be $100. If the manager were to act purely in the interest of all shareholders, he would not pursue this acquisition. If, however, the incremental utility the manager would derive from managing a larger asset base had a monetary equivalent that exceeds $100 (say $120), he or she would pursue the acquisition since his or her total personal utility would be increased, albeit at the expense of shareholders. The problem here is that the manager's incentives are not perfectly aligned with those of the outside shareholders. One way to improve this alignment is to increase the manager's equity ownership. For instance, if the manager in our example held 80 percent of the company's equity, he or she would eschew the value-dissipating merger.

Aligning the incentives of managers and shareholders was a major motivation for the leveraged buyouts (LBOs) of the 1980s. However, LBOs are not a panacea. The very high financial leverage used in an LBO is likely to spawn other conflicts of interest that could lower company value. In particular, Jensen and Meckling (1976) showed that agency problems between shareholders and bondholders are likely to flare up when the company's financial leverage is high enough. Other related agency problems have been documented in the finance literature. Jensen (1986) argues that managers whose companies have positive free cash flow (i.e., cash flow in excess of that needed to fund the operations and profitable investments of the company) tend to waste it. This implies that one way to improve performance is to have managers precommit to paying out excess cash flow (e.g., by increasing debt payments).

Another source of agency problems is the way organizations manage their talent pool processes to determine whom to promote. In every organization, managers compete for promotions, and the culmination of this implicit tournament is promotion to CEO of the corporation. This competition induces managers to engage in reputation-building behavior. Because the probability of being promoted increases as the *perception* of the manager's ability increases (since true ability is unknown and must be inferred from performance), he or she will often take actions that are likely to alter this perception favorably and, thus, enhance his or her reputation. These actions frequently dissipate firm value. This intuition is developed by Milbourn, Shockley, and Thakor (1997), who show that managers will exhibit *failure aversion;* that is, they will overinvest in information gathering about projects, leading to excessively long new-product development cycle times (see Chapter 8 in this volume). The authors argue that this is only one example of the many agency problems that are likely to arise from the managerial failure aversion that stems quite naturally from intrafirm tournaments among managers.

One way to alleviate agency problems is to design managers' compensation structures to reward them for increasing shareholder value. Such a compensation structure makes managers' pay contingent on an observable performance measure that is correlated highly with shareholder value. Two such measures, as noted subsequently, are EVA and Refined Economic Value Added (REVA). Examples of companies that have adopted EVA-based compensation structures include Coca-Cola, AT&T, CSX, and Briggs and Stratton.

Lack of Focus

Another reason for poor performance is a lack of focus in the asset portfolio of a diversified organization. Such diversification often results from the belief that there are "economies of scope" or benefits associated with diversification that make the whole greater than the sum of its parts (e.g., coinsurance of debt payments). Recent evidence, however, suggests that this belief lacks empirical merit. Mergers of unrelated companies have resulted in poor postmerger financial performance. Berger and Ofek (1995) show that during 1986–1991, diversification led to an average value loss of between 13 and 15 percent. Comment and Jarrell (1995) note that the 1980s witnessed a trend toward specialization. They also empirically document a positive relation between increased focus and stock returns. John and Ofek (1995) show that asset sales that increase the focus of the business have led to improved operating performance in each of the three years following the increase in focus. This implies that the total value of unrelated entities would be increased if each were allowed to operate as an individual, more focused entity. Alternatively, poor financial performance could result from a lack of strategic focus within the organization.

Consequences of Poor Performance

Sustained poor financial performance has numerous consequences. One is that talented employees tend to leave the organization. This loss of valuable human resources can have serious short- and long-run implications. In the short run, the loss of key talent hampers the company's ability to respond to adversity and achieve a successful turnaround. The problems therefore continue to persist, leaving less-skilled employees to guide the company during very trying times. This increases the likelihood of long-run difficulties, with the possibility of further exodus of talent and even more diminished competitive strength for the company.

Another consequence of poor financial performance is that it may lead to the ouster of the CEO. Although such management upheavals can lead to short-term turmoil within the organization, such actions can provide incentives to the CEO *ex ante* to engage in value-maximizing behavior. Denis and Denis (1995) find that forced resignations of CEOs tend to follow periods of large declines in operating performance. They also find that large improvements in performance tend to follow forced resignations. Furthermore, they find that the real threat to CEOs is from external pressures (e.g., takeovers, outside stakeholders) and not from the company's own board of directors. This finding suggests a potential lack of effective internal monitoring of the CEO, and emphasizes the importance of linking CEO compensation to a reliable measure of shareholder value creation. Linking CEO compensation to shareholder value is complicated by the fact that the same boards that tend to be lax about disciplining managers are also responsible for setting the CEO's compensation.

Of course, ineffective internal controls do not necessarily mean that CEOs would be undisciplined. The threat of being fired due to external corporate control pressures may be quite powerful. Agrawal and Walking (1994) show that CEOs who are forced to depart due to takeover bids find that it takes more than three years on average to find another senior executive-level job. A corporation that consistently underperforms financially is often likely to be the target of a hostile takeover bid. Such takeovers can cause a manager to engage in behavior consistent with shareholder value because not doing so invites a hostile takeover and increases the likelihood of his or her dismissal. The market for corporate control is a major factor in ensuring that executives maximize shareholder value, and an active outside market for corporate control is necessary to prevent managers from flagrantly pursuing their own interests at shareholders' expense.

Another mechanism for improving performance is via shareholder activism. In recent years, institutional investors, such as the Teachers Insurance and Annuity Association-College Retirement Equities Fund (TIAA-CREF) and the California Public Employees' Retirement System (CalPERS), have become quite active in the area of corporate governance. For example, both of these organizations have attacked H. J. Heinz's board of directors for not being sufficiently independent despite Heinz's apparently good financial performance because many of the board members were appointed by the CEO himself (see Byrne 1997b). To promote proper governance, the National Association of Corporate Directors has developed a series of guidelines for boards to ensure independence. But are such guidelines of value to investors? A recent study by McKinsey & Co., published in *Business Week,* found that institutional investors would pay a premium of 11 percent for a company with superior governance (see Byrne 1997a). Thus, given this pressure by investors, it is becoming more difficult for management and boards to ignore the interest of shareholders.

Although the market for corporate control is quite efficient in the United States, empirical evidence suggests that a company must destroy about one-third of its shareholder value on average before the market for corporate control kicks in to arrest further erosion of shareholder value. Some of the factors that impede the efficiency of the market for corporate control include high search costs for acquirers looking for appropriate targets, as well as the existence of "poison pills," "golden parachutes," and other antitakeover devices adopted by the managers of targets.

These difficulties aside, takeover attempts can also be discouraged because the target's shareholders have an incentive to free ride. To understand what is meant by free riding, consider a company that is worth $10 per share if its current management continues to run the company and worth $20 per share if the acquirer takes control. The acquirer's transaction costs of the takeover are $0.50 per share. For it to be in the best interest of the acquirer to take over the company, it must be able to buy the company for no greater than $19.50 per share. However, target shareholders will not sell their shares for less than $20 per share (if they can accurately assess the posttakeover value of the company). Consequently, the acquirer must bid at least $20 per share to induce the target company's shareholder to sell. But at that price it is better for the acquirer not to make a bid.

Measuring Financial Performance

So how do we measure poor financial performance? Given the limitations of using external measures (e.g., TSR) on evaluating financial performance, internal measures of realized performance are generally used. Examples of such measures are earnings per share (EPS), EPS growth, and sales growth. Although a company that exhibits high sales or earnings growth may be creating value for shareholders, this need not be the case. For example, one way to increase sales or earnings is simply to expand operations, which generally involves additional investments in fixed assets, human resources, working capital, and so forth. However, such expansion enhances shareholder value only if expansion is profitable. Income statement measures such as sales and earnings ignore one of the most important costs to investors—the cost of capital. Consequently, it is possible for a company to increase earnings and still destroy shareholder value if the cost of capital associated with new investments is sufficiently high. This implies that focusing on conventional measures such as EPS and growth may result in poor internal assessments of performance.

Recently, much attention has been focused on developing measures that capture all relevant benefits and costs, with one of the most popular measures being EVA. EVA, in its simplest terms, can be expressed as follows:

$$EVA = \text{Net Operating Profit After Taxes} - \text{Capital Charge}$$

Thus, EVA is simply adjusted accounting profit minus a capital charge, where the capital charge depends on both the amount of capital and the cost of that capital (i.e., the required rate of return on investments). Therefore, if one can properly measure net operating profit, the cost of capital, and the amount of assets invested, one can compute the amount of value the company created for its shareholders over a given period.

Because the effectiveness of an internal performance measure is ultimately judged by how well it correlates with shareholder value creation, the question is: How does this measure of shareholder value correlate with TSR? An answer is provided by Bacidore, et al. (1997), who show that EVA is positively correlated with *abnormal returns*—defined as the TSR minus the expected rate of return—accruing to shareholders over a given period.

Interestingly, in investigating the list of Stern Stewart 1,000 companies over the five-year period 1991–1995, we find that only 362 of the 1,000 companies generated an average EVA that was positive. The list of companies with positive EVAs includes Coca-Cola, Intel, Microsoft, and Wal-Mart. The average EVA for Coca-Cola, for example, was $1.35 billion per year. Coca Cola's average annual total shareholder return was

26.15 percent, which far exceeds its cost of equity capital. Such a finding is representative of the stocks with average positive EVA. The average annual TSR for the positive-EVA group was 24.52 percent, well above the average equity cost of capital for these companies.

On the other hand, 636 companies in the top 1,000 had a negative average EVA, which suggests that the majority of companies destroyed shareholder value over this period, according to EVA. Consistent with the predictive ability of EVA, the average TSR for this group was much lower, a paltry 13.94 percent. One example of a company experiencing poor financial performance was K-Mart. Its average annual EVA from 1991 to 1995 was − $813 million. Its average annual TSR was − 12.87 percent. The data indicate that EVA does correlate well with shareholder value creation.

This correlation notwithstanding, Bacidore et al. (1997) argue that EVA can be improved on as far as its consistency with shareholder value creation is concerned, because net assets in the EVA calculation are based on an adjusted book-value approach. This approach begins with the book value of assets and adds back items such as capitalized leases and goodwill amortization to get an estimate of how much economic capital is employed by the company. However, since these adjustments are based on accounting numbers, they may not accurately estimate the market value of the net assets or capital deployed by the company. Bacidore et al. (1997) propose an alternative measure, REVA, to overcome the problems associated with EVA as traditionally defined. REVA utilizes the market value of the capital invested in the company at the beginning of the period in estimating the capital charge for that period. This is important because individuals must pay the market value for investments in the company. Consequently, REVA is theoretically a better measure of value creation in that it better estimates the true cost of the capital employed in generating profits.

But what about the empirical merits of REVA versus EVA? Bacidore et al. (1997) confirm empirically that REVA is a superior measure to EVA in that REVA's correlation with abnormal returns is greater than EVA's correlation with abnormal returns. Given that REVA is a measure that is consistent with shareholder value creation both theoretically and empirically, REVA appears to be the better measure of period-by-period company performance.

Thoughts for Future Research

Many issues remain to be researched, including how shareholder value creation is impacted by the adoption of refined EVA measures on company performance, the effective communication of strategy, and pay-for-performance. Further research on such issues would provide insight as to whether some of the more popular corporate initiatives translate into improved company performance. As stated previously, it is essential that such initiatives ultimately link to shareholder value creation. The indisputable fact is this: No matter how well a company apparently serves its other stakeholders, it has little chance to survive in its existing form if its financial performance is poor and it fails to serve its shareholders.

Refined EVA Measures

The search for financial performance measures that correlate highly with shareholder value and correctly affect managerial behavior is far from over. REVA is an improvement over EVA and is simpler to compute, but because of its newness we know little about the practical issues that may arise when it is adopted as a corporate performance measure. An interesting avenue of future research would therefore be to evaluate the performance of companies that have adopted these newer performance measures and to determine whether these newly implemented measures lead to improved company performance. Such an evaluation, however, can only be done as corporations begin to employ these newer EVA metrics. Thus, it may be some time before the incremental benefit of these EVA refinements can be assessed.

Effective Communication of Strategy

Although we know empirically a great deal about some of the causes of poor financial performance, we know far less about others. For example, we know quite a bit about what lack of corporate focus does to a company's financial performance, but there is scant empirical evidence regarding the impact of poorly designed capital allocation systems or ineffective communication of corporate strategy on a company's financial performance. This is largely due to lack of good intrafirm data. Therefore, establishing a link between the need for better communication of strategy throughout the organization would first require identifying companies that have effectively communicated their strategy. The shareholder value creation of such companies could be compared with that of companies with poor communication of strategy. A strong positive correlation would be expected between effective communication and shareholder value creation. Such a study would not only help establish a link between shareholder value creation and effective communication of strategy, but would also help quantify the gains from effective communication of strategy.

Pay-for-Performance

Many of the causes of poor performance are due to the misalignment of the incentives of employees and those of shareholders. Much research has been devoted to understanding how CEO compensation, that is, CEO pay-for-performance, can improve performance (e.g., Jensen and Murphy 1990; Milbourn 1996). However, less attention has been focused on how to provide incentive for employees farther down the organizational ladder. An interesting area of research would be to determine how effective similar pay-for-performance contracts are for the other employees of the corporation. One potentially fruitful mechanism is to utilize some type of REVA- or EVA-based compensation, and, in fact, many companies are beginning to adopt pay-for-performance contracts for other employees. Therefore, it would be interesting to determine whether such contracts lead to improved performance.

One very real complication, though, is that compensating such employees on corporatewide EVA is inefficient in the sense that much of this EVA is out of their direct control. Attempting to correct this by utilizing a divisional or business unit EVA, however, may lead to individuals maximizing the value of the division, rather than maximizing total, or corporatewide, shareholder value.[4] Another interesting area of research, therefore, would be to compare the performance of companies that utilize corporatewide EVA, divisional EVA, and those that use no pay-for-performance contracts at all. This comparison would help determine whether pay-for-performance leads to enhanced performance and whether corporatewide EVA or divisional EVA is the most efficient means of compensation. Of course, the relative efficiency of the two types of EVA contracts depends on such factors as size of the company and scope of operations.

---

[4]Eli Lilly CEO Randall Tabias noted that Lilly decided it was best not to use business unit EVA for compensation for precisely this reason (see Martin 1996).

A detailed analysis that conditions on such factors may lead to a better understanding of which types of companies should utilize divisional EVA, which should utilize corporate EVA, and which, if any, would extract little benefit from altering their compensation systems to incorporate pay-for-performance.

Another problem in implementing a pay-for-performance compensation system is determining how far down the organizational hierarchy pay-for-performance should be utilized. Similarly, it is quite difficult to assess how sensitive compensation should be to performance as one moves down the organizational ladder. For example, if a company is considering adopting EVA for compensation, should this compensation be extended to all employees or should it be reserved for senior management? Furthermore, what percentage of, say, EVA improvement should accrue to each employee? Again, it would be interesting to evaluate those corporations that have incorporated EVA-based compensation at various levels throughout the organization and to determine which compensation systems lead to the greatest enhancement in company performance.

Conclusion

Poor financial performance is indeed a pressing problem for many organizations today. In this chapter we discussed several different organizational reasons for poor financial performance as well as some of the consequences of sustained poor financial performance. To address this problem, we suggested that attention must be paid to how companies measure financial performance and provide incentives to their top managers. In particular we suggest that Refined Economic Value Added (REVA) is a better measure of period-by-period company performance than Economic Value Added (EVA) and, thus, is a more appropriate measure to use as a basis for management compensation. Although much research still needs to be done, it is important for companies to begin evaluating whether their existing incentive systems actually translate into improved company performance.

References

Agrawal, A. and Walking, R. 1994. "Executive Careers and Compensation Surrounding Takeover Bids." *Journal of Finance* 49, 985–1014.

Bacidore, J., Boquist, J., Milbourn, T., and Thakor, A. 1997. "The Search for the Best Financial Performance Measure." *Financial Analysts Journal* 53, 11–20.

Berger, A. and Ofek, E. 1995. "Diversification's Effect on Firm Value." *Journal of Financial Economics* 37, 39–65.

Boquist, J., Milbourn, T., and Thakor, A. 1998. "How Do You Win the Capital Allocation Game?" *Sloan Management Review* 39(2), 59–71.

Byrne, J. A. 1997a. "The CEO and the Board." *Business Week* (September 15), 106–16.

———. 1997b. "Putting More Stock in Good Governance." *Business Week* (September 15), 116.

Comment, R. and Jarrell, G. 1995. "Corporate Focus and Stock Returns." *Journal of Financial Economics* 37, 67–87.

Deming, E. 1990. *The New Economics.* Cambridge, MA: MIT Press.

Denis, D. J. and Denis, D. K. 1995. "Performance Changes Following Top Management Dismissals." *Journal of Finance* 50, 1029–57.

Hamel, G. 1997. "Killer Strategies That Make Shareholders Rich." *Fortune* (June 23) 70–84.

Harris, M. and Raviv, A. 1996. "The Capital Budgeting Process: Incentives and Information." *Journal of Finance* 51, 1139–74.

Jensen, M. 1986. "The Agency Costs of Free Cash Flow, Corporate Finance and Takeovers." *American Economic Review* 76, 323–29.

———. 1991. "Corporate Control and the Politics of Finance." *Journal of Applied Corporate Finance* 4, 13–33.

Jensen, M. and Meckling, W. 1976. "Theory of the Firm: Managerial Behavior, Agency Costs and Ownership Structure." *Journal of Financial Economics* 3, 305–60.

Jensen, M. and Murphy, K. J. 1990. "Performance Pay and Top-Management Incentives." *Journal of Political Economy* 98, 225–62.

John, K. and Ofek, E. 1995. "Asset Sales and Increase in Focus." *Journal of Financial Economics* 37, 105–26.

Kaplan, R. S. and Norton D. P. 1992. "The Balanced Scorecard—Measures That Drive Performance." *Harvard Business Review* (January–February), 70(1), 71–79.

Martin, J. 1996. "Eli Lilly Is Making Shareholders Rich. How? By Linking Pay to EVA." *Fortune* (September 9) 173–174.

Milbourn, T. 1996. "The Executive Compensation Puzzle: Theory and Evidence." Working paper, London Business School.

Milbourn, T., Shockley, R., and Thakor, A. 1997. "Prestige, Intrafirm Tournaments, and Failure Aversion in Corporate Decisions." Working paper, University of Michigan, Ann Arbor.

Chapter 11

The Problems and Promises of Total Quality Management: Implications for Organizational Performance

KIM S. CAMERON *and* MICHAEL THOMPSON

S ince the mid-1980s, three approaches to organizational change have predominated. They are by far the most frequently used strategies by organizations trying to improve their effectiveness. These three approaches are total quality management (TQM), downsizing, and reengineering. This chapter focuses on TQM as a macromanagerial strategy for changing organizations and enhancing their performance. We consider TQM an ideal candidate for any discussion of macromanagerial problems because the concept of TQM was developed to serve as a kind of "weapon-of-mass-construction"—a universal performance enhancer. The broad-based initiatives that we have examined in our own research and consulting efforts, and many that we cite from the literature, were undertaken to respond to such fundamental problems as the following:

▲ Disappointing quality results in specific products or services
▲ Unmet quality expectations despite specific improvement efforts
▲ Customer satisfaction difficulties

As significant as these problems are, many of the responses organizations use to respond to them are not as broad based as the term *total*

215

quality management would lead us to believe. Some quality improvement efforts carry a TQM label but are really reengineering or downsizing efforts. Some are not really quality improvement efforts of any kind, but poorly disguised public relations efforts. The term *total quality management* thus suffers many misapplications. And research on TQM efforts is not encouraging. Although most of the research is not empirical, the studies that have attempted to evaluate the success of TQM efforts according to some standardized indicators of success do not inspire enthusiasm.

For example, a McKinsey survey of U.S. and European companies found that 67 percent of the TQM programs older than two years died for lack of results. Although quality processes and practices were pursued, there was an inadequate level of payoff in these companies to maintain support for change efforts associated with quality. In addition, a Rath and Strong survey of Fortune 500 companies found that only 20 percent reported having achieved their quality objectives. More than 40 percent indicated that their quality initiatives were a complete failure. Ernst and Young's study of 584 companies in four industries (autos, banks, computers, health care) in the United States, Japan, Germany, and Canada found that most companies had not enjoyed success as a result of their total quality practices. Most companies labeled TQM a failure and were actually cutting back their quality budgets. The American Quality Foundation's survey of companies found that most had adopted a randomized "shotgun" approach to quality improvement, as evidenced by more than 945 different quality tactics, tools, and techniques being employed, and such nonsystematic actions led to failure. Criticism of quality programs has thus begun to escalate, especially in the popular press, and some writers have even described it as an outdated management fad of the 1980s (Jacob 1993).

Thus, we have a pressing need to evaluate TQM as an approach to solving organizational problems. To clarify terms and set the stage for this discussion, we first provide some alternative definitions of quality, and then discuss TQM as a macro-approach to enhancing organizational effectiveness. We discuss some of the major problems that arise in implementing TQM as a method of change and, finally, pose some questions that can be applied to further research.

Definitions of Quality

The difference between the term *quality* and the more comprehensive term *total quality management* (or TQM) is neither precisely delineated in the literature nor obvious in practice. Both terms are used interchangeably in the literature, as is the case in this chapter, although TQM is generally regarded as encompassing a broad managerial philosophy and organizationwide principles. The term *quality*, on the other hand, is usually restricted to attributes of products or services. Quality is therefore an imprecisely defined term that encompasses a wide variety of approaches to enhancing organizational effectiveness.

Prior to the 1980s, the scholarly literature on quality used the term as an attribute of whatever organizations were interested in accomplishing, such as reducing error rates in manufacturing companies (Crosby 1979), enhancing the reputations of universities (Webster 1981), or shortening the recovery rates of patients in health care organizations (Scott et al. 1978). However, as global competitive pressures intensified and more attention was paid to the Japanese "quality revolution," quality increasingly became regarded as the *summum bonum* of organizational performance.

Managers and organization members became converts of the pursuit of quality as the single most important organizational objective (Deming 1986), and scholars scrambled to catch up by substituting quality as the dependent variable of choice. In 1993, for example, quality was the most frequently appearing topic in research papers at the Annual Meetings of the Academy of Management, the organizational studies professional association. Whereas, the term *organizational effectiveness* had largely disappeared from the organizational studies literature, articles and books published between 1985 and 1995 on quality numbered in the thousands (see Cameron and Whetten 1996; Peterson and Cameron 1995). This indicates, simply, that quality had begun to be elevated to a conceptual level formerly afforded only to effectiveness, that is, as a construct designated as the central objective of organizational action. It had begun to encompass multiple outcomes, effects, and processes (Cameron and Whetten 1996).

Just as quickly, however, attention to quality among organizational scholars began to wane. The rhetorical shelf-life of quality has diminished significantly in the last two or three years, even though the actual need for quality improvements remains critical. Although we may be discussing quality less often in scholarly journals, and even in operations meetings in organizations, the stated goals of the quality movement are far from realized. Most important, consensus has not been attained on the definition and scope of quality.

"Big Q" versus "Little q" Quality

Any discussion of quality improvement efforts or quality problems must be clarified at the outset. Are we talking about efforts to improve the cultural milieu in which all the work of an organization is carried out, or are we talking about efforts to improve specific products and services? Joseph Juran made this very distinction between what he calls a "big Q" approach to quality and a "little q" approach (Greene 1993). The former refers to quality as an overall, encompassing culture of the organization, and the latter refers to specific tools, techniques, activities, or product and service attributes within an organization. "Little q" is associated with quality as an attribute of a product or a process, whereas "big Q" is associated with the strategy and overall functioning of the organization in addition to the ultimate outcome produced by its products and services. The phrase *total quality management* (i.e., TQM) is generally substituted for big Q quality (Sashkin and Kiser 1993).

Only recently has quality taken on the TQM or big Q connotation. Traditionally, quality was treated as a reliability engineering or statistical control issue and appeared mainly in engineering, operations management, manufacturing, and applied statistics literature. It was limited to its application to products or processes, not to overall organizational performance. For example, Garvin (1988) identified four "quality eras" in the United States:

1. *An inspection era*—quality was associated with mistakes and errors detected in products or services after they were produced
2. *A statistical control era*—defects were reduced by statistical sampling and testing and by controlling variability in the processes that produced products
3. *A quality assurance era*—quality techniques and philosophies were expanded beyond the production of outputs to "total quality control" in which top management took responsibility for ensuring quality in all parts of the organization
4. *A strategic quality management era*—quality was defined from the customer's point of view and the organization's strategy became centered on quality.

This shift from the first era to the fourth was largely a shift from little q to big Q quality. It is this big Q or TQM use of quality that has begun to appear in the organizational studies literature and has begun to rival effectiveness as the key organizational-level dependent variable.

To illustrate, Cameron (1995), expanding on Garvin's (1988) discussion, summarized seven of the most frequently appearing definitions of quality in the literature (see Table 11-1). These definitions are for the following approaches to quality: transcendent, product-based, user-based, manufacturing-based, value-based, system-based, and philosophical.

Dimensions of Little q

As can be noted from the definitions in Table 11-1, one difficulty with studying quality is that its definition is neither precise nor consensual. *Quality,* similar to terms such as *effectiveness, satisfaction, empowerment,* and *leadership,* is a construct not a concept, and no objective referents exist. Its definition is constructed in the minds of definers (Cameron 1981), so no one definition is ever completely correct. For example, a common theme in the top five definitions in Table 11-1 is that they focus on quality as an attribute of products and services (little q). Garvin's (1988) eight dimensions of quality—performance, features, reliability, durability, serviceability, conformance, aesthetics, perceived quality—coupled with two from Teboul (1991)—safety, prestige—produce a near-comprehensive listing of aspects of quality associated with the top five definitions. Table 11-2 summarizes these ten dimensions, all of which relate to a product, service, or activity of an organization (little q quality) rather than to overall organizational performance.

Dimensions of Big Q

The last two definitions of quality in Table 11-1, on the other hand, focus on quality from a more comprehensive, organizational-level perspective (TQM or big Q quality). They incorporate a variety of organizational and individual attributes that supersede a single product or service or a single constituency's definition. In other words, TQM or big Q quality includes a more comprehensive set of characteristics in its definition. Some of the many attributes associated with big 'Q' quality or TQM (see Malcolm Baldrige National Quality Award 1992; Deming 1986; Juran 1992) are as follows:

(text continues on p. 221)

Table 11-1. Major Definitions of Quality

Approach	Definition	Example
Transcendent	"Quality is neither mind nor matter, but a third entity independent of the two . . . even though Quality cannot be defined, you know what it is" (Pirsig 1974).	▲ Innate excellence ▲ Timeless beauty ▲ Universal appeal
Product-based	"Quality refers to the amounts of the unpriced attributes contained in each unit of the priced attribute" (Leffler 1982).	▲ Durability ▲ Extra desired attributes ▲ Wanted features
User-based	"Quality is fitness for use" (Juran 1974). "Quality consists of the capacity to satisfy wants" (Edwards 1968).	▲ Satisfies customers ▲ Meets needs ▲ Fulfills expectations
Manufacturing-based	"Quality means conformance to requirements" (Crosby 1979).	▲ Reliability ▲ Adherence to specifications ▲ Variation within tolerance limits
Value-based	"Quality means best for certain conditions . . . (a) the actual use and (b) the selling price" (Fiegenbaum 1961).	▲ Performance at an acceptable price ▲ Value for the money spent ▲ Affordable excellence
System-based	"[Quality is] a system of means to economically produce goods or services which satisfy customers' requirements" (Japanese Industrial Standard Z8101 1981, p. 14).	▲ Utilizes accepted quality procedures ▲ Quality processes ▲ Integrated approach
Philosophical	"[Quality] means that the organization's culture is defined by and supports the constant attainment of mind-set customer satisfaction through an integrated system of tools, techniques, and training" (Sashkin and Kiser 1993).	▲ Management philosophy ▲ Lifestyle

Source: Cameron and Whetten (1996).

Table 11-2. Dimensions of Product, Service, or Activity Quality

Dimension	Description
Performance	Product operating characteristics
Features	Additional product characteristics
Reliability	Probability of a product's proper functioning over time
Durability	Measure of product life
Serviceability	Speed, competence, and ease of service
Conformance	Degree to which product meets prescribed standards
Aesthetics	Subjective opinion regarding product appeal
Perceived quality	Perception of quality, often influenced by advertising
Safety	Protection against malfunction and other problems
Prestige	Image of product associated with elevated stature

Source: Garvin (1988); Khurana (1994); Teboul (1991).

▲ Continuous improvement in all activities and in all individuals in the organization
▲ Customer satisfaction for internal and external customers
▲ Efficient deployment of resources
▲ Employee, supplier, and customer development and recognition
▲ Environmental well-being
▲ Exemplary, visionary, and aggressive leadership
▲ Fast response time
▲ Full participation of employees, suppliers, and customers
▲ Lifelong relationships with customers
▲ Long-range perspectives
▲ Partnerships upstream, downstream, and across functions
▲ Prevention of error by designing in quality
▲ Process mapping and process improvement
▲ Provision of customer value
▲ Quantitative measurement and management-by-fact
▲ Root cause analysis
▲ Shared values, vision, and culture
▲ Standard quality tools (such as statistical process control, quality function deployment, and design of experiment)
▲ Top management sponsorship and involvement
▲ Waste reduction and cost containment

Garvin (1988) and Teboul (1991) identified seven dimensions they associated with "strategic quality" or big Q quality. These dimensions were proposed as prerequisites to the quality-effectiveness relationship. That is, to achieve effectiveness, organizations must have the following attributes:

1. Quality as a competitive priority—quality is used as a differentiating factor.
2. Customer focus—special efforts are made to understand and satisfy the customer.
3. Quality deployment—quality is included in the planning process and management controls.
4. Quality incentives—rewards and recognition are available for quality performance.
5. Organizationwide commitment—responsibilities for quality are shared by all employees.
6. Top management commitment—top management inculcates quality values.
7. Progressive workforce practices—participation, multiskilling, and so on are implemented.

In 1988 the U.S. Department of Commerce established the Malcolm Baldrige National Quality Award (MBNQA) and developed a framework for quality that is claimed to be comprehensive in terms of the dimensions it incorporates. These dimensions are hypothesized to have a particular relationship to one another, as illustrated in Figure 11-1, although these relationships have never been tested empirically. The Leadership dimension is classified as a driver of quality. Four dimensions—Quality Information and Analysis, Strategic Quality Planning, Human Resource Development and Management, and Management of Process Quality—all are classified as process dimensions. Two dimensions are assumed to be desirable outcomes—Customer Satisfaction and Quality Results. The MBNQA program (and its counterparts, the more recent European Quality Award and the older Japanese Deming Prize) has probably had a more significant effect on organizational practices than any factor other than automation. Almost no organization in the industrialized world can be found that has not adopted some type of change in order to improve its quality, partially due to the impact of these national awards on business functioning. Whereas, until now the MBNQA award has been limited to

(text continues on p. 224)

Figure 11-1. The Malcolm Baldridge National Quality Award framework

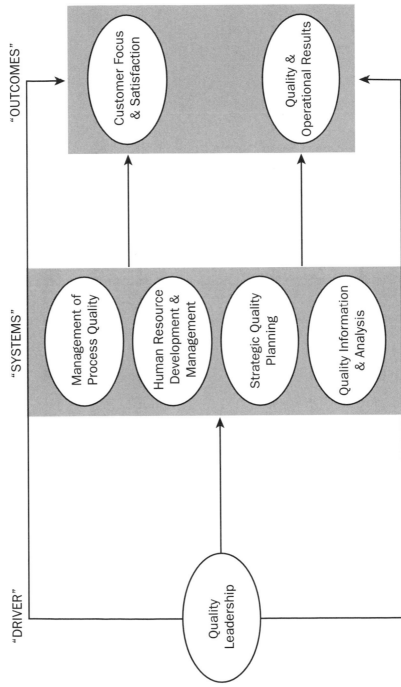

large businesses, small businesses, and service companies (two awards can be given in each category each year), the award is now being expanded to include educational organizations as well.

Still another approach to addressing TQM or big Q quality was proposed by Greene (1993), who, in a review of global quality practices, identified twenty-four "approaches to total quality" that describe a comprehensive set of processes comprising a TQM-based organization. Whereas, he argued that no single organization may be characterized by all twenty-four processes (inasmuch as the processes he described are all discussed neither in the U.S. nor in the Japanese literature, but are available if both are combined), these processes are, he asserted, nevertheless required for a total quality organization. Table 11-3 lists these twenty-four processes which focus primarily on the ways in which quality is achieved rather than on what is achieved.

Summary of the Dimensions and Approaches to Quality

We have presented the various approaches and dimensions to quality in order to point out that TQM is not yet a precisely defined construct. TQM encompasses many management practices and prescriptions that have been a part of the organizational literature for several decades. For example, Kahn (1993) pointed out that TQM is, for the most part, a practical restatement of many social science principles that have existed for a good many years, such as statistical measurement, teamwork, sharing power, service to customers, and flexible "System 4" structures and "linking-pin" designs, systems thinking, and culture change (see especially Coch and French 1948; Likert 1961; Seashore and Bowers 1970; Tannenbaum and Kahn 1958). TQM's multiple dimensions make it difficult to draw precise conclusions about its relationship to organizational effectiveness, although much anecdotal evidence exists that TQM is a prerequisite for organizational effectiveness for modern organizations.

Relationships between Quality and Effectiveness

The claim made by many advocates of TQM that implementing TQM principles improves organizational effectiveness has not been entirely

(text continues on p. 226)

Table 11-3. Greene's (1993) Twenty-Four Total Quality Processes

Category	Specific Process
Debuffering processes	Inventory buffers: just-in-time
	Tolerance buffers: statistical process control
	Authority buffers: quality circles
	Functional department buffers: total quality control
Scientific styling processes	Scientific prevention; total preventative maintenance
	Scientific design: Taguchi methods
	Scientific cognition: fourteen statistical and management tools
	Scientific application: high-technology circles
Workforce deployment processes	Automation deployment: buy time
	New technology deployment: buys customer satisfaction
	Quality function deployment: buys customer understanding
	Policy deployment: anticipates customer needs
Process engineering	Process architecting
	Process improving
	Process deployment
	Process execution automation
Organizational transparency processes	System inclusion of customers: customer-aided design
	Product inclusion of customers: customer-managed corporation
	Feeling inclusion of customers: Kansei engineering
	Generation inclusion: middle-up-down management
Cognitive competitiveness approaches	Learning organizations: cognitive quality of life
	Learning self-management: metacognitive organization
	University workgroups: social democratic quality
	Learning invention: democratic scientific management

confirmed in the literature. Everyday observations of the success of (especially) Japanese companies in productivity, market share, and competitiveness compared with U.S. companies have led most observers to point to quality as a key predictor of organizational success. For example, loss of market share and profitability in the U.S. automobile industry is widely attributed to poor quality relative to the Japanese; industry turnaround came only when quality problems were attacked aggressively. In retail, transportation, entertainment, banking, and other service industries, the most profitable companies are those that point to high-quality goods and customer service as the key to their success (e.g., Nordstroms, Wal-Mart, Disney, Morgan Bank, American Airlines).

Unfortunately, although a great deal of writing and storytelling has made a strong case for the importance of quality in ensuring organizational success, firm conclusions must be tempered by the fact that relatively little empirical work has been done to assess the relationships between TQM and organizational effectiveness. Of course, there is extensive literature on the topic of quality. For example, the American Society for Quality Control has more than 100,000 members, several publications are focused exclusively on the topic of quality (e.g., *Quality Progress, Quality Management Journal*), and quality has been the focus of writing in the United States and Japan for more than forty years (e.g., Fiegenbaum 1961; Juran 1951; Shewhart 1931). However, much of that focus has been either on processes and procedures associated with reducing or preventing mistakes and controlling variation, or on the dynamics associated with the production of quality products or services (e.g., via teamwork, lean manufacturing processes, quality circles, customer satisfaction, measurement, root-cause analysis, continuous improvement philosophy). That is, until recently quality writing was almost always associated with the manufacturing process related to producing goods or services, the nature of the goods or services themselves (e.g., defect rates), or the expectations and levels of satisfaction of customers. Organizational quality—the extent to which the organization itself reflects quality principles and practices—has been largely ignored in the empirical literature, has the extent to which organizational quality produces organizational effectiveness.

In other words, a notable characteristic of the scholarly literature on TQM is the dearth of empirical investigations. For example, in a broad review of TQM literature up to 1995 in higher education, Peterson and Cameron (1995) found that only 3 percent of the published articles were empirical studies of TQM, 59 percent were commentaries or editorials about TQM's merits or attributes, and 36 percent were case study descriptions of TQM's application in a single organization or setting. Hence, it seems that much more is known about the attributes and dimensions of TQM than about its impact on organizational performance.

Positive Results from the General Accounting Office

Despite criticism, the relationship between quality and several desirable outcomes is relatively well accepted, even though organizational effectiveness per se has been understudied. For example, a common criticism of quality as an approach to enhance organizational effectiveness is that quality processes are overemphasized to the exclusion of an analysis of outcomes and effects (e.g., Bowles 1992; Crawford-Mason 1992; Crosby 1992; Hammond 1992; McKoewn 1992). This overemphasis led the U.S. General Accounting Office to conduct a study of organizations that had implemented quality processes to a significant extent. The intent was to investigate the relationships between common quality process and desirable outcomes. The twenty companies investigated all were finalists in the MBNQA competition in 1988 and 1989. Each reported outcome data from the then-present time back to the time they initially embarked on a path to win the award by implementing quality processes. Table 11-4 summarizes the annual percentage of improvement in four categories of commonly desired outcomes associated with prescribed quality processes. The major conclusion of the study was that companies that implemented the quality process advocated by the MBNQA experienced continuous improvement in performance indicators and exceeded the industry averages in each of the four outcome categories—employee-related indicators, operating indicators, customer satisfaction indicators, and financial performance indicators. Of course, no causal or even statistical associations were made in this study, so whether successful companies tended to implement quality processes or whether companies that implemented these processes tended to become more successful is not known.

Relationships to Customer Satisfaction

In addition to the investigation of the MBNQA processes, other studies have focused on the relationships between particular quality dimensions

Table 11-4. Results of a U.S. General Accounting Office Study of
the Relationships between Quality Processes and
Desired Outcomes

Outcome Category	Reported Annual Improvement (%)
Employee-related indicators	
Employee satisfaction	1.4
Attendance	0.1
Turnover (decrease)	6.0
Safety and health	1.8
Suggestions	16.6
Operating indicators	
Reliability	11.3
On-time delivery	4.7
Order-processing time	12.0
Errors or defects	10.3
Product lead time	5.8
Inventory turnover	7.2
Costs of quality	9.0
Customer satisfaction indicators	
Overall customer satisfaction	2.5
Customer complaints (decrease)	11.6
Customer retention	1.0
Financial performance indicators	
Market share	13.7
Sales per employee	8.6
Return on assets	1.3
Return on sales	0.4

and organizational outcomes. For example, customer satisfaction has been
addressed in quite an extensive literature in the field of marketing. A
number of investigations have appeared examining the relationships between perceived quality and customer satisfaction (Anderson and Sullivan
1993; Anderson, Fornell, and Lehmann 1994; Churchill and Surprenant
1982; Oliver and DeSarbo 1988). In an empirical investigation of companies in the Swedish Customer Satisfaction Barometer database, Anderson,
Fornell, and Lehmann (1994) found that perceived quality had a strong
positive effect on customer satisfaction. In turn, the quality-customer satisfaction relationship had a strong positive effect on profitability as measured by return on investment. Fornell (1992) pointed out the advantages
of increasing customer satisfaction:

Though empirical evidence is limited, increases in customer satisfaction are generally believed to (1) shift the demand curve upward and/or make the slope of the curve steeper (i.e., lower price elasticity, higher margins), (2) reduce marketing costs (customer acquisition requires less effort), (3) increase marketing costs for competitors (satisfied customers are more difficult for competitors to take away), (4) lower transaction costs (contract negotiations, order processing, bargaining, and so on), (5) reduce customer turnover (fewer lost customers to replace), (6) increase cross-selling (more products, larger accounts), (7) lower employee turnover (satisfied customers affect the satisfaction of front-line personnel), (8) enhance reputation (positive customer word-of-mouth), and (9) reduce failure costs (reduction in downtime, rework, warranty claims, and so on). (p. 11)

Relationships to Productivity

The relationship between quality and productivity has also been investigated by many researchers. Since the early 1970s, several quality gurus have been writing extensively that "quality is free." This claim is based on the assertion that high quality eliminates the costs associated with lost customers, rework, excess time, indirect engineering, modified specifications, data collection and analysis, field service, reinspection, and waste (Cole 1993; Crosby 1979; Deming 1986; Ferdows and DeMeyer 1990; Imai 1986; Schonberger 1982). But empirical evidence to support the claim behind "free quality" remains spotty. Ittner (1992) found that nonconformance costs go down simultaneously with reductions in conformance costs, thus enhancing productivity. Various marketing studies (e.g., the Profit Impact of Market Strategy studies: Buzzell and Wiersma 1981; Anderson, Fornell, and Rust 1997; Philips, Chang, and Buzzell 1983) and field studies in manufacturing (e.g., Garvin 1988; Ittner 1992; Khurana 1994; Sluti 1992) found evidence that quality processes are associated with higher productivity, which, in turn, translates into high company value (Hendricks and Singhal 1996). Reynolds (1988) surveyed 69 companies and found that quality circles led to improved productivity, cost-effectiveness, and employee morale. Ansari (1984) surveyed 150 companies and found that just-in-time practices led to productivity improvements. Griffin (1988) found in a study of 73 companies that productivity initially improved as a result of quality circles, then fell back to previous levels. Krafcik and MacDuffie (1992) found that certain "lean production" techniques (all associated with TQM) led to higher productivity. And, Flynn, Schroeder and Sakakibara (1993) studied U.S. and Japanese companies and found seven critical dimensions of quality management to be associated with superior product quality.

Relationships to Competitiveness

The relationship between quality and organizational competitiveness has also received some attention by corporate strategists. Quality, they claimed, has a positive association with increased demand (Abbott 1955) and inelastic demand (Porter 1980). For example, Porter (1980) claimed that organizations differentiate themselves from their competitors mainly by providing more durable or reliable products, adding desirable features, providing high levels of customer service, or having an extensive dealer network (all aspects of TQM or big Q quality). He stated:

> Differentiation (on quality) provides insulation against competitive rivalry because of brand loyalty by customers and resulting lower sensitivity to price. It also increases margins which avoids the need for a low-cost position. The resulting customer loyalty and the need for a competitor to overcome uniqueness provides entry barriers. Differentiation yields higher margins with which to deal with supplier power, and it clearly mitigates buyer power, since buyers lack comparable alternatives and are thereby less price sensitive. Finally, the firm that has differentiated itself (through quality) to achieve customer loyalty should be better positioned vis-à-vis substitutes than its competitors. (p. 38)

The PIMS analyses confirm this competitive advantage by showing perceived product quality to be the most powerful predictor of corporate financial success when compared to market share, productivity, low-cost production, diversified product mix, and other common predictors of performance (e.g., Buzzell and Wiersma 1981).

Relationships between Big Q Quality and Effectiveness

On the other hand, as mentioned previously, few studies have investigated directly the relationship between organizational effectiveness and quality, particularly big Q quality or TQM. In one of the few investigations conducted, Cameron and colleagues (Cameron 1992, 1995; Cameron, Freeman, and Mishra 1991) studied the relationships between quality culture and organizational effectiveness among companies in the automotive industry, electronics businesses, and educational organizations. Quality culture represents a peculiar organizational mind-set or orientation toward quality—that is, a set of values, principles, and definitions related to quality. A cultural approach to quality is illustrated by a statement made by Bush (1992): "Quality management is not just a strategy. It must be a new style of working, even a new style of thinking. A dedication to quality and excellence is more than good business. It is a way of life, giving something back to society, offering your best to others." (Malcolm Baldrige National Quality Award 1992, p.1)

A quality culture, in other words, represents a way of working, a way of thinking, a personal commitment, and a lifestyle that is shared by members of an organization. It represents the ultimate big Q quality definition. A model explaining the characteristics of different quality cultures was investigated by Cameron and colleagues (Cameron 1992, 1995; Cameron and Peterson 1995; Cameron, Freeman and Mishra 1991) in studies in which four different cultures, mind-sets, or generalized orientations toward quality were assessed. They found that most of the several hundred organizations studied had developed their own unique cultural profile indicating various degrees of emphasis across these four quality cultures. Table 11-5 summarizes the attributes of each of the four types of cultures. No organization was characterized by a single quality culture, but most had one culture type that dominated the others.

These different quality cultures have emerged developmentally over the last few decades in for-profit organizations. Prior to the 1970s, quality was primarily the prerogative of reliability engineers, auditors, or others relegated to the checker or inspector function. Little attention was given to quality improvement as a value, and few organization members paid much attention to quality practices. This quality culture is labeled a status quo orientation. When this quality culture type is dominant, customers

Table 11-5. A Model of Quality Cultures: Four Stages

Status Quo

Products

▲ Keep the production and service processes moving.

▲ Root product and service design in convenience to the company and its workers; tradition and habit are strong, silent forces.

▲ Treat quality standards as an irritant, a hoop to jump through.

Customers

▲ Treat customers as "consumers" who will take what we offer them.

▲ Pay little attention to customer complaints.

▲ Resist suggestions for improvements that are inconvenient.

Error Detection

Products

▲ Avoid mistakes.

▲ Reduce waste, rework, and repair.

▲ Detect problems.

▲ Focus on outputs.

Customers

▲ Avoid annoying customers.

▲ Respond to complaints efficiently and accurately.

▲ Assess satisfaction after-the-fact.

▲ Focus on needs and requirements.

are treated as mere consumers of goods and services who will purchase virtually anything produced by the company. Attention to customer needs and service quality standards is largely seen as an irritant because the major objective is to get goods or services into the hands of customers in an efficient and profitable manner. Quality is delegated to a few specialty functions and has little to do with the day-to-day functioning of the organization.

On the other hand, during the 1970s, most U.S. organizations began to emphasize a quality culture centered on error detection. In this quality culture type, the organization as a whole stresses inspecting and detecting errors, avoiding mistakes, reducing waste, and finding and fixing errors. Quality control auditors inspect products and services after they are produced; that is, they "inspect in" quality. Regarding relationships with

Error Prevention

Products
- ▲ Expect zero defects.
- ▲ Prevent errors and mistakes.
- ▲ Hold everyone accountable.
- ▲ Focus on processes and root causes.

Customers
- ▲ Satisfy customers and exceed expectations.
- ▲ Eliminate problems in advance.
- ▲ Involve customers in design.
- ▲ Focus on preferences or "nice-to-have" attributes.

Perpetual Creative Quality

Products
- ▲ Constantly improve and escalate standards.
- ▲ Concentrate on things-gone-right.
- ▲ Emphasize breakthroughs.
- ▲ Focus on improvement in suppliers, customers, and processes.

Customers
- ▲ Expect lifelong loyalty.
- ▲ Surprise and delight customers.
- ▲ Anticipate customer expectations.
- ▲ Create new preferences.

Source: Cameron (1992).

customers, the organization's emphasis is to avoid upsetting or irritating internal and external customers in service delivery. Organizations develop systems that respond to customer requirements or specifications so that customer needs can be met. They determine after the product or service is delivered how satisfied customers are. By and large, this is a reactive or defensive approach to quality. It assures that organizations meet basic requirements, but errors are identified after-the-fact. Cameron and colleagues (Cameron 1992, 1995; Cameron, Freeman, and Mishra 1991) found that this quality culture type still dominates in a majority of organizations.

The 1980s saw a transition to an error prevention culture, or an emphasis on avoiding mistakes instead of correcting them after-the-fact. The main goal in this type of culture is to achieve zero defects (perfection) by doing work correctly the first time. Errors are prevented by focusing on how work is accomplished (the process) and by emphasizing root (common) causes of problems. Finding out why mistakes occur is more important than finding the mistake itself. All workers are held accountable for quality, not just end-of-the-line inspectors. Regarding relationships with customers, the emphasis is on pleasing and satisfying constituents (not just avoiding annoying them) and providing service that creates customer loyalty through exceeding customer expectations. This may be achieved by training customers before a product or service is delivered so that they know what to expect, obtaining customer preferences in advance of production, and monitoring customer satisfaction after goods and services are delivered so that customization can be offered.

A fourth quality culture emerged during the late 1980s and 1990s centered on perpetual creative quality. This culture, typical of only a few well-developed organizations, couples continuous improvement (small, incremental changes) with innovation (large, breakthrough changes), so that current standards of performance are constantly being raised. The focus on quality shifts to improvement in addition to prevention, or to designing and producing "things-gone-right" as well as avoiding "things-gone-wrong." The organization's standard changes from hitting a target to improving performance. Its objective is to achieve levels of quality in products and services that are not only unexpected but also unrequested. Problems are solved for customers and they receive unexpected benefits. Helping improve suppliers' and customers' quality is equally important to improving the organization's own work processes and employees. Solving customer problems that no one expected to be solved creates new expectations and surprises and delights customers.

Each type of quality culture is more advanced than its predecessor because each adds dimensions to the general approach of the former type. Error detection and inspection, for example, are not ignored nor necessarily abandoned; they are simply supplemented and made less necessary by an emphasis on error prevention and process improvement. Similarly, perpetual creative quality adds to the former two cultures by combining improvement and innovation in the quality objective. Several researchers have argued that the world's best organizations are typified by perpetual creative quality (Deming 1986; Garvin 1988; Kano 1995), but no empirical study has verified this assumption. However, the studies cited previously by Cameron and colleagues (Cameron 1992, 1995; Cameron, Freeman, and Mishra 1991) found that organizations that had developed an advanced quality culture (i.e., error prevention and perpetual creative quality) were more successful in their downsizing activities and had higher levels of organizational effectiveness than those with a less advanced quality culture. Organizations with a less advanced quality culture (status quo and error detection) are less successful in downsizing activities and have lower levels of organizational effectiveness.

For example, Cameron's (1992) research of more than 200 manufacturing and service organizations revealed that organizations in a status quo condition (paying little attention to quality) or dominated by an error detection culture were significantly lower performers on every process and outcome measure than were organizations dominated by error prevention and creative quality cultures.[1] Organizations dominated by a creative quality culture scored highest on all process and outcome measures. The error prevention companies scored second highest.

Khurana's (1994) study of the worldwide picture-tube manufacturing industry also confirmed this linkage between dimensions of quality culture and organizational effectiveness. He investigated the relationship among organizational efficiency, productivity, various indicators of product errors, and two dimensions of quality culture. He found that organizations with strong quality cultures performed better than those without strong cultures.

Summary of Relationships between TQM and Organizational Effectiveness

Empirical research has been conducted on the relationships between various aspects of TQM and organizational effectiveness, but it is both sparse and limited mainly to indicators of performance such as productivity, customer satisfaction, and error rates. Whereas, these limited findings provide support for a positive relationship between quality and effectiveness, the fact that the popular press is becoming more and more critical of TQM based on the rate at which quality improvement programs are

[1]The processes and outcomes used in the study included defect levels, financial performance over five years, ratings of organizational effectiveness, effective leadership, effective information gathering and analysis, appropriate structure, effective information use, effective planning, effective human resource utilization, customer satisfaction, use of quality tools, effective downsizing, and amount of past improvement.

being abandoned gives one pause. It is clear that many questions are yet to be addressed regarding this relationship, including those outlined in the next section.

Unanswered Questions Regarding TQM

It is ironic that the quality movement has been among the most powerful forces, if not the single most powerful force, in motivating organizational change in the last decade. Yet, with the dearth of empirical research on quality, particularly TQM or big Q quality, and the absence of theory regarding how and why TQM affects organizational performance, little clear understanding is available about the relationships between quality and organizational effectiveness. Thus, several key questions remain unanswered regarding TQM as a change strategy. These are not the only issues that need attention, of course, but they do represent some of the more important questions that deserve researcher consideration. It now appears that the term *TQM* is receding in currency; however, the organizational change efforts that have, for the past decade, been undertaken under the TQM flag will continue to be pursued under different terms and in different packages. Some of these questions are therefore more broadly applicable to macro-change efforts in general:

1. *What is TQM?* Is TQM a change strategy, a culture, a package of management principles, a set of values, a definition of an organization, a constituency's evaluation, or some combination of these alternatives? When writers use the term, what are they referring to? Is it the ultimate dependent variable or a fad that will likely fade over time?

2. *What are the key dimensions of TQM?* In light of the variety of models and definitions available (e.g., Deming's fourteen points, Crosby's fourteen points, Greene's twenty-four key processes), are some dimensions more crucial than others in defining quality? How would we know that we have a necessary and sufficient list of dimensions? On what basis would we select the core dimensions of TQM? For example, is TQM primarily a cluster of improvement efforts that focus "inward" on internal processes and operations, or is it, in its best applications, balanced by equal attention paid to external issues such as customer satisfaction and supplier involvement?

3. *What are the relationships among the dimensions of TQM?* Assum-

ing that we can identify core dimensions of TQM, what are the relationships among those dimensions? Do they have a temporal ordering as some models suggest (e.g., should leadership involvement precede the development of certain organizational processes as implied in MBNQA)? Do some dimensions subsume others?

4. *Are TQM principles universal or are they contingent on other factors?* Thus far, most TQM literature has adopted an "ideal type" approach, namely, that TQM is good under every circumstance for every organization. Are there situations in which TQM will not work or in which these broad-based efforts for change might be dysfunctional? What aspects of TQM are situationally dependent? Is a theory of TQM possible?

5. *What is new?* If TQM is a restatement of traditional social science principles, as argued by Kahn (1993), is there anything new here? Have we learned anything by talking about quality as a construct? Why not go back to basic principles of empowerment, system 4 thinking, teamwork, and so on?

6. *What is not TQM?* Almost every good management practice and prescription has been included in someone's definition of TQM. What is not a dimension of TQM? What are the conceptual boundaries of the construct? Without an understanding of what is and what is not TQM, no good theory or stream of research can be developed.

7. *What is the role of timing in TQM?* How much time does it take to implement TQM? Are the time estimates of leaders (the time by which they expect to see change) typically realistic or not? Is TQM a short-term change strategy, a long-term change strategy, both, or neither? What aspects of TQM should be addressed first, or last?

8. *What is the relationship between TQM and organizational effectiveness?* With the multidimensional nature of organizational effectiveness and the apparent multidimensional nature of TQM, how are the two constructs related? In what ways are they the same, predictors of one another, substitutes for one another, or independent of one another?

9. *How is TQM measured?* What are the key indicators of successful implementation of TQM or successful accomplishment of TQM? Whose perspective is the most legitimate is assessing TQM (e.g., customers, those involved in the operations of the organization, those leading the organization)? Do different constituencies use different measurement criteria? Does TQM require the use of a "balanced scorecard" of performance

measures that includes key stakeholders such as customers, suppliers, investors, and employees?

10. *What are the policy implications of TQM?* Is TQM an organizational specific approach, or could national policies be formulated to elevate output and customer service levels for an entire nation? What aspects of TQM are or are not legislatable? Does TQM represent a particular set of values making it impossible to superimpose on a diverse and eclectic set of industries and organizations?

Conclusion

Perhaps the greatest benefit derived from the TQM movement is that it seems to have helped organizational leaders and managers at many levels understand and appreciate both the "hard" and "soft" dimensions of organizational performance and quality improvement. Whatever its failures, the TQM movement has helped people take a broader, more comprehensive approach to improving organizational performance. Based on our experience in consulting and executive education, we see process experts who now understand the social and cultural dimensions of quality better than their predecessors. Similarly, the managers and consultants who work on organizational culture change are probably more sophisticated and informed about core process design—the technical and workflow issues—than ever. Perhaps the heaviest burden faced by those undertaking major change efforts, such as TQM initiatives, is the burden of unmet and unrealistic expectations. When genuine results lag behind expectations, the people responsible for delivering the results can easily become discouraged and cynical. For this reason, we urge organizational researchers to explore the role played by human expectations and collective optimism in sustaining change efforts. How well do organizational members understand why the effort is being made, and by what measures and indicators, be they unrealistic, practical, coherent, or hidden, are people to know if they are making progress? The pacing and flow of how much is attempted, how quickly, by organizations are important considerations in distinguishing the effective efforts from the failures.

The rather sudden abandonment of TQM initiatives in the late 1990s is perhaps as unwise as was the naive optimism with which the initiatives were undertaken in the 1980s. Call them by whatever name we choose, these large-scale efforts to enhance organizational performance will be with us for the duration. Our task, and opportunity, is to study such efforts with greater precision and thoughtfulness.

References

Abbott, L. 1955. *Quality and Competition.* New York: Columbia University Press.

Anderson, E., Fornell, C., and Lehmann. 1994. "Customer Satisfaction, Market Share, and Profitability: Findings From Sweden." *Journal of Marketing.* 58(3), 53–66.

Anderson, E., Fornell, C., and Rust, R. T. 1997. "Customer Satisfaction, Productivity, and Profitability: Differences Between Goods and Services." *Marketing Science* 16(2), 129–45.

Anderson, E. and Sullivan, M. 1993. "The Antecedents and Consequences of Customer Satisfaction for Firms." *Marketing Science* 12, 125–43.

Ansari, A. 1984. "An Empirical Investigation of the Implementation of Japanese Just-in-Time Purchasing Practices and Its Impact on Product Quality and Productivity in U.S. Firms." Ph.D. diss., University of Nebraska.

Bowles, J. 1992. "Does the Baldrige Award Really Work?" *Harvard Business Review* (January/February) 70(1), 127.

Buzzell, R. D. and Wiersma, F. D. 1981. "Modeling Changes in Market Share: A Cross-Sectional Analysis." *Strategic Management Journal* 2(1), 27–42.

Cameron, K. S. 1981. "Construct and Subjectivity Problems in Organizational Effectiveness." *Public Productivity Review* 7, 105–21.

———. 1992. "In What Ways Do Organizations Implement Total Quality?" Paper presented at the Academy of Management Meetings, Las Vegas, NV. August.

———. 1995. "Downsizing, Quality, and Performance." In R. E. Cole (ed.), *The Fall and Rise of the American Quality Movement.* New York: Oxford University Press.

——— and Peterson, M. 1995. *The Culture and Climate of Quality.* Ann Arbor: University of Michigan.

——— and Whetten, D. 1996. "Organizational Effectiveness and Quality: The Second Generation." In J. R. Smart (ed.), *Higher Education: Handbook of Theory and Research.* New York: Agathon.

Cameron, K. S., Freeman, S. J., and Mishra, A. K. 1991. "Best Practices in White-Collar Downsizing: Managing Contradictions." *Academy of Management Executive* 5, 57–73.

Churchill, G. and Surprenant, C. 1982. "An Investigation into the Determinants of Customer Satisfaction." *Journal of Marketing Research* 19, 491–504.

Coch, L. and French, J. R. P. 1948. "Overcoming Resistance to Change." *Human Relations* 1, 512–32.

Cole, R. E. 1993. "Learning From Learning Theory: Implications for Quality Improvements of Turnover, Use of Contingent Workers, and Job Rotation Policies." *Quality Management Journal* 1, 9–25.

Crawford-Mason, C. 1992. "Does the Baldrige Award Really Work?" *Harvard Business Review* (January/February) 70(1), 134–36.

Crosby, P. 1979. *Quality Is Free.* New York: New American Library.

Crosby, P. B. 1992. "Does the Baldrige Award Really Work?" *Harvard Business Review* (January/February) 70(1), 127–28.

Deming, W. E. 1986. *Out of the Crisis.* Cambridge, MA: MIT Press.

Edwards, C. D. 1968. "The Meaning of Quality." *Quality Progress,* October, 37.

Ferdows, K. and DeMeyer, A. 1990. "Lasting Improvements in Manufacturing Performance." *Journal of Operations Management* 9, 168–84.

Fiegenbaum, A. V. 1961. *Total Quality Control.* New York: McGraw-Hill.

Flynn, B., Schroeder, R., and Sakakibara, S. 1993. "A Framework for Quality Management Research: Definition and Measurement." Working paper, University of Iowa. Iowa City.

Fornell, C. 1992. "A National Customer Satisfaction Barometer." *Journal of Marketing* 56, 6–21.

Garvin, D. A. 1988. *Managing Quality: The Strategic and Competitive Edge.* New York: Free Press.

Greene, R. T. 1993. *Global Quality: A Synthesis of the World's Best Management Methods.* Homewood, IL: Business One Irwin.

Griffin, R. W. 1988. "Consequences of Quality Circles in an Industrial Setting: A Longitudinal Assessment." *Academy of Management Journal* 31(2), 338–58.

Hammond, J. 1992. "Does the Baldrige Award Really Work?" *Harvard Business Review* (January/February) 70(1), 132.

Hendricks, K. B. and Singhal, V. R. 1996. "Quality Awards and the Market Value of the Firm: An Empirical Investigation." *Management Science* 42(3), 415–37.

Imai, M. 1986. *Kaizen.* New York: Random House.

Ittner, C. 1992. *The Economics and Management of Quality Costs.* Cambridge, MA: School of Business Administration, Harvard University.

Jacob, R. 1993. "TQM: More Than a Dying Fad." *Fortune* (October 18), 128(9), 52–56.

Japanese Industrial Standards Committee. 1981. "Industrial Standards, 1981."

Juran, J. M. 1951. *Quality Control Handbook.* New York: McGraw-Hill.

———. 1974. *Quality Control Handbook,* 3rd ed. New York: McGraw-Hill.

————. 1992. *Juran on Quality by Design*. New York: Free Press.

Kahn, R. 1993. *M-Quality: A Brief Intellectual History*. Ann Arbor: Institute for Social Research, University of Michigan.

Kano, N. 1995. "A Perspective on Quality Activities in American Firms." In Robert E. Cole (ed.) *The Death and Life of the American Quality Movement*. New York: Oxford University Press.

Khurana, A. 1994. "Managing Complex Processes: Quality in the Global Color Picture Tube Industry." Ph.D. diss., University of Michigan.

Krafcik, J. and MacDuffie, P. 1992. "Integrating Technology and Human Resources for High-Performance Manufacturing: Evidence From the International Auto Industry." In T. Kochan and M. Useem (eds.), *Transforming Organizations*. New York: Oxford University Press.

Leffler, K. B. 1982. "Ambiguous Changes in Product Quality." *American Economic Review* 72(5), 956–67.

Likert, R. 1961. *New Patterns of Management*. New York: McGraw-Hill.

"Malcolm Baldrige National Quality Award Application Guidelines." 1992. Washington, DC: U.S. Department of Commerce.

McKeown, K. 1992. "Does the Baldrige Award Really Work?" *Harvard Business Review* (January/February) 70(1), 140.

Oliver, R. and DeSarbo, W. 1988. "Response Determinants in Satisfaction Judgments." *Journal of Consumer Research* 14(4), 495–508.

Peterson, M. and Cameron, K. 1995. *Total Quality Management in Higher Education: From Assessment to Improvement*. Ann Arbor: Center for the Study of Higher and Postsecondary Education, University of Michigan.

Philips, L., Chang, D., and Buzzell, R. 1983. "Product Quality, Cost Position, and Business Performance." *Journal of Marketing* 47, 26–43.

Pirsig, R. 1974. *Zen and the Art of Motorcycle Maintenance*. New York: Bantam Books.

Porter, M. 1980. *Competitive Strategy*. New York: Free Press.

Reynolds, R. B. 1988. "An Investigation into the Effectiveness of Quality Circles Applications in the United States." Ph.D. diss., University of Georgia.

Sashkin, M. and Kiser, K. J. 1993. *Putting Total Quality Management to Work*. San Francisco: Barrett-Koehler.

Schonberger, R. 1982. *Japanese Manufacturing Techniques*. New York: Free Press.

Scott, W. R., Flood, A. B., Wayne, E., and Forrest, W. H. 1978. "Organizational Effectiveness and the Quality of Surgical Care in Hospitals." In M. Meyer (ed.), *Environments and Organizations*. San Francisco: Jossey-Bass.

Seashore, S. E. and Bowers, D. G. 1970. "The Durability of Organizational Change." *American Psychologist* 25: 227–33.

Shewhart, W. A. 1931. *The Economic Control of Quality of Manufactured Product*. New York: Van Nostrand.

Sluti, D. 1992. "Quality, Cost, Price and Other Factors Influencing Quality: A

Study of Manufacturing in New Zealand." Ph.D. diss., University of Auk-
    land, New Zealand.
Tannenbaum, A. and Kahn, R. 1958. *Participation in Local Unions.* Evanston,
    IL: Row, Peterson.
Teboul, J. 1991. *Managing Quality Dynamics.* New York: Prentice Hall.
Webster, D. S. 1981. "Advantages and Disadvantages of Methods of Assessing
    Quality." *Change* (October) 13, 20–24.

The Perils of Responsiveness in Modern Organizations: A Framework for Problem Identification

LYNDA ST. CLAIR, ROBERT E. QUINN, *and* REGINA M. O'NEILL

W e began this book with the premise that truly useful organizational research is built on three supporting and equally important parts: theoretical conceptualization, methodological precision, and practical applications. A primary goal of this book is to help scholars find new fruitful research paths that take into account the interpenetration of theory, method, and practice by considering the pressing problems of modern organizations. Each chapter focuses on a pressing problem of importance to organizational practice and provides suggestions on how to advance research related to that particular problem. Thus, this book provides the beginnings of a productive research program that incorporates perspectives from both organizational scholars and practitioners.

The eleven problems discussed in this volume explore only a small subset of the pressing problems faced by organizations today. Recall that

---

*This Conclusion is based in part on work by Robert E. Quinn and Lynda St. Clair that appeared in *Consulting Psychology Journal: Practice and Research* 49(2), copyright © 1997 by the Educational Publishing Foundation and the Division of Consulting Psychology. Adapted with permission.

the book was organized around two primary categories of these problems: people problems and process problems. Interestingly, the people and process problems overlap in several ways. Therefore, while these two broad categories of problems introduce several promising topics, our hope is that future research will consider a more complex phenomenon of the wide range of problems that today's organizations face. This Conclusion presents a theoretical framework that can be used to identify other pressing organizational problems to expand research avenues further. Specifically, we suggest that in future research the complex and comprehensive set of pressing problems of modern organizations can be viewed through the lens of the responsive organization framework developed by Quinn and St. Clair (1997).

Consistent with the emphasis on blending theory and practice outlined in the Introduction, the framework presented in this Conclusion was developed, in large part, as a result of the recognition that in many instances, theory was not particularly helpful for practice. This is true despite the fact that both practitioners and theorists agree that organizations today face enormous competitive pressures and must be highly responsive to rapid changes in the external environment if they are to survive. The problem is twofold. First, as discussed in the Introduction, the academic literature is often focused on issues that derive from theory but have little grounding in the practical problems facing organizations today. Second, even when theory and research consider important problems of practice, it is often difficult to interpret the different perspectives and concepts that should, in theory, be helpful to practice. Here, we focus on the second of these issues.

Our goal is to synthesize a diverse set of organizational perspectives and provide a framework, derived from competing values theory (Quinn 1988; Quinn et al. 1990), that provides insight into the positive and negative aspects of "responsive" organizations with a particular emphasis on the problems that they face in practice. We present the framework of the responsive organization with the hope that it will prove helpful to researchers contemplating the study of pressing organizational problems that are beyond the scope of this book.

We begin by introducing the concept of responsiveness and establishing its importance for modern organizations. Next, we briefly describe the original competing values model that serves as the foundation for this framework. We consciously modify the original model by looking at the entire framework through one of the four lenses of the framework. By viewing the entire model through the lens of the open systems model, we bias it toward responsiveness. This modification leads to the development of a new theoretical framework that allows us to consider better the emerging responsive organization. We then classify a variety of recent management practices and emerging organizational problems according to that new framework, thereby illustrating the positive and negative characteristics of the responsive organization.

Next, we use the eleven problems addressed in this book to illustrate the dynamic nature of the responsive organization framework. In illustrating how these problems fit into this framework, we accomplish two things. First, we summarize the chapters in a new and meaningful way through the lens of the responsive organization framework. Second, we demonstrate how the responsive organization framework can be utilized in the future to help researchers identify other pressing problems of modern organizations that are beyond the scope of this book. We conclude with a call for more rigorous research on how to balance the competing values required for organizations to be responsive in today's highly competitive global environment. In line with a primary premise of the book, we emphasize how such future research should be conceptually rich, methodologically rigorous, and practically significant.

The Modern Organization and Responsiveness: An Introduction

The genesis of the responsive organization framework is grounded in both practice and theory. From practice comes the recognition that today's world of constant change and increasing global competition requires more responsive forms of organizing. Responsive organizations are sensitive to stimuli and are able to act quickly. Responsiveness is more than simply being reactive; it requires that the organization anticipate change and move proactively. A responsive organization is one in which structures and procedures enhance the organization's ability to take advantage of changes in the environment to enhance its competitive advantage.

To cope with the incessant demand for change, managers, researchers, and consultants have proposed a variety of new concepts and ideas on how organizations can become more responsive. Around the world companies are engaging in thousands of organizational experiments designed to make their organizations more responsive. As these experiments are conceptualized, executed, and evaluated, numerous new words, concepts, and theories enter the management domain. For example, people now speak of empowerment, cycle times, right sizing, boundaryless organizing, process reengineering, and cross-functional teams. These ideas are intended to help organizations become more flexible and better able to adapt to their ever-altering environment—in essence, to become more responsive.

Unfortunately, the language and concepts that have emerged from both practice and theory have not been linked together in any coherent way. As the domain of concepts and ideas grows, it becomes increasingly complex and ever more difficult to understand. One purpose of this Conclusion is to embed the ideas and concepts of practice into a meaningful theoretical framework or map that can help people make sense of this territory that demands more responsiveness from modern organizations.

The Responsive Organization

Theoretical Foundations

As we began seeking to develop a framework of that modern, responsive organization, we followed the same path that Max Weber (Gerth and Mills 1946) took, when, at the end of the last century, he sought to identify the general characteristics of what was then a newly emerging form of organization—the professional bureaucracy. Today the emerging form is nearly the opposite. It might be called the responsive or virtual organization. We sought to identify the most general characteristics of this emerging form. Although we were in fact generating an "ideal type," we instead used the term *framework* to avoid the implication that we are being proscriptive, rather than descriptive. Like Weber, our intention has not been to advocate for a particular form of organization but to describe the core characteristics of an emerging organizational form. In keeping with this notion, we have sought to be explicit about both its positive and negative characteristics.

Work on the competing values approach to organization (Quinn 1988; Quinn et al. 1990) provides the underpinning for the framework that we derive here (see Figure 1). The competing values model maps out four different quadrants on two dimensions. The vertical axis reflects a

(text continues on p. 248)

Figure 1. The competing values framework.

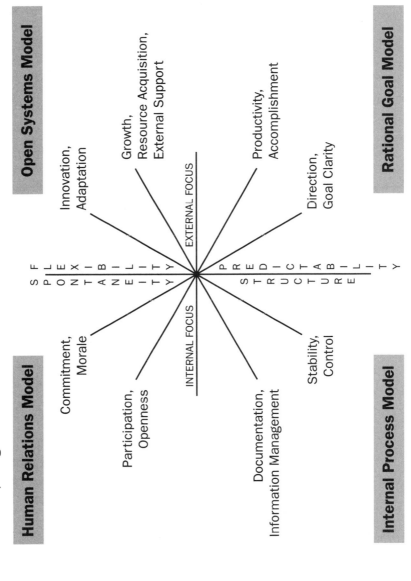

Human Relations Model

Open Systems Model

Internal Process Model

Rational Goal Model

FLEXIBILITY

CONTROL

EXTERNAL FOCUS

INTERNAL FOCUS

Innovation,
Adaptation

Growth,
Resource Acquisition,
External Support

Productivity,
Accomplishment

Direction,
Goal Clarity

Commitment,
Morale

Participation,
Openness

Documentation,
Information Management

Stability,
Control

dimension that is anchored by flexibility at one extreme and control at the other. The horizontal dimension is defined in terms of focus of attention, ranging from internal to external. The four quadrants reflect different combinations of these underlying dimensions. For example, organizations need to acquire resources and external support, reflecting the external focus and need for flexibility that characterizes the open systems quadrant. They also need effective information management and formal communication and control systems, consistent with the internal focus and emphasis on control found in the internal process quadrant. Organizations need to value and develop human resources, consistent with the human relations quadrant's focus on internal issues and flexibility. And they need to be effective in planning and achieving goals, as suggested by the emphasis on external issues and control in the rational goal model quadrant.

The values that underlie each of the four quadrants of the competing values model are positive. What the overall framework makes clear is that some of the quadrants complement each other whereas some offer a stark contrast. By highlighting these apparently paradoxical relationships, the framework recognizes the inherently difficult nature of effective organizing. These paradoxes become even more pronounced when organizations attempt to become more responsive, as we discuss subsequently.

Organizations and their managers must learn to balance those opposites. Unfortunately, for the practitioner, it is quite difficult to maintain an awareness of all four quadrants and to see the value in all four perspectives simultaneously. The need for intentional action on a timely basis leads people to choose a desired end state such as increased orders or faster change, increased trust or more productivity. Once an end state is specified and pursued, it is difficult to value simultaneously the criteria specified in the opposite quadrant. That quadrant tends to get neglected or ignored. The competing values framework leads to more complex thinking and it helps surface the values of the other quadrants. Thus, the competing values framework is intended to help managers and organizations find the proper balance among the quadrants by clarifying the underlying assumptions of different areas on the map and the tools that can be used to advance in those directions.

Developing the Framework

Competitive pressure to become more responsive has forced theorists and practitioners to try to invent an organizational form that is flexible and externally oriented. Thus, one quadrant of the original competing values framework, open systems, is particularly central. The quest for responsiveness, however, does not eliminate the importance of the other three quadrants. We still must consider internal processes and structures, organizational goals, and people. What must change, if we are to create a more flexible externally oriented organizational form, is how we think about each of these quadrants.

The elements in each quadrant must be conceptualized so as to increase organizational responsiveness. Rather than contributing to slow and costly bureaucratic practices, the structures and processes in the internal process quadrant, for example, must lead to increased speed and adaptability. Rather than destroying the goodwill of employees, the practices in the rational goal quadrant must align the internal and external conditions in such a way as to inspire rather than destroy the human commitment necessary for constant adaptation. Rather than turning the organization into a permissive country club, the practices in the human relations quadrant should contribute to the achievement of the collective purpose and increase the capacity of the organization to continually engage changing external realities.

To see what assumptions might be needed in designing a more responsive organization, we used an iterative process. We began with a thought experiment, using the open systems quadrant as a lens through which to view the entire model and asking ourselves what we thought the key assumptions of each quadrant would be if that quadrant were reoriented to be more adaptive and responsive. Next, we reviewed the literature to look for descriptions of old and new management practices or ways of doing business. Drawing from a variety of sources, we located several articles that referred to old and/or new business practices (Arthur, Claman, and DeFillippi 1995; Byrne 1986; Carnevale 1995; Davis 1995; DeMeuse and Tornow 1990; Rousseau 1990; Rousseau and Wade-Benzoni 1995; Tichy and Sherman 1993; Wall and Jackson 1995). We then attempted to relate the old management practices to the original competing values framework and the new management practices to the responsive organization framework that we had derived from our thought experiment. Old and new ideas were categorized by Quinn and St. Clair, who then discussed and resolved any disagreements about classification. The following descriptions of each quadrant of the responsive organization framework resulted from this blending of theory and practice. The resulting framework can be a valuable tool for researchers and practicing managers alike as they attempt to predict and control the positive and negative consequences of organizational responsiveness.

Human Relations Quadrant

The key assumptions addressed by the human relations quadrant relate to individuals and groups. In the original competing values model, individuals were assumed to serve the organization by following orders (compliance) and cooperating with the mandates of the organization. It was also assumed that individuals needed direction so that they could competently do the tasks that they were assigned. Rewards were allocated to individuals even if their performance took place in group activities. Groups tended to be relatively homogeneous and were expected to require supervision and decision making from outside the group.

In theory, the human relations quadrant is defined by flexibility and an internal orientation, whereas in practice these dimensions have not always been evident. As the global economy has placed more demands for responsiveness on organizations, evolving practices associated with the human relations quadrant have led to a new understanding of the roles of individuals and groups in organizations. At the individual level, the emphasis has moved from compliance and cooperation to more proactive forms of involvement and participation. For example, interpersonal skills are becoming as valued as technical skills. At the group level, teamwork has increased and teams are often self-managing, allowing the group to make their own decisions. Permanent, homogeneous teams give way to temporary teams that are diverse and oftentimes global in terms of membership. These practices suggest that the quadrant continues to be defined by a need for flexibility while the focus moves from internal to more external and global concerns. Table 1 highlights these old and new practices and includes some problems that are emerging as a result of the push toward responsiveness in the human relations quadrant.

Open Systems Quadrant

The original open systems quadrant emphasized flexibility, innovation, and an external focus. It was characterized by the traditional management practices given in Table 2. Many of these practices, however, tended to be reactive, incremental, short-term, and limited nationally. For example, when external trends indicated that change was needed (e.g., customer

Table 1. Classification of Management Practices Related to Assumptions about People and Groups in the Human Relations Quadrant

Traditional Management Practices	Emerging Management Practices	Emerging Management Problems
Compliance (people as subordinates)	Involvement (people as partners)	Loss of authority
Cooperation (people as employees)	Empowerment (people as owners)	Unintegrated effort
Direction (people as machines)	Participation (people as contributors)	Loss of efficiency
Loyalty (people as long-term employees)	Self-reliance (people as contractors)	Unpredictable behavior
Task competence (people as technicians)	Emotional intelligence (people as technically and interpersonally competent)	Self-authorization
Individual performance	Teamwork	Collusion
Supervision	Self-managing work teams	Unproductive discussion
Permanent, homogeneous work groups	Temporary, diverse, global terms	Conflicting cultural assumptions
Managing groups	Coaching and facilitating	Low expectations
Nonconfrontational relationships	Continuous challenge of ideas	Unresolved conflict

satisfaction was declining), efforts were made to complete the change as quickly as possible and return to a stable state. Because the culture of the organization was assumed to be homogeneous, the types of changes initiated tended to be incremental, rather than radical. Growth was viewed in terms of constraints, rather than opportunities, with a focus on bottom-line profitability. If opportunities to grow emerged, they were embraced, but they were not sought out and were typically limited to growth in a single country.

Table 2. Classification of Management Practices Related to Assumptions about Change and Growth in the Open Systems Quadrant

Traditional Management Practices	Emerging Management Practices	Emerging Management Problems
Living with change	Creative, proactive change orientation	Too many initiatives
Monitoring customer satisfaction	Anticipating unarticulated customer needs	Change overload
Incremental improvements	Quantum breakthroughs	Sense of chaos
Change completion mentality	Commitment to continuous realignment	Loss of direction
Individual learning	Organizational learning	Loss of productive focus
Single focus on bottom-line profit	Focus on bottom-line profit and top-line growth	Increased differentiation
Opportunistic growth orientation	Long-term growth planning	Functional conflict
Parochial growth orientation	Global strategy for market expansion	Regional conflict
Cautious merger and acquisition strategy	Proactive merger and acquisition strategy	Headquarters field conflict
Growth through internal expertise	Growth through partnerships	Interorganizational conflict

By magnifying the necessary flexibility and innovation required of organizations to become responsive, assumptions about change move toward the perspective that continuous realignment is desirable as well as necessary. Attention is still focused on the external environment, but the emphasis shifts to anticipating (rather than reacting to) customer needs. With respect to growth, responsive organizations are constantly looking for ways to expand their markets, especially in the global arena. In addition to generating more bottom-line profits, increasing revenues becomes a focus of attention. Rather than viewing growth as something to be attained through opportunism, the responsive organization takes a long-term planning approach to growth. Thus, with the advent of a more global economy, the practices of the open systems model have become more proactive, radical, long-term, and global. Table 2 presents the emerging practices associated with the open systems quadrant and their related problems in the last two columns.

Rational Goal Quadrant

The rational goal quadrant in the original competing values model focused on productive accomplishment. Critical assumptions were related to how performance should be encouraged and evaluated (performance discipline) and what should determine the direction of the organization. Performance discipline was assumed to be best achieved by using analysis and planning to generate achievable goals. Direction was viewed as requiring clear goals and specific rules and policies to ensure that those goals were met. Economically realistic objectives, data analysis, logical decisions, controlled action, and measured success were key elements of this model.

As organizations are forced to shift their thinking to more innovative and flexible means of establishing the performance discipline and direction for the organization, these earlier orientations begin to change. For example, new assumptions about performance discipline must now include stretch goals that are not guaranteed to be achieved. Attention must be focused on customers (outside the organization) to help determine what decisions are in the best interests of the organization. Because everything tends to be in a state of constant flux, ensuring a consistent direction for the organization requires that specific rules and procedures give way to broad principles that can guide the action of organizational members under constantly changing circumstances. To accomplish this, an overarching vision of the organization must continuously be presented in the organization to achieve a common strategic mind-set. These changes, although intended to make the organization more responsive, have also had some unintended negative consequences. Table 3 presents traditional practices, emerging practices, and problems related to these emerging practices for the rational goal quadrant.

Internal Process Quadrant

The internal process quadrant in the original competing values model assumed that organizations were best served when stability and control

Table 3. Classification of Management Practices Related to Assumptions about Performance Discipline and Direction in the Rational Goal Quadrant

Traditional Management Practices	Emerging Management Practices	Emerging Management Problems
Data gathering, analysis, and planning	Decisive, action-focused decision making	Unrealistic work expectations
Achievable objectives	Stretch goals	Perpetual exertion
Rewards for effort	Rewards for performance	Erosion of life balance
Low-risk decisions	Customer-driven decisions	Employees equal commodities
Focus on productivity	Focus on adding value	Erosion of teamwork
Command and control	Charismatic leadership	Dependency
Management by objective (MBO)	Compelling, persuasive vision	Groupthink
Specifying a clear direction	Continuous selling of a vision	Death of dialog
Written goals	Embodiment of a vision, "walk the talk"	Undiscussable minority opinions
Control through rules and policies	Commonly held strategic mind-set	Restricted thinking

were maximized. To ensure stability, it was assumed that organizations should be designed hierarchically with clear chains of command and independent staff functions. Control was seen as best achieved by planning, followed by production, and finally the routinization of production processes.

The central characteristics of stability and control in the internal process quadrant appear to be direct opposites of the characteristics of a responsive organization. In fact, today's highly competitive environment has put extreme pressure on the practices traditionally associated with the internal process quadrant, and consequently, new practices have emerged. These new practices are still appropriately included in the internal process quadrant because they relate to the fundamental issues of structure, design, and process that distinguish the internal process quadrant.

Unfortunately, even with their emphasis on responsiveness, these new practices have not turned out to be a panacea (e.g., five of the eleven problems discussed in this book relate to the internal process quadrant). Rather, new problems have emerged, in many cases as a direct result of the practices instituted to become more responsive. Table 4 summarizes

Table 4. Classification of Management Practices Related to Assumptions about Organizational Structure and Process in the Internal Process Quadrant

Traditional Management Practices	Emerging Management Practices	Emerging Management Problems
Functional focus	Boundaryless organizing	Ambiguous roles
Hierarchical levels	Flat organizational design	Unclear expectations
Clear chain of command	Matrix organizations	Multiple accountabilities
Vertical information flow	Cross-functional information sharing	Internal conflict
Independent staff functions	Staff functions as integrated business partners	Internally focused politics
Linear planning and production	Simultaneous design and parallel processes	Impending crisis
Inventory control	Just-in-time processes	High anxiety
Routinized processes	Reengineering processes and improved speed	Extensive analysis
Downsizing processes	Right-sizing processes	High stress
Efficiency of work processes	Elimination of work; new workout programs	Continuous reengineering

these trends. The first column shows some of the practices that have traditionally been associated with the internal process quadrant. The second and third columns list, respectively, many of the new practices that are associated with this quadrant and the emerging problems that have emerged in the wake of these new practices.

Summary of the Responsive Organization Framework

The responsive organization framework can be summarized using two figures. In Figure 2, we integrate the emerging management practices

Figure 2. The responsive organization: The positive zone.

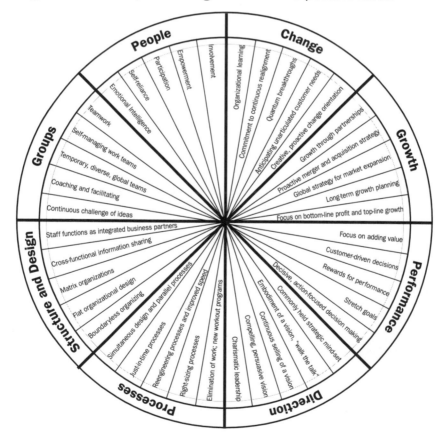

from Tables 1–4. This positive view of the responsive organization reflects the kinds of practices that theoretically should help organizations be more responsive. By contrast, Figure 3 integrates the emerging management problems given in Tables 1–4. This negative view of the responsive organization reflects what has been happening in practice as organizations attempt to become more responsive, in many cases by adopting the practices shown in Figure 2. In each figure, the selected forty practices (Figure 2) and problems (Figure 3) are not intended to be comprehensive. Nor would all these practices or problems be expected to be manifest in any given company. They simply represent the general types of management

Figure 3. The responsive organization: The negative zone.

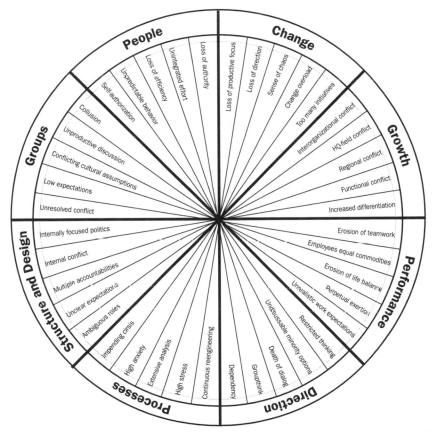

practices and problems that are emerging today. Any particular practice or problem might be removed and replaced with another that is consistent with the general dimensions underlying that quadrant of the framework. The framework is itself highly flexible.

The responsive organization framework as represented in Figures 2 and 3 is based on two related assumptions. The first concerns connectedness and change, and the second concerns balance. First, in the responsive organization, everything involves process, and all processes are assumed to be connected to all others. That is, all processes continually co-evolve. It is assumed, for example, that organizations both create and are created by their environment: When the environment changes, the organization changes; when the organization changes, the environment changes. Likewise, the individual within the organization is both determined and determining. In the responsive organization, everything is linked by a series of mutual feedback loops that operate simultaneously. Actions x and y are both causing and being caused by each other.

Second, because the characteristics associated with the four quadrants of the responsive organization co-evolve, if one is neglected, they are all endangered. To build or maintain a responsive organization requires attention to all of the characteristics associated with the four quadrants of the framework. The executive's task is to balance creatively these characteristics while attending to the practices that flow from them.

The balancing act that we are proposing is particularly difficult because pushing too hard in the direction of any of the quadrants can lead to unintended negative consequences, as shown in Figure 3. The interconnectedness necessary to make the framework responsive also implies that the system will become unbalanced and, thus, dysfunctional if the goal of responsiveness in any one of the quadrants is pushed too far. The universal rule of "everything in moderation" is also true for becoming more responsive.

This "negative zone" provides a worldview that is seldom represented in the rhetoric of modern organizing, yet it captures many of the problems that are taking center stage in the global economy, including conflicting cultural assumptions, loss of efficiency, loss of direction, functional conflict, erosion of life balance, undiscussable issues, continuous reengineering, and ambiguous roles (to name only a few of the forty). Again, these forty problems are not in any way sacred; they simply articulate what might emerge if balance is lost. Any particular problem can be removed and replaced by an alternative problem that is consistent with the general dimensions of that quadrant of the framework. Thus, the responsive organization framework provides a method for identifying potentially pressing problems beyond those discussed in this book for future research. We caution, however, that merely fitting within the framework does not imply that a problem is a critical concern in practice. Establishing the relative importance of problems requires input from practitioners who may have experienced these problems and can assess their significance for organizational practice.

The Dynamics of Responsiveness: Sample Problems

In theory, the responsive organization framework suggests that organizations can find the appropriate balance among the four quadrants of the framework. In practice, however, we recognize that problems can develop as a consequence of pursuing responsiveness in one area at the expense of other areas. In addition, however, the interconnected nature of organizational processes also makes it likely that a practice originally intended to improve responsiveness in one quadrant may paradoxically result in problems associated with that same quadrant.

In this section, we use the eleven pressing problems described in this book to illustrate the dynamic nature of responsive organizations and how these types of paradoxical results might occur. The scenarios suggested here for how these problems might have developed are necessarily speculative, but they are derived from both existing theory and anecdotes of practice. Future research is needed to document specific examples of these complex dynamic processes.

Problems in the Human Relations Quadrant

The problems of communication and cultural misunderstanding described by Alnot and Brannen (Chapter 5) may result in part from a very appropriate emphasis in the human relations quadrant on increasing diversity within the organization. With diversity comes the opportunity to create diverse global teams. In theory, this should spark innovation and lead to creative breakthroughs. Without appropriate training and development to take advantage of workforce diversity, however, organizations are likely to be beset by all the problems of diversity without any of its benefits. This is especially true if, in an effort to remain flexible, teams are temporary. Employees have little incentive to build close relationships and improve their communication with individuals if those relationships are destined to be short-term in nature.

Problems in the Open Systems Quadrant

Three chapters focus on problems that result when organizations attempt to become too responsive to the external environment in the open systems quadrant. Wells and Bantel (Chapter 9) consider the problem of loss of direction that results when organizations attempt to become too expansive in their attempts to find strategic competitive advantages. Similarly, in Chapter 10 Bacidore and Thakor discuss loss of direction (as manifest in poor capital allocation decisions) as one of the reasons that organizations experience poor financial performance. Cameron and Thompson (Chapter 11) note that companies are often unsuccessful in meeting quality expectations because they embrace too many initiatives and consequently fail to achieve any of them. Each of these problems appears to derive from making a commitment to continuous realignment in response to the ever-changing external environment. This proactive change orientation should theoretically help companies take advantage of new trends and prepare for shifting expectations. In practice, however, constantly trying to reinvent the organization may undermine organizational processes and overwhelm the people in the organization.

Problems in the Rational Goal Quadrant

When organizations focus solely on increasing shareholder value (overemphasizing the rational goal quadrant), they may begin to make excessive demands of employees, as discussed by Welch, Ebert, and Spreitzer in Chapter 3. By trying rewards to performance and instituting stretch goals, employees may often feel as though they are forced to choose between their work and their lives outside of work. This could result in the type of perpetual exertion in the workplace and erosion of life balance discussed in Chapter 3. Although the immediate effect of these problems is on the individuals employed in the organization, over time as employees' performance deteriorates, organizational processes are likely to be impaired as well.

A contrasting way that overemphasis on performance may potentially manifest itself is, ironically, through the underuse of employees. Following Morgan and Feldman's (Chapter 4) arguments, organizations may fail to take advantage of employees' skills because those skills either do not add apparent value for customers or would raise the cost of employees to the organization. In such a case, the failure to take advantage of employees' skills would be consistent with viewing employees as commodities. If too much emphasis is placed on customers, then employees may begin to be viewed as interchangeable, and therefore their specialized skills will be less highly valued.

Problems in the Internal Process Quadrant

Five chapters in this book focus on problems associated with the internal process quadrant. Three emphasize structure; two focus on process directly. Interest in this quadrant is undoubtedly high because of the numerous experiments with organizational structure and processes that have been taking place in recent years. This heavy concentration of problems is also fitting from the perspective of the responsive organization framework because it is the internal process quadrant that is directly opposite the open systems quadrant, the lens that Quinn and St. Clair (1997) used for modifying the original competing values model in deriving that new framework.

The problems of internally focused politics and internal conflict are described by Williams and Dutton in Chapter 1. Although issues of power and politics have always been a factor in organizations, one emerging management practice that might result in an increase in political activity in organizations is the attempt to make staff functions integrated business partners. Such a shift in structure may be threatening to employees who traditionally have not had to share power with advisory staff in areas such as human resources that have historically been excluded from the strategic decision-making processes of organizations.

The issues of multiple accountabilities and chaotic job rotations are also related to structural aspects of the organization. Multiple accountabilities can occur in other organizational structures, but are built into the design of matrix organizations. Despite the fact that organizational textbooks generally consider matrix structures as improvements over older functional forms, when they are implemented they can create problems for employees and organizational processes, as Arlington and Baker note in Chapter 2. Likewise, the ambiguous roles that are likely to result from chaotic job rotations (Snyder and Duarte, Chapter 6) may possibly result from attempts to become "boundaryless," a more recent and even more abstract concept of organizational structure. In both these cases, the benefits of these structural innovations from theory have rarely been fully realized in their practical implementations.

Martin and Carlile (Chapter 7) look at the problems that result when processes are continuously reengineered but not well designed. Leading this reengineering drive is the desire to eliminate work and reduce costs—a goal that managers and theorists would both applaud. The reality of reengineering, however, is that it is often costly in and of itself, as many companies are now discovering. Furthermore, redesigned processes, even if they do succeed in eliminating work, do not necessarily reduce costs. One potential solution to this problem is to do a better job of estimating the benefits and costs of reengineering. That solution, however, may turn into a new problem—overemphasis on analysis, as discussed by Vodosek and Sutcliffe (Chapter 8).

Balancing the Quadrants

The preceding examples serve to demonstrate the dynamics of responsiveness. The nature of the competing values model on which the responsive organization framework is based suggests that the balancing process is likely to lead to a pendulum effect as different management practices are implemented over time to respond to changes in the environment. In some cases, those management practices will be in the same quadrant, as demonstrated by the preceding examples. In other cases, if a problem emerges from the application of a management practice in one quadrant, a new management practice from the opposite quadrant may be applied to resolve the original problem. However, because there is a tendency to overcompensate, the new focus of attention is likely to be applied to excess, leading to problems in the original management practice's quadrant. Understanding this dynamic tension is crucial to the development of theories and practices that can predict and control the consequences of organizational responsiveness in the future.

Conclusion

In concluding our book, we have attempted to increase understanding of the responsive organization and its related management philosophies and practices to help guide future research efforts. We have explored the idea that different assumptions about the necessary capabilities of organizations in the future can be understood as a new competing values framework for responsive organizations. We have integrated a number of emerging practices into a single overarching framework that is consistent with classical frameworks in the management literature. In exploring both the positive and negative aspects of becoming increasingly more responsive, we have attempted to demonstrate both the complexity of the responsive organization and some of the practical implications that flow from this form of organization. Finally, to illustrate that the responsive organization framework is useful for identifying pressing problems that can be examined in future research, we have shown how the problems in this book fit within that framework and help illuminate different aspects of it.

Organizational responsiveness is becoming a necessity, rather than a competitive advantage. By articulating the characteristics of the responsive organization and pointing out potentially negative consequences of responsiveness, the ideas outlined in this Conclusion can help organizational theorists and practitioners alike. By identifying both the potential benefits and problems that are likely to be characteristic of more responsive organizations in the future, we hope that this framework will serve as a guide for future research on pressing problems of modern organizations that is theoretically grounded, methodologically rigorous, and practically important.

References

Arthur, M. B., Claman, P. H., and DeFillippi, R. J. 1995. "Intelligent Enterprise, Intelligent Careers." *Academy of Management Executive* IX(4), 7–20.

Byrne, J. A. 1986. "Business Fads: What's In—and Out." *Business Week* (January 20), 52–61.

Carnevale, A. P. 1995. "Enhancing Skills in the New Economy." In A. Howard (ed.), *The Changing Nature of Work*. San Francisco: Jossey-Bass.

Davis, D. D. 1995. "Form, Function, and Strategy in Boundaryless Organizations." In A. Howard (ed.), *The Changing Nature of Work*. San Francisco: Jossey-Bass.

DeMeuse, K. P. and Tornow, W. W. 1990. "The Tie That Binds—Has Become Very, Very Frayed!" *Human Resource Planning* 13(3), 203–213.

Gerth, H. and Mills, C. W. 1946. *From Max Weber: Essays in Sociology.* New York: Oxford University Press.

Quinn, R. E. 1988. *Beyond Rational Management: Mastering the Paradoxes and Competing Demands of High Performance.* San Francisco: Jossey-Bass.

Quinn, R. E., Faerman, S. R., Thompson, M. P., and McGrath, M. R. 1990. *Becoming a Master Manager: A Competency Framework.* New York: Wiley.

Quinn, R. E. and St. Clair, L. 1997. "The Emerging Professional Adhocracy: A General Framework of Responsive Organizing." *Consulting Psychology Journal: Practice and Research* 49(2), 152–61.

Rousseau, D. M. 1990. "New Hire Perceptions of Their Own and Their Employer's Obligations: A Study of Psychological Contracts." *Journal of Organizational Behavior* 11, 389–400.

Rousseau, D. M. and Wade-Benzoni, R. A. 1995. "Changing Individual-Organization Attachments: A Two Way Street." In A. Howard (ed.), *The Changing Nature of Work.* San Francisco: Jossey-Bass.

Tichy, N. M. and Sherman, S. 1993. *Control Your Destiny or Someone Else Will.* New York: Currency Doubleday.

Wall, T. D. and Jackson, P. R. 1995. "New Manufacturing Initiatives and Shopfloor Job Design." In A. Howard (ed.), *The Changing Nature of Work.* San Francisco: Jossey-Bass.

Appendix |

Pressing Problems of Modern Organizations

The following twenty-one problem categories were derived based on data from a survey of managers from 117 organizations. Following each problem category is a list of the specific variables that the managers were asked to rate in terms of importance. The list is shown in decreasing order of importance, so the most important problem identified by these managers was Competitive External Pressures.

Competitive External Pressures: intense competition in the industry; pressures from external competitors; inability to cope with outside competition; lack of a distinct competitive advantage.

Lack of Strategic Direction: unclear direction from top management; conflicting messages from members of the top management team; ambiguity about what is truly valued at the top of the organization; shifting organizational priorities; ever-changing initiatives in the organization; absence of a compelling corporate vision.

Multiple Accountabilities: frustrating multiple-reporting relationships; conflicting accountabilities; confusing matrix relationships.

Chaotic Job Rotations: rapid movement of people from one assignment to another; continuous movement of people in and out of jobs; frequent movement of managers from job to job; length of time in job assignments keeps shrinking.

Unmanaged Growth: unrealistic planning assumptions in entering new markets; difficulties managing the entry into new markets; denial of the realities associated with new markets; unmanaged organizational growth; chaotic patterns of growth; lack of vision in managing the growth process.

Poor Financial Performance: poor financial performance; disappointing earnings; high operating costs; overrunning budgets; spending too much money; low net income; inadequate cost control.

Process Problems: ineffective internal processes; processes that are too complex; difficulties in resolving process problems.

Dissatisfaction with Quality: disappointing quality results; unmet quality expectations; customer satisfaction problems; inability to get quality improvements; difficulty responding to the voice of the customer; failure to meet customer expectations.

Inadequate Resources: organizations that are too lean; inadequate resources to get the job done; lack of capacity necessary to complete assignments.

Disappointing Sales Performance: poor sales performance; unmet sales quotas; disappointing total sales.

Difficulties in Partnering: difficulties in partnering with other companies; disappointing results from external partnerships; difficulties in making mergers and acquisitions work.

Overworked People: conflicts between personal and professional life; difficulty integrating work and professional life; loss of personal life balance; feeling overworked; working close to the point of burnout.

Conflict and Intimidation: hesitation in challenging the ideas of others; avoidance of exploring honest differences of opinion; reluctance to confront others' ideas constructively; turf protection between functions; unwillingness to coordinate across functions; cross-functional conflict; reluctance to take initiative; hesitance in making decisions; fear of making mistakes.

Corrosive Political Climate: lack of cohesiveness in group efforts; divisiveness among team members; lack of teamwork among peers; people who personally benefit at the cost of the organization; a political climate that undermines trust; self-serving behavior that hurts the organization; unclear linkages between individual performance and the rewards given; people who put personal power ahead of the organizational good.

Underemployed Human Resources: too many people who are not contributing; difficulty getting ineffective people out of the organization; people who are not adding value to the organization.

Cultural Misunderstanding: interpersonal conflicts due to different global backgrounds; communication problems between people of different national cultures; misunderstandings due to language problems.

Unresponsive Headquarters: headquarters has difficulty aligning with changing local needs; inability of the home office to respond to feedback from the field; policies generated at the corporate offices do not match local realities; people at the main office are unwilling to give up control.

Lack of Innovation: discouraging the introduction of new ideas; inhibiting innovative practices; lack of creativity in problem-solving efforts; insufficient emphasis on innovative ideas.

Overemphasis on Analysis: too much emphasis on measurement and control; too much emphasis on measurement data; too much time devoted to forms and reports; too many resources devoted to information analysis.

Inaccessible Information: limited access to information held by direct supervisors; bosses who tightly control data on key issues; difficulty getting facts from the next level up.

Resisting Globalization: absence of worldwide reporting requirements; internal resistance to a global management system.

Index